(Con)Fusing Signs and Postmodern Positions

I0646615

LATIN AMERICAN STUDIES
VOLUME 15
GARLAND REFERENCE LIBRARY OF THE HUMANITIES
VOLUME 2136

LATIN AMERICAN STUDIES

DAVID WILLIAM FOSTER, *Series Editor*

THE CONTEMPORARY PRAXIS
OF THE FANTASTIC
Borges and Cortázar
by Julio Rodríguez-Luis

TROPICAL PATHS
*Essays on Modern
Brazilian Literature*
edited by Randal Johnson

THE POSTMODERN IN LATIN
AND LATINO AMERICAN
CULTURAL NARRATIVES
Collected Essays and Interviews
edited by Claudia Ferman

READERS AND LABYRINTHS
*Detective Fiction in Borges,
Bustos Domecq, and Eco*
by Jorge Hernández Martín

MAGIC REALISM
Social Context and Discourse
by María-Elena Angulo

RESISTING BOUNDARIES
*The Subject of
Naturalism in Brazil*
by Eva Paulino Bueno

LESBIAN VOICES
FROM LATIN AMERICA
Breaking Ground
by Elena M. Martínez

THE JEWISH DIASPORA
IN LATIN AMERICA
*New Studies on
History and Literature*
edited by David Sheinin
and Lois Baer Barr

JEWISH WRITERS
OF LATIN AMERICA
A Dictionary
edited by Darrell B. Lockhart

READERS AND
WRITERS IN CUBA
*A Social History
of Print Culture,
1830s–1990s*
by Pamela Maria Smorkaloff

BORGES AND THE
POLITICS OF FORM
by José Eduardo González

VOICES OF THE SURVIVORS
*Testimony, Mourning, and Memory
in Post-Dictatorship Argentina
(1983–1995)*
by Liria Evangelista
translated by Renzo Llorente

GENDER AND IDENTITY FORMATION
IN CONTEMPORARY
MEXICAN LITERATURE
by Marina Pérez de Mendiola

(CON)FUSING SIGNS AND
POSTMODERN POSITIONS
*Spanish American Performance,
Experimental Writing, and the
Critique of Political Confusion*
by Robert Neustadt

CHICANO/LATINO HOMOEROTIC
IDENTITIES
by David William Foster

(Con)Fusing Signs and Postmodern Positions

Spanish American Performance, Experimental Writing, and the Critique of Political Confusion

Robert Neustadt

Routledge
Taylor & Francis Group

NEW YORK AND LONDON

This edition Published 2011 by Routledge
711 Third Avenue, New York, NY 10017
2 Park Square, Milton Park, Abingdon, Oxfordshire OX14 4RN

First issued in paperback 2014

Routledge is an imprint of the Taylor and Francis Group, an informa business

Library of Congress Cataloging-in-Publication Data

Neustadt, Robert Alan, 1961–
    (Con)fusing signs and postmodern positions : Spanish American performance, experimental writing, and the critique of political confusion / by Robert Neustadt.
      p.   cm. — (Latin American studies ; v. 15)   (Garland reference library of the humanities ; v. 2136)
    Includes bibliographical references and index.
    ISBN: 0-8153-3272-6 (alk paper);
    1. Spanish American literature — 20th century — History and criticism. 2. Literature, Experimental — Latin American — History and criticism. 3. Postmodernism — Latin America. 4. Arts and society — Latin America. 5. Art — Political aspects — Latin America. I. Title. II. Series: Latin American studies ; vol. 15. III. Series: Garland reference library of the humanities ; vol. 2136.
PQ7081.N48   1999
860.9'98—dc21   99-15047
                                                 CIP

Cover photograph by Lotty Rosenfeld.

ISBN 13: 978-1-138-86443-6 (pbk)
ISBN 13: 978-0-8153-3272-5 (hbk)

For Cacea Marie and Tasha Moselle.

And in memory of O.J. Cooper, running on the other side.

CONTENTS

ILLUSTRATIONS

Series Preface

The monographs in Garland's Latin American Studies series deal with significant aspects of literary writing, defined broadly and including general topics, groups of works, or treatments of specific authors and movements. Titles published have been selected on the basis of the originality of scholarship and the coherency of the theoretical underpinnings of the critical discourse. Cognizant of the fact that literary study is an ongoing dialogue between multiple voices, authors in the LAS series have chosen topics and approaches that complement attempts to revise the canon of Latin American literature and that propose new agendas for their analysis. These critical works focus on interdisciplinary approaches to Latin American issues: the bridging of national and linguistic divisions, subaltern studies, feminism, queer theory, popular culture, and minority topics, and many others topics that continue to gain increasing exposure in academic and popular culture.

David William Foster

ACKNOWLEDGMENTS

I would like to thank the many colleagues, professors and friends who read and commented on various sections of this text at various times and in various drafts: Melvyn S. Arrington, James Barrett, Rosamel Benavides, O.J. Cooper, Juan Armando Epple, Jennifer Fink, Jean Franco, Leonardo García-Pabón, Erika E. Hess, Horacio Legras, Forest Pyle, Michael P. Lynch, Cecilia Ojeda, Elisa Rosales, Gustavo Verdesio, Liliana Trevizán and Gareth Williams. As could probably go without saying, any and all of this work's weaknesses and inadequacies are my responsibility.

I would also like to acknowledge the Office of Research at the University of Mississippi for granting me summer support stipends, which provided the time necessary to complete the manuscript.

I am grateful to Diamela Eltit, Alejandro Jodorowsky, Lotty Rosenfeld and Marcela Yentzin for helping me to acquire materials that made this project possible.

Thank you to Louella Holter of the Bilby Research Center at Northern Arizona University for carefully editing my manuscript and preparing it for publication.

I appreciate the help of the entire editorial team at Garland, especially Kristi Long and James Morgan.

Thank you to my parents for years of love and support.

And thank you to Cacea and Tasha, for more than words can say.

Sections of Chapters 2, 3 and 4 have appeared in earlier drafts as individual essays in the following journals: "Diamela Eltit: Clearing Space for Critical Performance," *Women and Performance: A Journal of Feminist Theory. New Hybrid Identities: Performing Race/Gender/ Nation/Sexuality* 7:2–8:1 (1995): 219–239.

"Alejandro Jodorowsky: Reiterating Chaos, Rattling the Cage of Representation," *Chasqui: Revista de literatura latinoamericana* 26.1 (1997): 56–74.

"(Con)Fusing Cultures: Guillermo Gómez-Peña and the Transgression of Borders." *Mattoid: A Journal of Literary and Cultural Studies* 52–53 (1998): 65–79.

INTRODUCTION

This book explores confusion. I use the term to evoke several ideas in Latin American culture, art, politics and literature. In the broadest sphere, I employ the word "confusion" to describe the generalized disorientation associated with Latin America in the age of postmodernity. In Latin America the coexistence of indigenous, mestizo and European cultures—juxtaposed with the uneven effects of mass media and high technology—combine to create a particularly diverse phenomenon. Guillermo Gómez-Peña refers to the postmodernity of Mexico City with irony: "From Aztec to post-punk, all styles, eras, and cultural expressions are intertwined in this megapastiche" (*Warrior* 18). I visualize postmodernism as a (con)fusion of cultural, economic and political signs that could combine but will never quite mix, like petroleum and vinegar or *huitlacoche* and caviar, served in a cyber café.

Contemporary Latin American cultural texts—film, literature, music and art, as well as the expressions of new social and political movements—reveal widespread disorientation with regard to issues of identity, history, political process and culture. At a time when the power of the modern nation-state appears secondary to that of the mass media and transnational corporations, questions of identity collide with reassessments of history, historical veracity and justice. Where and how far back in time do Latin Americans look to trace the signs of their identity? What roles do technology, free trade, neoliberalism, dictatorship, revolution, literature, the Catholic church, the Spanish language, the Conquista and traditional belief systems play in determining the identities of present-day Chileans, Mexicans or Chicanos? Whether one might be an Indian living in the Amazon, a peasant from El Salvador, a Marxist revolutionary with a web page or a banker in Santiago, the postmodern world system surrounds and, to a certain extent, defines the limits of one's existence. There is a saying in Spanish, *ni chicha ni limonada*, that means "neither one thing nor another." Postmodernism is *chicha* and lemonade, Inca Cola and *Televisión Azteca*. And it includes best-selling magic realism and neo-avant-garde "novels" that refuse to tell a story with a plot. Popular literature includes *fotonovelas* for the semi-literate and *telenovelas* for housewives. Meanwhile, revolutionaries send e-mail, and Indians perform "authentic" dances for change outside museums. A growing class of Latin Americans takes diet pills and Prozac and works by cell phone while nearly 40 percent of the population lives in extreme poverty.[1] The confusing symptoms and contrasts of postmodernity are everywhere. Although we may never uncoil the perfect string of signifiers with which to represent and define the phenomenon, it is now and we are in "it." I use "confusion," consequently, to signify the entire postcolonial and postmodern complex of spatial, temporal, historical and subjective disorientation.

And more. We are in the midst of what many thinkers refer to as a "crisis of representation" that is both aesthetic and political. One critic posits the concept of a crisis of representation—"a deeply felt loss of faith in our ability to represent the real"—as the common denominator in the conflicting array of theoretical postmodernisms: "No matter whether they are aesthetic, epistemological, moral, or political in nature, the representations that we used to rely on can no longer be taken for granted."[2] How can we represent and critique any political situation through art or literature when "truth and reference," to quote Linda Hutcheon, "have ceased to be unproblematic issues" (*Poetics* 223)? Jean Baudrillard, French philosopher-turned-cult hero, assesses the crisis apocalyptically. For Baudrillard representation no longer exists in the traditional sense of signs and referents, because it has been transcended by simulation wherein the original referent has been replaced with simulated signs: "Art is dead, not only because its critical transcendence is gone, but because *reality* itself, entirely impregnated by an aesthetic which is inseparable from its own structure, *has been confused with its own image*" (emphasis added, 151–2). Although an extreme example, Baudrillard's image of reality confused with its image signals a conundrum of positionality that plagues all theories of postmodernity. That is to say, postmodern critics elaborate theories of postmodernity in order to describe postmodernity. We are *within* the aesthetic and political swamp that we wish to express. Confusion represents a sign of our condition, and our place, in time.

"(Con)fusing signs," on the other hand, means something different. Throughout this study I refer to works—whether literary, performative or videographic—as *texts* that can be read and analyzed. A text is a collection of *signs* that articulates meaning through internal and intertextual juxtaposition. Because meaning is constituted through difference (De Saussure), and *différance* (Derrida), textual articulation does not arise from a simple cumulative addition or concretion. Based on its Latin root, *confundere*—meaning "to pour together" or "mix"—one could visualize any text as a (con)fusion of signs and their interstitial traces. This (con)fusion constitutes a necessary part of both textual production—writing—and interpretation. Writers structure texts from a myriad of linguistic, visual and political signs. Reading implies a process during which the reader's preconceived expectations become progressively validated, dismissed, and most of all, realigned with the signs of the text. Meaning evolves through a process of (con)fusion and that process begins in a state of relative confusion.

This book analyzes experimental texts by three Spanish American artists-writers-performers—Diamela Eltit, Alejandro Jodorowsky and Guillermo Gómez-Peña—who critique our confusing postmodern predicament through the (con)fusion of various multimedia representations. During the 1960s, Jodorowsky led a series of "happenings" in the streets of Mexico and Europe, *efímeros pánicos*, questioning the divisions between life and art, actors and the viewing public, and the relationship between popular theater and politics. In addition to street theater, Jodorowsky has written unorthodox texts in virtually every genre from novels and poetry to comic books, pantomime, theater and film. Depicting characters involved in quests to find themselves, truth and true representation in a world run amok, Jodorowsky obsessively reiterates themes of postmodern violence and disorientation. Eltit and Gómez-Peña have also attempted to blur the lines between art, performance and contemporary politics via unconventional and difficult to interpret gestures. In 1980, for example, Eltit scarified her arms and performed a reading of her novel manuscript in a brothel while projecting a video image of her face onto an exterior wall. This confusing performance contests the traditional representation of women in society as well as the pain inflicted on Chileans by the Pinochet dictatorship. An author of eight books, Eltit continues to write in an experimental vein, exploring the margins of society from a place well to the margins of mainstream literature. Gómez-Peña, who began his career as a member of a performance collective that mounted interventions on the U.S.–Mexico border, moved away from the region after winning, in 1991, a MacArthur "Genius" award. In 1992 he and fellow performer Coco Fusco enclosed themselves in a cage in Madrid's Columbus Plaza claiming to be Indians from an undiscovered island in America. Fusco's video, *The Couple in the Cage*, documents the performance and the public's reaction, many of whom believed that Fusco and Gómez-Peña were really Indians. Fusco and Gómez-Peña's performance underscores the manner in which popular culture and the media construct minority identities with a series of stereotypical representations. In more recent performances Gómez-Peña has enclosed himself inside of a Plexiglas box in museums, embodying again the role and position of an object on display.

I should stress from the outset that I am not attempting to propose either a new theory of postmodernism or the dynamics of textual reception. I am exploring the critical and political dimensions of contemporary Spanish American artistic practices that are often explained away in the vague name of postmodern fragmentation. Highlighting experimental techniques and their political implications is particularly important today, at a time when best-seller formula-books dominate both Latin American and world markets. Literature requiring an active reader became a well-known trademark of Latin American *nueva narrativa* in the 1960s and 1970s. In spite of the influence of the canonical great works of the "Boom," such as Cortázar's *Rayuela* or Vargas Llosa's *La ciudad y los perros* to name just two, narrative fragmentation cannot be limited to any historical moment or style. There exist many ways to fragment a text. And "fragmentation," furthermore, is an ambiguous term that refers to many different aesthetic practices and strategies. Though many Spanish American writers create fragmented texts, this by no means implies that each does the same *thing* to narratives. All texts that I have studied demand an actively participating reader in contrast to a passive recipient. What unifies them, however, is not so much the fact that they experiment with narrative and the role of the reader, but rather the manner in which they situate their experimental texts within the political contexts of narrative, language and representation. I analyze texts that explicitly foreground semiotic (con)fusion as a strategy to formulate political critiques of cultural and political confusion.

Recurrent themes such as the loss of memory, the search for an origin, scrambled communication systems and confused cultural identity reaffirm a desire to reorient. Fredric Jameson has written about a hypothetical aesthetic practice, "cognitive mapping," in order to "map the great global multinational and decentered communicational network in which we find ourselves caught as individual subjects" (*Postmodernism* 44). The disorientation of postmodernity, according to Jameson, has "succeeded in transcending the capacities of the individual human body to locate itself, to organize its immediate surroundings perceptually, and cognitively to map its position in a mappable external world" (44). If for Jameson postmodernism connotes a world gone mapless, my view is that the works of Eltit, Gómez-Peña and Jodorowsky constitute cultural efforts toward mapping a position from which to articulate a critique. Their efforts take place at the margins of traditional representation wherein they engage with the confusion of postmodernity by the practice of fusing signs. These writers emerge from and articulate different positions via related strategies of multiple media, fragmentation, performance and (con)fusion. Following common threads and exploring significant differences, this book aims to provide perspective as to how contemporary art and literature cope with and respond to the confusion inherent in a crisis of representation.

Chapter 1 examines the theoretical issues that frame the process of (con)fusing signs within the context of a concept that I call a "postmodern position." I explore the difficulty of articulating critiques of political and social conditions at a time when poststructuralist sensibilities have rendered the idea of critical distance obsolete. Although distance may appear flattened in the new space of postmodernism, critique remains viable. Critical distance has not eroded so much as the spatial metaphor has been exposed. I apply Michel Foucault's concept of the Panopticon as a model to describe our perpetually *internal* orientation. We cannot get outside of a culture, or for that matter a text, anymore than a text can be extracted from the world. To constitute critique, then, it is necessary to articulate critique internally, to construct and to speak from a perspective on the inside. I call this type of interior perspective a postmodern position.

Chapter 2 consists of close readings and analyses of the controversial work of award-winning Chilean novelist, Diamela Eltit. Writing under the repression of the Pinochet regime, Eltit found herself within the societal incarceration of (neo)fascism. The military coup of 1973 represented a violent and unambiguous attempt to impose rigorous and regimented discipline throughout Chile. Furthermore, while the regime represented a thoroughly visible model for discipline, a multitude of transparent discursive structures functioned in tandem with the authoritarian government. Eltit was and is aware that she could no more escape representational discourse than she could remove herself from the confines of her body. In Chapter 2, I propose reading Eltit's first novel *Lumpérica* (1983), her gesture of self-mutilation and her videographic recording *Maipu* as a multimedia perfomance action. (Con)fusing images from performance art, literature and video, Eltit simultaneously mutilates her body and discourse. By tracing a spiral series of *mises en abyme* I argue that she clears a space for politically viable critique. I conclude the chapter with an account of Eltit's recent novel, *Los vigilantes* (1994), to show how her view of contemporary democratic

Chile evokes an image of a society locked inside of a transparent "seeing machine."

Chapter 3 focuses on the work of Alejandro Jodorowsky, a controversial Chilean writer who experiments with a variety of media and art forms. Jodorowsky also writes within and against the partitions of disciplinary society. According to Foucault, the most sinister aspect of disciplinary society lies in the fact that it functions by itself. It is not that the guards in the Panopticon forcibly control the prisoners but rather that the machine converts a prisoner into the subject of his or her own constraint. In contrast to Eltit, Jodorowsky's concerns reflect a more generalized critique of contemporary society. Jodorowsky represents characters in a loop of circular quests to highlight the manner in which "man" effectively imprisons himself. In Chapter 3, I read across Jodorowsky's oeuvre of pantomime, novels, film, theater and comics to demonstrate how he reiterates circular narratives of chaos to reveal the self-imposed structures inherent in paradigms of order.

Chapter 4 explores written texts and performances by Mexican artist Guillermo Gómez-Peña, and focuses on the manner in which his work moves between national and conceptual borders. Gómez-Peña's performance art challenges the social, political and geographic implications of a construct known today as the "New World Order." Foucault describes discipline as "an anti-nomadic technique" (*Discipline* 218). Gómez-Peña's theatrical nomadism raises questions about the borders between artistic, generic and political disciplines. In critical writings and performance art Gómez-Peña embodies a (con)fusion of stereotypes that corrodes the notion of national, ethnic and sexual identity. In Chapter 4, I read Gómez-Peña's poetry and performances to demonstrate the manner in which he simultaneously underscores and transgresses cultural, discursive and linguistic boundaries.

I have chosen Eltit, Jodorowsky and Gómez-Peña because of the manner in which they (con)fuse signs, as well as for the fact that their texts encounter and allegorize the dimensions of postmodern positionality. An overview of their work, furthermore, traces significant temporal and geographical trajectories. With regard to literary history, a progression from Jodorowsky to Eltit and Gómez-Peña reiterates what Octavio Paz has called *la tradición de ruptura*. Jodorowsky's direct contact and conflict with André Breton and Salvador Dalí in Paris directly links him to the close of the historical avant-garde. Eltit pertains to a neo-avant-garde generation of the 1980s. Gómez-Peña, in turn, works in a contemporary genre of issue-oriented performance art and is a central voice in the current debate on multiculturalism.

I refer repeatedly in this book to nonlocalizable locations, "positions" of thought, culture, critique and power. While it is true that none of these positions occupy a point in space, the relational differences that grant them meaning and significance do emerge in concrete places. Whereas each of these writers articulates different types of texts and hence different positions, they write from specific geographical locations. Eltit's work is rooted in Chile, opposing most vehemently the Pinochet dictatorship (and legacy) but also firmly contesting the simplistic conventions of socialist realism. Although her writing specifically addresses the situation of Chile, her denunciation of order resonates with dictatorships throughout Latin America during the 1970s and 1980s. Rather than focusing on one country, Gómez-Peña centered his earlier work on the border between the United States and Mexico. He then moved away from this specific geopolitical zone, expanding his critique to the phenomenon of discursive and ideological borders. Jodorowsky, who has worked in Chile, Mexico and Paris, conjugates his representations of contemporary disorientation through the optic of mysticism and hence tends to focus more on universal rather than regional issues.

(Con)fusing signs across a constellation of diverse media and discourses, Eltit, Jodorowsky and Gómez-Peña articulate a series of extraordinary political critiques. Analyzing and mapping these encounters with(in) various configurations of a postmodern position, this book aims to reconsider the implications raised by the theoretical liquidation of critical distance arising in our contemporary crises of representation. Ultimately, I hope to highlight a theoretical ground on which to explain the powerful internal critiques made possible by an awareness of postmodern positions.

NOTES

1. This figure is according to Gert Rosenthal, executive secretary of ECLAC (the United Nations Economic Commission for Latin America and the Caribbean), from his speech of October 3, 1997 at the Meeting of Latin American and Asian Ministers of Economy and/or Trade and Industry. Online: www.eclac.cl/english/news/Pressrelease/PECC.html

2. Hans Berthens, *The Idea of Postmodernism: A History* (1995), 11.

(CON)FUSING SIGNS AND POSTMODERN POSITIONS

CHAPTER 1

(Con)Fusing Approaches to a Postmodern Position

There exist myriad ways to fragment texts, to conflate images and to (con)fuse signs, and this book identifies and explores the strategies and political consequences of many of these techniques in Spanish American art, performance and literature. Diamela Eltit, Alejandro Jodorowsky and Guillermo Gómez-Peña each employ multiple media in conjunction with writing to position themselves within contemporary crises of representation. Each experiments with conflated imagery and fractured narrative to stake a position within, and to develop a critique of, the politics of representation. In addition to fragmentation, their (con)fusing strategies include the simultaneous manipulation of multiple genres and media. In this chapter I explore the theoretical underpinnings of positionality that unite three disparate artists, each of whom realizes that he or she cannot escape from the systems that each strives to critique. Aware that no place outside of language, culture, discourse or representation exists, these artists explicitly call attention to this situation. The purpose of this chapter is to theorize a critical locus—a postmodern position—from which political critique remains possible.

Because Jodorowsky has worked in film and Eltit and Gómez-Peña in video, the aesthetics of *montage* play an important role in my analyses. Once a celebrated arm of the avant-garde in the modernist mission to break the conventions of representation and to create critical distance, montage no longer signals any particular ideological tendency. Rather than looking back to the avant-garde to explain contemporary aesthetic practices, I would like to consider first the effect of montage in contemporary popular culture. It is crucial to acknowledge that since the 1960s montage has been appropriated by the mainstream media and the advertising industry. Nestor García Canclini writes that postmodern video

3

clips jumble images from so many texts that they distract the viewer and eclipse any notion of plot, context or history: "En la mayoría de los casos toda acción es dada en fragmentos, no pide que nos concentremos, que busquemos una continuidad. No hay historia de la cual hablar. Ni siquiera importa la historia del arte o los medios; se saquean imágenes de todas partes, en cualquier orden" (284–5). Texts by Eltit, Gómez-Peña and Jodorowsky invoke a slightly different aesthetic of montage. Their texts do flatten the notion of *historia* in the sense of plot, but at the same time these writers call attention to historical issues previously edited out by dominant representations of history. Using montage to construct political critique today proves problematic for at least two reasons: First, the technique and technology of montage belongs at least as much to the culture industries as to radical artists. And second, extreme montage complicates interpretation. To put it another way, (con)fusing signs confuses the audience.

To underscore the manner in which a montage of images can critique the politics of representation while simultaneously undermining any such critique, we can use an example from contemporary popular culture, Dominican pop star Juan Luis Guerra's music video, *El costo de la vida* (1992). This is an MTV-style production that has received substantial play on television in Latin America and the United States, as well as in bars and nightclubs throughout the world. As the video begins we see Guerra, who plays the role of a newscaster, aligning his tie and putting on a suit jacket in the studio before taking his place at the news desk. A globe with a news logo spins across the screen to the soundbite of news-announcement music. The viewer immediately recognizes the context; this is the scene of televised world news.

In his musical news report, Guerra sings *las noticias del día*, making reference to the cost-of-living index, which continues to rise. The lyrics evoke the problems of inflation and monetary devaluation so commonplace throughout Latin America: "El costo de la vida sube otra vez, el peso que baja ya ni se ve y las habichuelas no se pueden comer, ni una libra de arroz, ni una cuarta de café." Elsewhere in the song he alludes to the rising cost of gasoline, political corruption, unemployment and the lack of health care. The singer's hypothesis hints at, in rather simplistic terms, the cultural divisions accompanying colonial and neocolonial control in Latin America: "Será porque aquí no hablamos inglés ... Será porque aquí no hablamos francés." The song calls attention to the fact that language plays a key role in the delineation of class lines.[1]

And yet while the song lyrics point to the uneven dispersion of resources in Latin America, the video projects a conflicting montage of images. These images initially appear on the news monitors behind Guerra in a highly fragmented exposition. Ultimately the images take over the entire visible space of the video. Interspersed between images of misery and violence (starving children, Chilean military repression, deforestation of the Amazon, boat people and so on) the video inserts quick scenes of erotic modern dance and footage of Japanese sumo wrestlers.[2] The video also flashes loose words across the screen that vary from the titles of other Guerra songs ("Ojalá que llueva café") to politically charged ideas, such as "Descubrimiento" and "500 Años."

The rapid movement from image to image de-emphasizes the historical context, reducing true cases of human suffering to a surface of glossy images. The hermeneutic experience that *El costo de la vida* suggests seems more akin to a spectacle of sports highlights of the day than a rigorous political critique. The highly polished presentation and synchronization of the images with the musical score essentially aestheticizes pain and suffering. More than raising consciousness about conditions in Latin America, the video sells Juan Luis Guerra's product—the compact disc *Areito*.[3] The dance scenes fetishize the human body as an image of sexual desire. I would argue that even the explicitly "political" images work to fetishize violence and misery more than to document the conditions in Latin America.

There remains, nevertheless, a critique sandwiched between the glitz and glamour of *El costo de la vida*. If we step back from the splash of imagery and read the plot, the video parodies the manner in which the media distract us from political issues by aestheticizing, magnifying and spectacularizing political images. Parody constitutes but one example of how a text can formulate criticism from the inside of the representational system that it critiques. The problem is that the video operates by the same spectacularizing aesthetic that it critiques. If one were to casually view the video on television, it would be all too easy to miss its political statement. I have given this example because it graphically demonstrates that the very act of formulating a critique can simultaneously reproduce the problem. In critiquing specific discourses by (con)fusing the signs of that discourse, Eltit, Jodorowsky and Gómez-Peña run similar risks of confusing their audiences. Eltit has been accused of writing hermetic novels that fetishize the lives of homeless and marginalized individuals. Jodorowsky's work might be perceived as a glorification of violence and sexism. Gómez-Peña receives complaints that his performances propagate the same mass media stereotypes that he attempts to foreground. Perhaps in part because all three do not work in highly commercial mediums, their work nevertheless effectively acknowledges the complicitous relationship between that which they critique and the texts that they produce. For this reason I see their texts as particularly appropriate examples to explore the dimension of postmodern positionality. By (con)fusing signs, these writers reproduce the confusion that renders critical distance impossible, and yet they manage to produce a critique of the politics underpinning the confusion.

READING THROUGH THE SIGN FIELD

Reading, writing and performing, perhaps even thinking, can be understood as processes of manipulating signs. Derived conceptually from the fields of philosophy as well as linguistic, literary and cultural theory, a sign can represent, and hence signify the place, or trace, of anything from a particle of language to an unconscious performance of culture. In *Mythologies*, Roland Barthes analyzes signs of mass culture in an effort to demonstrate the semiotic process by which signs combine to create cultural myths. Barthes reads diverse events—from professional wrestling matches to striptease, from trends in advertising to the public perception of Einstein's brain—as collections of signs. Part of the beauty of Barthes's classic study derives from the fact that he analyzes signs of manifestly different sizes and types: "A whole book may be the signifier of a single concept; and conversely, a minute form (a word, a gesture, even incidental, so long as it is noticed) can serve as a signifier to a concept filled with a very rich history" (120).

I have chosen to analyze texts by Eltit, Jodorowsky and Gómez-Peña because they manipulate various types of signs from a range of different positions. Eltit's de(con)struction of language, Jodorowsky's allegorical quests for an original language and Gómez-Peña's embodiment of social stereotypes constitute complex signifying practices that should not be merely subsumed under the name of postmodern fragmentation. The signs that comprise each of these texts call attention to larger problems and diverse issues in Spanish American culture. Eltit, Jodorowsky and Gómez-Peña (con)fuse issues and images of spectacle, narrative, gender and nation to critique the confusing signs of postmodern disorientation. Each of these writers strategically embraces the experimental aesthetic techniques that David William Foster summarizes as the most salient features of postmodern conduct: "The mixing or blending of categories, the decentering and 'anarchicalization' of cardinal points of reference, and simply the flouting of all definitions that attempt repressively to hold the line" (4). I am exploring, in other words, the manner in which Eltit's, Jodorowsky's and Gómez-Peña's experimental texts engage and situate themselves within "the disjunctive cultural signs of these (postmodern) times" (Bhabha 222).

I should emphasize, nevertheless, that I make no claim that the texts or authors I study should necessarily be qualified as postmodern per se. Efforts to define postmodernism in terms of pure aesthetic, formal or historical characteristics inevitably self-destruct when matched up to an extended spectrum of literary history. The *Quijote*, for that matter, with its programmatic problematization of historical truth, its complex meta-textual structure, its parodic intertextuality (fusing genres of popular fiction and high art) and its fragmentation could pass for postmodern *avant la lettre* were it not completed in 1615. For my purposes, arguing about whether these texts should be classified as postmodern would constitute an irrelevant sidetrack, not to mention the fact that other critics have addressed that issue.[4] Rather than defining what kinds of texts these are, I am interested in charting how these three artists-writers-performers strategically deploy a series of unconventional texts from across a spectrum of different media—from corporeal mutilation and performance art to novels, videos and comic books—to critique and encounter aspects of contemporary political disorientation.

My use of confusion as a metaphor of postmodernity derives from an extensive corpus of critical theory. Fredric Jameson, in *Postmodernism or the Cultural Logic of Late Capitalism*, employs Baudrillard's image of "schizophrenic vertigo" to describe the cultural and political disorientation characterizing the conditions of late capitalism. For Jameson postmodernism evolved with the global atomization of capital whereby hegemonic power became redistributed from individual nations to a worldwide network of multi- and transnational corporations. The massive proliferation of electronic media has resulted in a confusing overload of information and signs called "semiotic glut." Reality can no longer be distinguished from simulation, postmodern "pastiche" has subsumed modern "parody," and superficial streams of images project a "culture of simulacrum" (15–16). Jameson sees postmodern art as a nonaesthetic mass of writhing signs that paradoxically do not signify anything except themselves: "We are left with that pure and random play of signifiers that ... ceaselessly reshuffles the fragments" (96). For

Jameson postmodern aesthetics constitute a confusion of hollow signs that are devoid of meaning.[5]

Another critic of contemporary cultural sensibilities, Celeste Olalquiaga, also employs the metaphor of confusion as a sign of our time. Olalquiaga begins her study of postmodernism by comparing contemporary modes of perception to a psychological disorder called psychasthenia, "in which being and surroundings fuse into one" (1). Olalquiaga's description of postmodern perception as psychasthenia is particularly relevant to my thesis in that her definition conflates the experiences of perceptual disorientation, identity and narrative: "Defined as a disturbance in the relation between self and surrounding territory, psychasthenia is a state in which the space defined by the coordinates of the organism's own body is confused with represented space" (1–2). By represented space, Olalquiaga refers to visual images, signs and texts, such as those propagated by the advertising industry. Note the narrative specificity of this confusion: Confusing the body with *represented* space correlates to (con)fusing the body with signs. Olalquiaga goes on to say that postmodern psychasthenia leads the subject to abandon its identity: "Incapable of demarcating the limits of its own body, lost in the immense area that circumscribes it, the psychasthenic organism proceeds to abandon its own identity to embrace the space beyond" (1–2). Identity, of course, is itself constructed of signs. Here I am referring to identity in the broadest sense. Identity may include a subject's self-perceived identity (i.e., who one thinks he or she is), as well as the label of identity ascribed by dominant society (i.e., who everyone else thinks he or she is). Alternatively, one might argue that one's identity, namely his or her tastes, preferences and predilections (foods consumed, sexual practices, clothing, modes of transportation and so forth) are constituted by publicity images created by the advertising industry. Regardless of the extent to which each scheme of identity may be true, identity is predicated on thought and language, in other words, signs. "Thinking," muses Wittgenstein in his dictation on the location of thought, "is essentially the activity of operating with signs" (6). From the languages with(in) which one thinks and the national, social, ethnic, sexual, religious, political and literary symbols with which he or she identifies (or is identified externally), identity is a fundamentally semiotic construction. Olalquiaga's description of a subject in the process of exchanging its identity with represented space exemplifies a subject that is incapable of transcending the realm of signs. Any crisis of identity involves a textualizing exchange or reconfiguration of signs at many different levels. The epistemological, political and aesthetic crises of postmodern representation have always already been (con)-fusions of signs.

Olalquiaga compares the psychasthenic phenomenon to the scattering of images taking place in postmodern cities. Specifically, she describes the subject's experience of urban architecture, replete with mirrored windows and trompes l'oeil as a jumbled quagmire of ever-reflecting disorientation: "The postmodern confusion of time and space ... transforms urban culture into a gigantic hologram capable of producing any image" (19). The electronic nature of these images plays a key role in reshaping contemporary perception. According to Olalquiaga, "high technology has induced a confusion between spatial and temporal boundaries, collapsing the conventions that formerly distinguished fantasy from reality and creating ... simulation" (xix). Electronic media have not merely penetrated communication networks but have flattened the contemporary perception of time, space, reality and self. As our perception of space becomes reorganized into "flatness," the postmodern subject's sense of self scatters on the surface like images in a house of mirrors. How writers and artists can simultaneously inscribe themselves in the house, shatter the mirrors and engage in politics constitutes the subject of this book.

THE MYTH OF CRITICAL DISTANCE

> El contexto parece estar más cerca del Todo que la idea. Pero en realidad todo está a igual distancia del Todo. Más aún: entre la parte y el Todo no hay distancia.
>
> —Alejandro Jodorowsky

Although critics generally agree to read postmodernism as political and aesthetic fragmentation (with variable emphasis on politics and aesthetics), the relative vulnerability or untouchability of contemporary political dominance continues to divide opinions. For many critics the lynchpin of the debate centers around a concept of critique called *critical distance*. My interest in this problem was initially inspired by Jameson's often-cited remark that critical distance is no longer possible:

> "Critical distance" has very precisely been abolished in the new space of postmodernism ... Political interventions ... are all somehow secretly disarmed and reabsorbed by a system of which

they themselves might well be considered a part, since they can achieve no distance from it. (*Postmodernism* 48–9)

Here, Jameson describes postmodernism as a space that takes on the shape of an insurmountable all-encompassing monster. His declaration that the late capitalist giant has eaten up critical distance continues to provoke an enormous debate among theorists.[6] Opposing scholars counter that critical distance has been not so much reified as it has been democratized.

Proponents of popular culture celebrate postmodernism, evoking images of carnivals (Bakhtin) that subvert hegemony through pluralism.[7] Carlos Fuentes endows his reading of postmodernity with a heavy dose of political optimism:

> ¿no promete la multiplicación de los multirrelatos del mundo poli-
> cultural, más acá del dominio exclusivo de la modernidad occiden-
> tal? La "incredulidad hacia las metanarrativas" puede ser sustituida
> por la credulidad hacia las polinarrativas que nos hablan de
> proyectos de liberación múltiples, no sólo occidentales. (25)

This statement by Fuentes responds to Lyotard's influential reading of postmodernism as "incredulity of meta-narratives." For Fuentes the fragmentary nature of postmodernism—a multiplication of multiple versions of a multicultural world—promises true democratic pluralism. Other thinkers, such as Nestor García Canclini, observe a potential for "good" resistant postmodern work and "bad" noncritical art that is lost in the middle of the market economy:[8]

> Pienso que la visión fragmentaria y diseminada de los experimen-
> talistas o posmodernos aparece con un doble sentido. *Puede ser una*
> *apertura ... cuando mantiene la preocupación crítica* ... En cambio,
> si eso se pierde, la fragmentación posmoderna se convierte en
> remedo artístico de los simulacros de atomización que un mercado
> ... juega con los consumidores dispersos. (emphasis added, 347)

García Canclini negotiates an "exit" for politically resistant postmodern art provided that it maintains its critical sensibility. Exactly how writers and artists are to insure the integrity of this *preocupación crítica* remains unclear. Notice the spatial metaphor that characterizes García Canclini's description of the potential effect of postmodern fragmentation in art: "Puede ser una apertura," an opening. Assuming that some writers and artists achieve this critical *opening*, the question remains as to where they, and we, will go. Unsure if there is a ground to support the presence of weightless postmodern signs, we approach the millennium without a sense of clear direction. Jodorowsky evokes this kind of multicultural and polytemporal confusion in the opening scene of his play, *El túnel se come por la boca*: "Flechas de metal, oxidadas y nuevas, con letras de distintas épocas y en diversos idiomas, indican hacia todas direcciones '¡Salida!'" (*Teatro* 23).

Curiously, although the concept of critical distance plays a crucial role in both celebrations and accusations of postmodernism, it has yet to be fleshed out critically. What exactly does critical distance mean? How can a spatial-temporal concept such as "distance" function in conjunction with narrative? Wayne C. Booth uses the term "aesthetic distance" as a measure of the illusion of fiction: "The degree to which the reader or spectator is asked to forget the artificiality of the work and 'lose himself' in it; whatever makes him aware that he is dealing with an aesthetic object and not real life increases 'aesthetic distance'" (276). There are obviously many reasons for highlighting the constructedness of art. Bertolt Brecht's (avant-garde) "alienation effect" is perhaps the best-known example of a writer who foregrounds the artificiality of the work for the political purpose that the reader-spectator not lose himself in it. Brecht's modernist aesthetic aims to highlight the representational apparatus of theater in order to break a viewer's unquestioning acceptance of the narrative scene. Brechtian alienation effects serve to produce critical distance by accentuating the aesthetic—underscoring, in other words, the fact that the play is composed of signs. This distance, according to Brecht, motivates a viewer to question the authoritarian discourse that lies hidden beneath representation.

Highlighting the semiotic bones of theater, then, Brecht attempted to enhance a critical distance that would ultimately lead to political change. But where does this strategy position the writing subject with respect to the problem that he or she aims to critique? To answer this question entails a discussion that situates the subject in its place in culture and discourse. I address the issue of subjectivity later, but would first like to analyze the spatial notion of distance. Where, in other words, is the subject? Visual and temporal interruptions in Brechtian theater underscore the distance between viewer and spectacle, distinguishing and distancing reality from representation. The (vanishing) point of this distance has more to do with politics than aesthetics. The ultimate goal is to change the political structure of society. The spatial image of critical distance, the concept that Jameson calls "our most cherished and time honored formula," constitutes a metaphor for isolating and confronting the political site of hegemonic power (*Postmodernism* 48). The problem becomes one of isolating the *location* of power from which one might mark off (critical) distance. Michel Foucault, nevertheless, argues against a spatial localization of power: "The idea that there is either located at—or emanating from—a given point something which is a 'power' seems to me to be based on a misguided analysis, one which at all events fails to account for a considerable number of phenomena. In reality power means relations, a more-or-less organized, hierarchical, coordinated cluster of relations" (*Power/Knowledge* 198). Foucault's understanding of power as a matrix of relations and not an identifiable locus situates the issue of critical distance within the impossible realm of utopia.

If we read power as a text, a parallel with language becomes apparent. Ferdinand de Saussure demonstrated that language functions through the differences that emerge when signs relate to other signs: "The important thing in the word is not the sound alone but the phonic differences that make it possible to distinguish this word from all others, for differences carry signification" (118). De Saussure elaborates on the graphic, phonetic and conceptual distinctiveness of the signs "horse," "tree," "sister" and "ox" (65–8). Along similar lines "postmodernity" signifies postmodernity (whatever it may actually mean) because the word-sign differs (phonetically, graphically and conceptually) from the words "modernity," "paternity" and "virtual postmen drink herbal tea." Language derives meaning from difference; power derives from the differential generated by a cluster of social and economic relations. Relations, whether social, sexual or economic are predicated on difference. Like language, power obtains its meaning from difference. How is it possible, then, that technology and late capitalism have eclipsed the possibility to construct a critique through art or literature today? Postmodernity may indeed provoke confusing crises of representation, but if one thing is certain, socioeconomic difference and unbalanced hierarchies of power relations remain ubiquitous. It is not that postmodernism has clipped away the potential for critical distance, but rather that contemporary (poststructuralist) sensibilities no longer accept the theoretical notion of distance as valid. Distance may appear to have been abolished in the new psychasthenic space of postmodernism. Critique, on the other hand, remains problematic yet viable. The strategic juxtaposition and (con)fusion of signs constitutes one approach to articulating this kind of critique. We cannot really see power because it does not exist in one place but rather emerges through relational difference. Wittgenstein's assertion about the location of thought—thinking "is essentially operating with signs" (6)—might apply as well for the location of power. Instead of power one can see *signs of power* that acquire meaning through social, sexual, cultural and political relations. Some of these signs are nearly impossible to miss. In post-coup Chile, a soldier carrying a U.S.–made machine gun constituted an unambiguous "text." Military installations on the U.S.–Mexico border convey a related message, although the border-text is punctuated with "holes" and countersigns that simultaneously discourage and encourage illegal migrants to provide cheap labor in the United States. In difficult texts readers must sometimes discover partially obscured differences that are implied contextually. A plaza in Santiago de Chile in Eltit's *Lumpérica* may not be recognized as a sign until one realizes that this space remains conspicuously empty in a country isolated by a military regime. Bodies, as well, can convey or obscure differences. Though we tend to think of our bodies as substantive biological realities, they can certainly function as indicators of relational difference and power. The body is a bearer of signs, a text, that can be "written" on and with by altering, marking and at times violating its appearance. Eltit's scarification of her arms, Jodorowsky's pantomime texts (which he wrote for Marcel Marceau) and Gómez-Peña's vestimentary manipulation of kitsch represent three very different examples of performances that use body language to "write" about power. Power is essentially operating with signs—to write about power is to reconfigure these signs. In chapters on Eltit, Gómez-Peña and Jodorowsky, I attempt to show how three Spanish American writers-artists-performers (con)fuse the signs of power.

Within a poststructuralist paradigm, critical distance has not been eroded to the extent that the spatial metaphor has been exposed. In *The Politics of Postmodernism*, Linda Hutcheon describes critical distance as an "illusion" that can be strategically generated and effaced by irony: "It is the function of irony in postmodern discourse to posit ... critical distance and then undo it" (15). Though it may be tempting to attribute this illusion to postmodernity, earlier cultural critics have pointed to the paradoxical status of cultural critique. Theodor Adorno discussed this years ago when studying the complicitous relationship between a cultural critic and the presumed object of study: "The cultural critic is not happy with civilization, to which alone he owes his discontent ... Yet he is necessarily of the same essence as that to which he fancies himself superior" (19). Feminist writers struggle to escape from patriarchal order while writing within language, a system that they themselves often perceive as patriarchal. How is it possible to critique culture, discourse or language when one lives within culture, discourse and language? Hutcheon correctly observes that this "crisis of representation" corresponds more to a renewed awareness than to an ontological change: "Everything always was 'cultural' in this sense, that is, always mediated by representations ... Notions of truth, reference and the noncultural real have not ceased to exist ... but ... they are no longer unproblematic issues" (34). We cannot get *outside* of culture, or for that matter, a text, anymore than a text can be extracted from the world. The only possible position from which to offer critique is internal.

A postmodern crisis of representation does not preclude representation but rather complicates the process of interpretation. Signs can still be read in the confusing present of postmodernity, though their meanings, as Nelly Richard observes, have become unfixed and destabilized: "La postmodernidad ... busca deshacer el compromiso de tener que *fijar* significaciones ... Desconfía incluso de toda estructura monológica o unisignificante, y reclama la *desestabilización del sentido* como producto de la deslegitimación del saber universal" (*La estratificación de los márgenes*, emphasis original, 43). Whereas the destabilization of meaning carries with it a degree of confusion, it also asserts the possibility of unfolding the signifying potential of signs. Here I am intentionally choosing the metaphor of *unfolding* over opening to avoid the untenable suggestion of a space external to signification. Richard points out that postmodern "technoculture" has awakened an interest in aesthetic and theoretical recycling, *reciclaje* (54). Artists do not create "new" signs so much as they recycle, rearticulate, deform, parody, resignify, and most of all, interrogate the dogma of the signs' original meanings (55). This strategy of semiotic recycling is probably not a specifically Spanish American practice, but rather is postcolonial. Richard describes it as a byproduct of Latin America's "peripheral" relationship to the First World: "La periferia ha tenido que perfeccionarse en el manejo de una 'cultura de la resignificación'" (55). By (con)fusing signs, in other words, Spanish American writers, artists and performers unfold the semiotic meaning of discourse without pretending to get outside. Postmodern crises of representation need not be seen as irrevocable. Reinterpreting the traditional concept of linguistic representation from a postmodern position, we might say that signs still *reflect*, but the "mirrors" simultaneously blur, distort and fragment images. No writer, artist or critic can get outside of the house of mirrors. Fortunately, though, there exist opportunities to move and rehang the mirrors. The questions of where and how, nevertheless, remain crucial.

It is precisely this problem of unlocalizable positionality that I explore throughout this book. Eltit, Jodorowsky and Gómez-Peña evoke images of confinement to systems that they attempt to critique internally. In Derridean terms, they *solicit*⁹ the foundations of a structure from which there is no escape. Rendering literary, visual and performance representations, Eltit, Jodorowsky and Gómez-Peña solicit the "prisonhouse" of representation. And yet, as useful as deconstruction might be (and I believe it is most useful), many different techniques exist for "shaking the system." Furthermore, whereas all hegemonic structures depend on language and discourse, hegemony does not correlate to any single idea, concept or unique ruling group. When reading Gramsci through Foucault and Wittgenstein, hegemonic power becomes a hierarchical cluster of uneven power relations, of differences and of signs. Eltit's, Jodorowsky's and Gómez-Peña's approaches are as diverse as the oppressive systems that they critique. What they bear in common is a *situation*—they gnaw against the hegemonic systems to which they themselves belong. The confinement that they inevitably encounter and articulate in their writing is part of what I refer to as a *postmodern position*. For Jameson, the idea of effective political art that can survive postmodern confusion lies pending in the nonspatial no-place of utopia: [It is a] "yet unimaginable mode of representing ... in which we may again begin to grasp our positioning as individual and collective subjects and regain a capacity to act and struggle which is at present neutralized by our spatial as well as our social confusion" (*Postmodernism* 54). My contention is that an awareness of their internal position allows Eltit, Jodorowsky and Gómez-Peña to constitute viable positions of critique. These positions are neither fixed nor spatial, and by no means do they pretend to exist on the "outside." As writers, they must articulate the positions from which they speak from *within* the discourses with which they engage. The postmodern position with(in) which Eltit, Jodorowsky and Gómez-Peña situate themselves realigns different "clusters of relations" (Foucault), negotiating differences of power through signs.

INSIDE IN THE SEEING MACHINE

> Outside of a book, a dog is a man's best friend. Inside of
> a dog, it's too dark to read.
>
> —Groucho Marx

Foucault's treatise, *Discipline and Punish: The Birth of the Prison,* provides a schematic analysis of social structure that helps demonstrate my view of a perpetually internal postmodern position. Specifically, Foucault's paradigm of the "Panopticon" provides an architectural and theoretical model that links physical incarceration to the transparent power mechanism of discipline. Explained simply, the Panopticon was a ring-shaped building with a tower in the center that was designed by Jeremy Bentham in the eighteenth century as a model institution of discipline, or prison. Inmates would occupy individual cells "like so many cages, so many small theaters, in which each actor is alone ... and constantly visible" from the central tower (200). Because the plan of the Panopticon prevents the prisoners from ever knowing whether or not they are currently under observation, the prisoners essentially guard themselves. By situating each confined person in a constant position of potential and nonconfirmable surveillance, Bentham's cage redefines the prisoner as the subject of his or her own incarceration. The jailed subjects effectively police themselves within a panoptic mechanism of power.

The implications of this machine are at least as striking as the efficiency with which it operates. As Foucault points out, Bentham's concept of the Panopticon included applications far vaster than penal justice: "The celebrated, transparent, circular cage, with its high tower ... also set out to show how one may 'unlock' the disciplines and get them to function in a diffused multiple, polyvalent way throughout the whole social body" (208–9). Bentham's model of discipline is immediately applicable to schools, hospitals, mental asylums, army barracks and so forth. In Foucault's words, this multipurposed instrument "programmes ... the basic functioning of a society penetrated through and through with disciplinary mechanisms" (209). Panopticism, then, is an interdisciplinary institution, or organization, that functions in the formation of what Foucault calls our "disciplinary society" (209). Eltit, Jodorowsky and Gómez-Peña each work in multiple media and genres, within and against the well-ordered partitions of the panoptic machine. The interdisciplinary productions of these artists-writers-performers challenge various tiers of the panoptic mechanism. Whereas discipline in Foucault's paradigm "clears up confusion" (219), Eltit, Jodorowsky and Gómez-Peña attempt to utilize (con)fusion against discipline. Superimposing literary, artistic and theatrical signs, they contest the compartmentalizing confinements of discipline. They create, to coin a phrase, "antidisciplinary" texts.

It is crucial to note the pervasiveness of the disciplinary society. Not merely interned individuals—inmates, prisoners and soldiers—live within the constraints of immobilizing institutions. "It's a machine," Foucault explains, "in which everyone is caught, those who exercise power just as much as those over whom it is exercised" (*Power/ Knowledge* 156). Whether rich or homeless, paying taxes, attending school, teaching, performing, writing criticism or essentially partaking in any social activity, we all assume our (unequal) places within the partitions of the panoptic machine. These partitions construct social "order." As Foucault writes, "Discipline fixes; it arrests or regulates movements; it clears up confusion; it dissipates compact groupings of individuals wandering about the country in unpredictable ways; it establishes calculated distributions" (*Discipline* 219). Discipline, in other words, both defines and represents the ordering structure of society.

One might argue that my use of the Panopticon as a metaphor for the postmodern situation is inappropriate; that the Panopticon relegated the inmate to prison, the student to school and the worker to his place in the modern factory. The Panopticon, one could object, is emblematic of the institutional structure of modernity, not postmodernity. I would maintain, nevertheless, that the panoptic mechanism of self-imposed discipline, a form of *virtual* control, functions similarly in the context of postmodernity. Foucault emphasizes that panopticism, the mechanism whereby individuals assume responsibility for constraining themselves, transcends the historical dimensions of the Panopticon-as-building: "The external power may throw off its physical weight; it tends to the noncorporal; and, the more it approaches this limit, the more constant, profound and permanent are its effects" (*Discipline* 203). Perhaps part of the confusion associated with postmodernity derives from the fact that transnational (in some ways noncorporeal) corporations are superseding the more visible (external) powers of the nation-state. Yes, we are living a postmodern condition that is defined by late capitalism and the dissolution of the nation-state, and is intimately associated with high technology, mass media, electronic simulation and a confusing preponderance of cultural, political, literary and virtual signs. But this postmodern society still functions through the hierarchical divisions and application of discipline. My point is that postmodern consumer society, with its weightless high-speed information, can still be visualized as a kind of panoptic, self-disciplining cage. The confines of the cage may at times be virtual, but its structure remains essentially disciplinary.

Consider, for example, an advertisement for *Etcétera*, an on-line weekly magazine from Mexico, dedicated to cultural and political analysis (see Figure 1-1). "La seducción está en línea," the ad reads, "En Internet, lectura inteligente." The obvious thrust of this advertisement text is to seduce the reader to read *Etcétera* and to discover the pleasure (as Barthes might have said) of the virtual text. This in itself is not unusual, the gesture of advertising being to entice the reader to consume a product. What is different here is that the product is virtual, an on-line *semanario de política y cultura*. In addition to "intelligent reading," *Etcétera*'s reader will discover, consume and take pleasure in images— textual and visual—of postmodern entertainment, the news. Of course this ad text functions in tandem with the image of a scantily clad woman who is surrounded by the coiled loops of a glowing rope representing the Internet. The phrase "la seducción está en línea" forms a multiple message: Virtual news magazines will seduce you on-line. To lasso a woman and bind her will seduce her for you. Finally, if you read *Etcétera*, you will be intelligent, well informed about politics and culture and able to seduce women with your knowledge.

An initial glance at the ad portrays a caged woman. It does not matter that her bodily posture looks more like she is about to fall down or become ill than seduce you; the interplay with the text says it all: "La seducción está en línea." Her hands appear fettered, allowing only enough movement to spread her unconstrained legs farther apart. Since her cage is virtual, we might consider what the image looks like beneath and between the *lines*. Is there a referent beneath this sign? The woman's complexion and body lines certainly do not correspond to the majority of Mexican women, or women anywhere for that matter. She is a Madison Avenue-style construction that represents sexual enticement. The model's neck and wrist are surrounded by beads and necklaces, reiterating the effect of the coiled rope that ties her up. Her dress wraps tightly around her body, covering little but accentuating her curvaceous body lines. Although I have read this ad thus far from a (stereotypical) male perspective, the text's implied reader can also be

Figure 1-1 Advertisement for on-line magazine, *Etcétera*

female. Women, the advertising agencies teach us, should seduce men by emulating these images. High-heeled shoes, jewelry, makeup, waist and bust lines all add up to "La seducción está en línea." The prisoner in the Panopticon and the worker in the factory are well behaved because they can never know when someone might be observing them. Women today who attempt to inhabit stereotypical images of sexuality do so precisely because of the panoptic structure of society—someone always may be watching. Rather than walk out of the image, men and women continue to perpetuate and consume the image. Advertisers exploit images of women as sexual prisoners to sell anything, from cars to the news. "The characteristics of the total system of contemporary world society," writes Jameson in the *Political Unconscious*, are "not the iron cage, but rather the *société de consommation*" (93). The images may be virtual but the cage is real.

Eltit, Jodorowsky and Gómez-Peña each explore the connections between gender and image, observer and observed. In *Lumpérica*, Eltit shreds the image of the ideal woman. In his comic book, the *Incal*, Jodorowsky parodies the masculine role in this dynamic by populating the city with mass-produced holographic prostitutes. While performing Gómez-Peña sometimes cross-dresses, inhabiting the feminine position as the object of the gaze. I discuss in the chapters to come the manner in which these writers strategically (con)fuse these issues. And yet the "prisonhouse of images" that I am discussing does not apply only to issues of gender. Each of these writers deconstructs the discourse of representation in general, underscoring the manner in which power structures manipulate images. When discussing the crisis of representation it is important to note that the *crisis* only troubles those on the other side of the image. The mainstream media, for example, clearly have no problem in representing the interests (economic, social and political) of those in power. By homogenizing, stereotyping and colorizing the images of Others, the media constitute transparent surface identities that appear natural and legitimate. Only when one attempts to contest these apparently legitimate images—to create a counterdiscourse—does the lopsided crisis of representation emerge. Eltit, Jodorowsky and Gómez-Peña do not attempt to substitute a correct image or group of signs that, to their view, more accurately represents a referent, but rather they denaturalize the process of representation through the (con)fusion of signs. Instead of resigning themselves to an insurmountable crisis of representation, these artists position their texts inside of the crisis.

Jodorowsky and Gómez-Peña explicitly highlight the role that the media and television play in shaping the constituent images of contemporary postmodern reality. In several of his works Jodorowsky depicts a world inundated with televisions—the news media literally manufacture the news as entertainment. Gómez-Peña often parodies the voice of a newscaster in his performance art, stereotyping the media in the act of creating stereotypes. Eltit, Jodorowsky and Gómez-Peña resign themselves, in other words, so as to exploit and intensify the urgent political consequences masked by mainstream representation.

Through its analyses of the texts of three writers-artists-performers, this book constitutes an initial attempt at theorizing the critical potential for articulating an effective postmodern position of political critique through literature and performance art. To establish the *locus* of this position entails situating the relation between the subject and his or her position within postmodern culture. Departing from Foucault's conceptualization—"[The subject is] not the author of the formulation, but a position that may be filled in certain conditions by various individuals" (*Archaeology of Knowledge* 115)—I am attempting to articulate a paradoxically unlocalizable position that changes "places" according to the subject's shifting situation with(in) the signs of hegemonic discourses.

The perennially fluid and unfixable character of this subject position is particularly noteworthy in the context of Latin American history and culture. Nelly Richard traces the fragmentation of Latin American identity to the traumatic experience of the Conquest, which imposed a European cultural paradigm and language system (European sign systems, in other words) on top of indigenous bodies:

> Desde el primer corte operado por la Conquista que escinde la conciencia del territorio y divide su nombrar entre significante (el cuerpo indígena) y significado (la palabra española), el sujeto latinoamericano habita un universo de representaciones estigmatizado por el trauma de una identidad fracturada por el conflicto entre el paradigma europeo de la cultura universalizante y un sustrato de experiencias declarado irreductible a esa lógica impuesto de racionalización histórica y simbolización cultural. (*La estratificación de los márgenes* 72)

Elsewhere, Richard reassesses the Latin American subject and stresses its conflictive and fragmentary constitution as a byproduct of uneven modernity:

Sujeto que nace del cruce entre los múltiples lenguajes transcritos y circulantes que se superponen fragmentariamente en la definición de una identidad cultural asumida como zona de colisiones: producto fracturado y tensional de la sintaxis de la modernidad, internacionalmente reguladas por el mercado euro-norteamericano de la información. (*La estratificación de los márgenes* 46)

The Latin American subject's linguistic and cultural fragmentation has become further fractured by the economic and political dynamics of late capitalism. In light of so much fragmentation one wonders whether it makes sense to speak of a Latin American subject at all. This problem becomes especially manifest upon acknowledging that the history of Latin America has been punctuated by a (con)fusion of colonialism, postcolonialism and also internal colonialism, which usually functions with the financial and military support of external powers. The imposition and overlapping of diverse power and sign systems has resulted in the simultaneous (con)fusion of diverse Latin American subjects as well as their disarticulation along ethnic, class and gender lines. For related theoretical reasons (that are not specifically Latin American), Ernesto Laclau and Chantal Mouffe have argued (from a post-Marxist standpoint) that it no longer makes sense to speak of a unified "working class revolution." Mouffe and Laclau speak of a nonessentialized range of democratic struggles that occupy an ensemble of subject positions: "Any democratic struggle emerges within an ensemble of positions, within a ... political space formed by a multiplicity of practices that do not exhaust the referential and empirical reality of the agents forming part of them" (132).

Similarly, the postmodern positions of which I speak cannot be definitively localized. "Resistance to the Panopticon," writes Foucault, "will have to be analyzed in tactical and strategic terms ... It is a matter ... of establishing the positions occupied and modes of actions used by each of the forces at work" (*Power/Knowledge* 163–4). It makes sense to speak not of an ontologically unified Spanish American "subject" but rather of an ensemble of interrelated, and often conflicting, subject positions. Though some of these positions are prescribed by society, a minority or alternative view often carries with it the potential of constituting a political critique. Liliana Trevizán argues that, in the case of Spanish American women writers, a marginalized position affords them an alternative and potentially transformative perspective:

El sujeto que experimenta el desplazamiento del centro, se coloca obviamente en una posición que le permite observar desde otro ángulo. Es esa postura diferente la que le otorga cierta capacidad crítica—e incluso autocrítica—que, dadas ciertas circunstancias, puede convertirse en fuerza transformadora. (2)

Decentered and potentially transformative positions exist not on the outside but rather at the margins of a system from which there is no escape. As Jodorowsky writes, "entre la parte y el Todo no hay distancia" (*Canciones* 153). Writers must carve a place for critique within the discourses surrounding them.

The concept of a postmodern position conveys an awareness that one cannot remove oneself entirely from the hegemonic system that he or she wishes to critique. This awareness allows contemporary writers, artists and performers such as Eltit, Jodorowsky and Gómez-Peña to construct the subject positions from which they speak. In the next chapters I analyze specific texts and performances to highlight the manner in which their writing demonstrates an awareness and articulation of an internal position. The notion of a postmodern position represents an interior perspective that allows artists and writers to create a conceptual locus from which to perform political critique.

NOTES

1. Clearly the song oversimplifies the issue of language by focusing solely on the hegemony of English and French. The Spanish conquest of Latin America was a linguistic imposition and a military invasion. What the song does not consider is the internal linguistic colonialism in Latin America today—the fact that indigenous peoples who do not speak Spanish suffer a double discrimination.

2. The sumo wrestlers perhaps symbolize the embattled multinational corporations that don't care about our opinion: "A nadie le importa qué piensa usted ... ni a la mitsubishi ni a la chevrolet."

3. *Areito* had purportedly sold more than five million copies less than a year after its release.

4. Julio Ortega, Juan Carlos Lértora and others describe Eltit's narrative as "postmodern." Fernando Burgos presents Jodorowsky's notion of *teatro pánico* as a paradigmatic example of postmodern sensibility (75–9). Gómez-Peña is not only mentioned in discussions of postmodernism by Homi Bhabha, Jean Franco and Nestor García Canclini, but he actually situ-

ates himself (theoretically and aesthetically) within a postmodern context. See the "critical texts" section of Gómez-Peña's *Warrior for Gringostroika.*

5. I should specify that Jameson sees postmodern signs as devoid of meaning in a traditional (modernist) sense. Although he finds individual signs and texts empty, Jameson reads the matrix of postmodern symptoms as a cultural dominant that arises, quite logically, from late capitalism.

6. By privileging this quote I am portraying Jameson's theory in an oversimplified, one-dimensional manner. At a later point in his study, Jameson dialectically recognizes a limited space for counterhegemonic resistance:

> The totalizing account of the postmodern always included a space for various forms of oppositional culture: those of marginal groups, those of radically distinct residual or emergent cultural languages, their existence being already predicated by the necessarily uneven development of late capitalism. (159)

I have highlighted Jameson's denial of critical distance to explain the evolution of my own theoretical approximation.

7. Jim Collins, for example, in *Uncommon Cultures*, celebrates postmodernism as a kind of democratic competition: "struggles of individual discourses to 'clear a space' within a field of competing discourses and fragmented audiences" (27). For Collins, postmodernism can be viewed in terms of a Bahktinian carnival encompassing multiple struggles for hegemony. See also Angela McRobbie's *Postmodernism and Popular Culture* for another view of the positive potential of postmodern pluralism.

8. Hal Foster, similarly, posits a binary opposition recognizing both the negative trend of "reactionary postmodernism" and an emancipatory version, "postmodernism of resistance." See Foster's preface to *The Anti-Aesthetic: Essays on Postmodern Culture.*

9. "This operation is called (from the Latin) *soliciting*. In other words, *shaking* in a way related to the *whole* (from *sollus*, in archaic Latin 'the whole,' and from *citare*, 'to put in motion')" (emphasis original, 6). Jacques Derrida, "Force and Signification," *Writing and Difference*, trans. Alan Bass (Chicago: U of Chicago, 1978), 3–30.

CHAPTER 2

Diamela Eltit:
Clearing Space For Critical Performance

(CON)FUSING IMAGES: THE BODY AND THE TEXT

La superficie está en todas partes y el centro en ninguna. Un
pedazo de piedra, un pedazo de carne, una inundación, un incendio,
una masacre, el mismo juego hipócrita del vacío.

—Alejandro Jodorowsky

Born in 1949 in Santiago, Chile, Diamela Eltit examines the violent
fracturing of post-coup Chile through novels,[1] video and performance
art. She exposes and problematizes discrete social, artistic and political
boundaries by overlapping the issues of gender, class, ideology and
discourse. In a variety of contexts Eltit explores themes of confused
identity, the body, and subjectivity. *Lumpérica* (1983), Eltit's first
novel, represents a bizarre spectacle in which a protagonist mutilates
her own body. Eltit herself performs an analogous expression in which
she scarifies her own arms and then reads her manuscript in a brothel.
This performance, in turn, engenders another "text," the video *Maipu*.[2]

In this chapter I trace the projection of Eltit's *performance* across
multiple genres, media and texts. My reading of *Lumpérica* and *Maipu*,
with Eltit's action of self-effacement, suggests a transtextual and multimedia continuum that spirals between fictional, corporeal and visual
performances. I use the concept of performance not only in terms of
theatrical or dramatic representation but also in the literal sense of
accomplishment, achievement and success. Consequently, a reading of
Eltit's performance will take into account how the work performs narratively as well as politically.

The context of the Chilean dictatorship imbues Eltit's work with a
sense of social and political urgency. Following the military coup of

September 11, 1973, anyone who even remotely supported Salvador Allende's socialist *Unidad Popular* lived under serious threat of "disappearance," torture, imprisonment and murder. During the early years of dictatorship, censorship gagged literary and artistic dissension, creating a state of cultural blackout, *apagón cultural*. In addition to physical repression, the regime fought to secure hegemony on ideological and discursive grounds. Women played a key role in this ideological struggle. The military government organized groups of mothers and wives (General Pinochet's wife headed the most important national organizations) who worked for the dictatorship by espousing the traditional values of family and patriotism. On a day-to-day level, women were encouraged to serve the country by working as volunteers for charitable organizations that maintained familiar and ecclesiastical institutions. Socially, these women did not act as autonomous subjects but rather they participated as auxiliary support within a hierarchical family paradigm.[3] Nuclear families were to support the great "national family," *la patria*, directed by the father figure Pinochet, purportedly to serve the will of God. Ultimately, the *discurso pinochetista* projected an image of the ideal woman within the symbolism of the Catholic Church, the Madonna.

Eltit addresses these concerns with a particularly eclectic brand of artistic activism. Rather than spearheading a clearly defined agenda, Eltit projects fragmented images of self-mutilating bodies. On one level, Eltit's narrative fragmentation evokes what one might call a realistic image of life under dictatorship. In his essay *La mala memoria*, Marco Antonio de la Parra insists that any accurate account of life during the dictatorship would have to be fragmented: "Todo relato de esa época si intenta ser lineal es falso, es un artificio posterior. Hemos sido fragmentados por la historia, convertidos en esquirlas, nos aferramos a la historia privada porque la pública ha sido volada en mil pedazos" (111). One way to read Eltit's experimental style, then, would posit that she mimetically represents the confusion of a society that has been blown to pieces. This is a plausible scenario, and the resulting imbroglio raises serious questions about the effectiveness of experimental art in politics. One must ask whether the interpretive "difficulty" of these texts undermines their subversive power. What does it mean to mutilate one's own body while living under a military dictatorship? And why write a novel ostensibly devoid of plot and apparent meaning?

My analysis twists together the formal and aesthetic elements of Eltit's experimentation with the political and literary notions of *repre-*

sentation. From a strictly literary perspective, Eltit's style situates her in opposition to any and all formulations of realism. In other words, her neo-avant-gardism resists the traditional status quo rendering of the literary canon as well as the easygoing plot constructions of popular literature. She turns the dominant representation of a novel inside out, rejecting even the possibility of representing reality in a clear unbiased viewpoint. It is crucial to note, nevertheless, that her approximation of literary deconstruction is inextricably related to a political agenda.

Eltit's novels constitute an extreme case of what René Jara in *Los límites de la representación* calls *novelas del ciclo del post-golpe*:

> Teorizando el golpe como un problema discursivo, estas novelas buscan plantearse como un contradiscurso que desplaza la coherencia aparente del discurso oficial, cuestionan los límites retóricos de ese discurso, y se proponen como una representación deliberada de los límites de la representación histórica tradicional y oficial. (6)

By accentuating the "limits of representation," Eltit discursively opposes the neo-fascistic sense of order imposed by the military dictatorship. The aesthetic, formal and structural fragmentation that is so pervasive in Eltit's work articulates a paradoxically coherent agenda of narrative obliteration. As Jara writes of post-coup narrative, "La literatura se viste de antilenguaje en oposición distópica al mito oficial para desplazarlo" (52). Through a process of narrative mutilation, Eltit displaces the narrative of national order. Needless to say, her strategy remains extremely controversial. At stake here is the role of fiction in politics. How can Eltit oppose the discursive order of the dictatorship via the medium of narrative fiction? If those in power project spurious images, can literature perform correctively? Can literature proliferate anything but analogous fictions?

Jean Franco describes Eltit as a writer who is "obliged to separate the political from the aesthetic" (70). For Franco, Eltit's literary experimentation pursues a different, less blatantly political tangent:

> Consider, for example, the case of the Chilean writer Diamela Eltit. She actively collaborated with the *Por la vida* movement, which stages demonstrations to publicize disappearance; she wrote novels that are so hermetic they seem to baffle critics, and she staged public performances such as kissing a homeless man or

reading her novel in a brothel in a poor section of Santiago. In this one author, we find a tangle of conflicting intentions: to act against the authoritarian state, to take literature symbolically into the most marginal of spaces, to work against the easy readability of the commercial text, to foreground the woman's body as a site of contention, to increase or exaggerate the marginality of art, and juxtapose literature's marginality to that of prostitutes, vagabonds, and the homeless. ("Going Public" 70)

Franco's summary, while critically insightful of Eltit's agency, starts from, what seems to me, a misguided preconception. Rather than separating "the political from the aesthetic," Eltit explicitly conflates the two realms. Highlighting the aesthetic nature of politics, she actively politicizes her exceedingly experimental fiction. In my view, Eltit's "tangle of conflicting intentions" reveals an understanding of the political and the aesthetic as inextricably related both to each other, and significantly, to narrative.[4] This is by no means an example of frivolous "postmodern" pastiche but rather is a complex political critique that opposes authoritarian predication. It is crucial to interpret Eltit performatively—to read not only what she "says" but what her work "does." Re-presenting authoritarian order through narrative confusion, Eltit produces antidisciplinary chaos in the regimes of literature and politics.

This chapter explores the way in which Eltit explicitly merges political and fictional issues within the discourses of performance and representation. She modifies the mimetic code not to reflect reality but rather to refract the "fiction" enveloped within the hegemonic image of reality. On a basic level *Lumpérica* constitutes a kind of narrative photo album. The novel represents the perpetual re-presentation of a woman in a series of different perspectives, viewpoints and media. *Lumpérica* continually rotates and superimposes this multitude of divergent images. The resulting confusion—scenes of schizophrenic vertigo— recall Jean Baudrillard's image of hyperreal implosion. There is no longer any distance between binary opposites. Referents and signs, images, bodies and texts overlap on the same depthless surface.

Lumpérica describes the plaza as a writhing entanglement of splintered words inscribed on bodies:

Nombres sobre nombres con las piernas enlazadas se aproximan en traducciones, en fragmentos de palabras, en mezclas de vo-

cablos, en sonidos, en títulos de films. Las palabras se escriben
sobre los cuerpos. (12)[5]

Superficially the novel inscribes a hyperreal palimpsest where reality
has been subsumed under fiction: "We live everywhere already in an
'esthetic' hallucination of reality. The old slogan 'truth is stranger than
fiction,' is obsolete. There is no more fiction that life could possibly
confront ... it is reality itself that disappears utterly in the game of
reality" (Baudrillard, *Simulations* 146–7). Eltit's layered series of representations of representations, nevertheless, stops short of adopting
Baudrillard's conclusion that everything is simulation. For Baudrillard,
"the contradictory process of true and false, of real and the imaginary, is
abolished in this hyperreal logic of montage" (122). Eltit re-presents
"this hyperreal logic of montage" precisely to reveal the convoluted
complexity inherent in political domination. In other words, she realizes, like Baudrillard, that "law and order themselves might really be
nothing more than a simulation" (38).[6] Rather than jettison the notion
of truth, however, Eltit distorts the "fiction," or simulacrum, of order.

Incapable of escaping discourse, Eltit turns to the representation of
spectacle as a means to clear performance space within representation.
Narratively she diffuses a hyperreal montage, superimposing bodies,
images and texts on the plane of *Lumpérica*'s plaza. What are the consequences of this "flat" compression of body, image and text? Are we left
with politically meaningless confusion? In Eltit's case I argue against
this dismissal. An aesthetic of flattening does not necessarily result in a
critical road kill, smashed by postmodernism on the side of the high-
way. As Olalquiaga writes, "The postmodern flattening of meaning does
not imply its disappearance but rather a shifting of registers that allows
the formation of new ways of signifying" (xvi). Eltit's (con)fusion of
signs leads to the formation of a practical space from which to perform
and project political resistance.

Eltit's (re)articulation of the discursive body corresponds to a performance that also performs. Eltit's performance *clears a critical space*
for critique and subsequent political/artistic performance. In maintaining
this position, I am not merely rehashing the theoretical cliché of a
subaltern resistance from within the monster's belly. Obviously, "literature" did not topple the neo-fascist military regime in Chile. Nevertheless, Eltit's critical performance creates a political opening, allowing
for writers and artists (including herself) to express and perform political
resistance in increasingly blatant defiance.

The bulk of this chapter focuses on Eltit's texts, particularly *Lumpérica*, in relation to the technological, discursive and political representation of her "performance." Of course her multimedia mode of expression did not merely emerge spontaneously. Before beginning my analysis of *Lumpérica*, then, I first sketch the historical context in which Eltit develops her poetics of political performance. Comprehending the ideological conflicts within the Left, both before and during the dictatorship, establishes the theoretical framework of Eltit's political and artistic strategy.

PERFORMANCE ART–POLITICAL PERFORMANCE

Eltit's intertwining of politics and art within performance developed while writing *Lumpérica* and collaborating with other artists in an avant-garde artistic collective. The group CADA (Colectivo de Acciones de Arte) denounced General Pinochet's authoritarian regime through radical performance actions and interventions.[7] CADA's manifesto aspired to marshal *real* political resistance and to mobilize popular unity while performing culturally—redefining the exclusionary parameters separating artistic creation from public interpretation and the corresponding production of meaning.

Nelly Richard, in her book *Margins and Institutions: Art in Chile since 1973*, contrasts CADA's interventions with the less sophisticated approach of Social Realism:

> El caminante chileno ya no dirige la mirada hacia los muros para ver adornadas sus superficies en el lugar usurpado de los graffiti, ni para suscribir los mensajes destinados a adoctrinarlo: ya no es solicitado como espectador de imágenes, sino como operador de arte, puesto que él mismo se encuentra corporalmente involucrado en la materialidad de una obra viva que lo hace parte de su trans-curso intercomunicativo. Y que lo convoca en torno a la urgencia de intervenir la red de condicionamientos sociales de la que es prisionero. (137)

For CADA, art "works" as a political tool, inspiring dialogue in the praxis of public life. In radical interventions, artists were to collaborate with their participating public to produce re-coded meaning in alternative paradigms. By dismantling the hierarchies implicit in both "high art" and the military dictatorship, CADA attempted to simultaneously subvert military authority and cultural hegemony.

Critics debate the effectiveness of CADA, both in eliciting popular participation and in facilitating "meaning." Hernan Vidal, for example, criticizes CADA's approach, which in his view reinscribes the vast material difference between classes, and respectively, between art and reality: "Las contradicciones del creador vanguardista se exacerban y aceleran, puesto que las necesidades del medio poblacional tienden a la sensibilidad realista" (*Poética* 144). Vidal criticizes a specific action, "¡Ay Sudamérica!" (1981), during which CADA dropped 400,000 flyers from airplanes into lower-class neighborhoods:

> Los creadores del *happening* pudieron haber entregado los vo-
> lantes en persona a los pobladores, si realmente querían estar
> próximos a ellos; mucho más cerca de los pobladores habrían
> estado si hubieran invertido el dinero gastado en los bimotores en
> el bienestar ... una escuadrilla de seis aviones toma aspecto de raid
> aéreo militar y no de aproximación amistosa. (146)

Nelly Richard, on the other hand, writes approvingly of this same action and the earlier, "Para no morir de hambre en el arte" (1979): "Son trabajos que se van conformando en la pluridimensionalidad social de sus soportes de materialización artística" (*Margins* 138). For Richard, CADA successfully integrates the popular classes and artists into a joint project aimed at politically redefining the function of art and community toward the betterment of quotidian conditions.

The ideological rift separating Vidal and Richard evokes a long-standing conflict that divided the Chilean Left in its struggle against the Pinochet regime. Richard describes two divergent branches of the Left—orthodox traditionalists and neo-avant-garde artists.[8] Whereas the former privileged open protest and political testimony, the neo-avant-garde aspired to reformulate dominant cultural standards:

> La ortodoxia militante de la izquierda tradicional privilegió aque-
> llas estéticas del testimonio ... Contra ese expresionismo de la
> contigencia batalló un segmento artístico y literario de corte neo-
> vanguardista empeñado en la reconceptualización crítica del pen-
> samiento cultural. ("Tres funciones de escritura" 37)

This critical debate remains far from resolved.[9] Vidal's call for realism echoes the opinion today of critics who celebrate the political efficacy of testimonial and reject nonlinear narrative as irresponsible distraction.[10] I am troubled by this opposition. Why should testimonial be lined up a priori against experimental fiction? Rather than placing fragmented narrative in opposition to testimonial, I would argue that nonlinear discourse provides an alternative mode of expression, which potentially can articulate coherent critiques of reality.[11] Diamela Eltit's experimental literature represents a prime example of this process. Although Eltit sidesteps testimonial's notion of a clear, univocal message, she does call attention to the "voiceless" and unrepresented inhabitants of the *lumpen*.[12]

In other texts, Eltit experiments with a radical form of "fictional" avant-garde testimonial. In her second novel, *Por la patria*, she uses a testimonial mode to relate the deliria of a group of women who survive prison and torture by the military. In *El padre mío*, Eltit literally transcribes the testimony of a schizophrenic street person. Although she deconstructs narrative stability, Eltit by no means abandons meaning and structure to an aesthetic hedonism, "anything goes." As Juan Carlos Lértora observes, Eltit does not refuse reality but rather renounces the illusion of realism: "Es de una ruptura respecto de la representación al modo de la ilusión realista tradicional, de una renuncia a la composición sistemática y racional" ("Categorías posmodernistas" 7). Occluding the realist image, Eltit leaves testimonial's concept of reality intact. In other words she accurately conveys the disorientation of life under dictatorship. She reproduces in narrative the incoherencies of oppression.

In spite of Eltit's infamous "hermeticism" many critics (including Richard, Ortega, Brito and others) have rigorously and correctly interpreted her texts as polyvalent narrative deconstructions of hegemonic power. At times, nevertheless, critics seem to isolate specific themes from her multifaceted critique. Her reinscription of the gendered body cannot and should not be separated from her political re(dis)articulation of discourse, her poststructuralist awareness of language nor the repression of the Pinochet regime. My analysis, then, aims to reconfigure these disparate interpretations (deconstructions of patriarchy, language and political power) together within the wider context of cultural, narrative and political performance.

Performance represents the common denominator of Eltit's work. Not only does spectacle play a key role in each of Eltit's "texts," but each of these respective performances dialogues intertextually. I do not claim that biographical analysis can "explain" *Lumpérica*, but Eltit's self-effacement, her public reading and the video *Maipu* function as formative episodes for the *mise en scène* that culminates with the publication of *Lumpérica*. I analyze key passages, seldom studied by critics, as significant components of Eltit's transtextual multimedia *performance action* in order to show that the ensemble of Eltit's work, like De Lauretis's conception of a critical feminist reading, "changes the representation into a performance which exceeds the text" (36).

LUMPÉRICA: READING BETWEEN THE SIGNS

Although all of Eltit's novels develop unconventionally, *Lumpérica*'s fragmented exposition surpasses them in terms of denying its reader a narrative line to follow. As readers we are severely disoriented—at times it seems impossible to determine who narrates and what exactly occurs. As the novel is virtually plotless—a transient woman, L. Iluminada, spends the night staring at a neon sign in a Santiago plaza—the action takes place on the level of narrative perspective. Third-person description alternates with first-person narration, ambiguous dialogue, and a kind of impersonal, often lyrical, textuality. How, then, in the midst of so much confusion, does one read *Lumpérica*?

Lumpérica, through all of its complications, explores the notions of narrative and language: "Libro que muestra al luminoso que vende: lenguaje será" (40). In many ways *Lumpérica* re-presents the interpretive process of reading *ad infinitum*. While the reader struggles hermeneutically to make sense out of the novel, diegetic characters "read" L. Iluminada's gestures for meaning. L. Iluminada, meanwhile, sits staring in the plaza trying to read the *luminoso*. The novel's conclusion corresponds to a literary epiphany: L. Iluminada, illuminated in the plaza, becomes "enlightened" as she decodes the luminous sign's message.

The *luminoso*, like a reversible hinge, plays a double role with relation to *Lumpérica* and L. Iluminada. The novel, in one respect, coincides with the illuminating apparatus of the *luminoso*, casting light on a street person in a Santiago plaza. *Lumpérica*, like the *luminoso*, projects L. Iluminada's image onto the printed page: "Y ella misma, que ha tomado su lugar, se va lentamente hasta su imagen y se pone bajo él para imprimirse" (31). L. Iluminada, printed in the plaza, coincides metaphorically with the text itself—the body, as it were, of the novel. Illuminated by the light and projected by *Lumpérica*, L. Iluminada reflects the enigmatic light: "Sus ropas grises reciben los tonos del luminoso. Le sirven de tela para su proyección" (31). Reading the sign, then, L. Iluminada teaches the reader how to read *Lumpérica*.

L. Iluminada specifically avoids the neon sign's immediate commercial advertisement: "Había recibido el mensaje, no del producto sino

del luminoso mismo, de su existencia como tal" (202). The commercial
messages represent mistaken, superficial readings: "evitando los men-
sajes aparentes que podrían haberla inducido a un errror por quedarse en
la superficialidad de la letra" (203). *Lumpérica*, nevertheless, seems
devoid of any apparent meaning. How can the reader decipher this narrative scramble? Significantly, L. Iluminada *constructs* her text by uniting elements from two consecutive signs: "Lo había logrado uniendo
las letras más distantes; las encendidas y las apagadas los cruces de
ambas, los signos que se construían en el medio, los aparentes vacíos,
el intercambio entre mensaje y mensaje" (203). To read *Lumpérica* the
reader, like L. Iluminada, must read "between the lines," constituting a
text by uniting the signs and traces of signs located at the interstices of
contiguous messages.

The *luminoso*'s flickering emissions evoke the narrative fragments
that oscillate throughout *Lumpérica*. Furthermore, what the text
neglects to expose, "los aparentes vacíos," is as important as what the
novel specifies. The irony of the situation expresses a hidden, subtex-
tual, political critique that, by going unsaid, becomes manifest symbolically. *Lumpérica*'s lack of plot can be explained on an immediate level
as a practical response to neo-fascist repression. By not naming the
military, Eltit writes around the dictatorship, and *Lumpérica* escapes
governmental censure. The novel, accordingly, revolves around a series
of voids. We never see the *luminoso* but only L. Iluminada, who reads
between the signs from an evacuated plaza.

L. Iluminada sits in a plaza staring at an advertisement whose commercial referent she cannot afford to buy. Her presence and the fact that
she (and *los pálidos*) are the sole recipients of the message infers the
repression of post-coup Chile. Interpreting contextually, the plaza
remains "empty" because of the military-imposed nocturnal curfew: "La
inutilidad de ambos—plaza y luminoso—en la noche la golpeó de
pleno" (203). Only the homeless remain in the plaza, precisely because
they have no home. Circumscribing its central referent, *Lumpérica* casts
light on the public plaza under the Pinochet regime. In other words the
novel inculpates the military dictatorship.[13]

It would be wrong, nevertheless, to reduce *Lumpérica* to a unified
"empty" allegory of post-coup Chile. The novel, like the *luminoso*,
proposes other concomitant messages that constitute its complex, and
ultimately open, polyvalency: "El luminoso caía con más fuerza
alcanzando a denotar incluso letras que, muy diluidas, no llegaban a
formar palabras. Pero allí estaban los grafismos que aceptaban más de

una interpretación" (204). Reading *Lumpérica* obliges a cumulative process, superimposing narrative fragments and re-presentations of these fragments, constructing, in Barthes's terminology, *un texte scriptible*,[14] "entre mensaje y mensaje" (203). And *Lumpérica* presents even more signs than the *luminoso*. Whereas L. Iluminada merges the components of two separate signs, *Lumpérica* barrages the reader with an array of different *grafismos*. How can the reader navigate through *Lumpérica*'s flickering sign field? Even if the novel signifies, via traces, the "holes" between signs, there must be something surrounding these symbolically loaded voids. What allows *Lumpérica* to function cohesively as a novelistic whole?

READING A MULTIMEDIA NOVEL

Although *Lumpérica* subordinates plot, reading between the fragments reveals a carefully coordinated structure. Literally a stack of paper, the book amasses a series of images superimposing each other and L. Iluminada in the plaza. Blurring and shifting the point of view, Eltit overlaps representations of diverse representational media. The challenge of reading *Lumpérica*, in this regard, corresponds to the task of reading a multimedia novel. It is significant that the media that Eltit evokes narratively in *Lumpérica* coincide with Eltit's multimedia performances. These performances both contribute toward the development of *Lumpérica* and extend the novel beyond its narrative boundaries. Later in this chapter I analyze Eltit's work in other media—video and skin—in relation to *Lumpérica* and Eltit's overall performance. Now, however, I would like to explore *Lumpérica*'s internal structure, as a novelistic continuum of multimedia representation.

Early in *Lumpérica*'s first chapter, after having established a rigorously detailed image of L. Iluminada in the plaza, the narrator evokes theatrical and filmic terminology:

> Ella, plenamente teatral por la observación de sus movimientos, camina erguida hasta el centro de la plaza para detenerse bajo la luz del luminoso ... Así se gesta su primera toma fílmica. (14)

Immediately following this *toma fílmica*, *Lumpérica* begins to read like a screenplay. Not only does the text re-present the image of L. Iluminada, *el luminoso* and *los pálidos* in the plaza, but the image widens to include cameras: "Ella está en el centro ... Una larga toma de tres minutos de duración en la que intervienen dos cámaras" (14–5). At this point it seems as if the novel's plot represents the process of making an experimental film.

This peculiar "film" underscores the theatrical aspects of society and social interaction.[15] The "actors," *los desarrapados*, are a group of impoverished transients. L. Iluminada performs for *los pálidos*, the cameras and the reader: "Ella se frota en su madera por el puro placer del espectáculo" (10). *Los pálidos*, as well, are on stage: "Han llegado ahora hasta ese mismo centro y empiezan su particular representación" (13). The neon sign, "esa luz que vende" (11) "baptizes," or represents the street people by giving them names: "El letrero que se encenderá y se apagará, rítimico y ritual ... les dará la vida: su identificación ciudadana ... Así serán nombrados genéricamente pálidos" (9). This "scene," then, represents a group of marginalized characters, a politically unrepresented *lumperío*, within the visual frame of cinema.

The narrative focus expands outward to include a level of meta-narrative criticism in which an implied director offers *comentarios, indicaciones* and *errores* of the first three scenes.[16] *Lumpérica*, from the first chapter, incorporates three narrative strata: *text*, presenting the image of L. Iluminada in the plaza; *textualization*, representing the process of filming L. Iluminada in the plaza; and *meta-text*, critiquing the performance and cinematography.

This narrative scheme, however, only scratches the surface of *Lumpérica*'s representational imbrication. In Chapters 4 and 5 ("Para la formulación de una imagen en la literatura" and "¿Quo Vadis?"), the visual image modulates to a specifically written, or literary, format: "Situación ahora no fílmica sino narrativa ... es una imagen completamente distinta para el que la lee ... como un zoom es la escritura" (99). Within this *escritura*, the plaza-as-stage metaphorically becomes text. *Los pálidos* and L. Iluminada align themselves, "como líneas ordenadas sobre la página" (105). These alternating perspectives, nevertheless, frequently transcend their boundaries: "Mirada y texto, cuerpo y mente se refrotan" (106). The novel itself, while constituting the exterior layer, or meta-text uniting the smaller fragments, fits conversely within the space of the "fictional" plaza: "Se abre así la novela, surgen los personajes, se los lee bajo la iluminación de la plaza" (106). At a later point this novel about a film becomes an essay that interprets a photograph (included within the text).

Lumpérica, accordingly, is composed of a collage of interrelated texts and self-reflexive meta-texts. Each of these layers embodies a narrative concretion, *mise en abyme*, that re-presents *Lumpérica*'s representation of L. Iluminada. The novel traces its own evolution, from the creative process(es) of its conception to the multiple readings produced through subsequent interpretation(s). In essence, *Lumpérica* self-reflexively interrogates the process of image construction. L. Iluminada corresponds to an ever-changing chain of fragmented images. Yet while her identity seems to be in a continual state of flux, her *situation* remains relatively fixed. A changing image remains always an image, regardless of its format. Film theory provides a theoretical paradigm— appropriate for interpreting both *Lumpérica*'s film and L. Iluminada's perpetually "moving" image. Examining L. Iluminada through the lens of feminist film theory, furthermore, focuses her situation within the crucial context of subjectivity.

SITUATING L. ILUMINADA: THE EMPTY
SPACE BETWEEN THE SIGNS

Laura Mulvey, in a well-known essay written in the early 1970s, pro-poses an aesthetic break with mainstream film in order to subvert patri-archal tradition in cinema. Her avant-garde agenda proposes an ambi-tious initiative to achieve critical distance in and through cinema. How can film, a medium predicated on the dynamics of voyeurism, shatter the voyeuristic gaze? For Mulvey, feminist film makers should destroy this element of "pleasure" (scopophilia) that is associated with narrative and that is oriented through the look of a male gaze.[17] *Lumpérica*'s film—focusing on an infected homeless woman, bleeding and convuls-ing in a plaza—might fulfill the endeavor Mulvey calls for.

The novel's film, with its faded colors and its lack of action, would provide limited "pleasure" to a viewing audience. The fractured narra-tive, furthermore, eschews the classical concept of symmetrical beauty: "Cayó en constantes equívocos, desconectando los diálogos, rescatando el tiempo en escenografías poco importantes. Se propició el desvarío en el lenguaje para alejar así la solución de la belleza" (83). In the Holly-wood films that Mulvey criticizes, voyeurism functions as a transparent apparatus of male libido. The viewer does not see the gaze but rather follows it unconsciously on the screen. The spectators then reinscribe the gaze from their places in the audience. In *Lumpérica*, while the reader voyeuristically observes L. Iluminada's spectacle, the novel markedly diagrams a network of intersecting gazes. In this case, how-ever, the gaze does not function as an invisible apparatus but rather calls attention to itself, constituting an obvious visual theme.

While L. Iluminada focuses on the neon sign, she herself represents the object of the gaze. Although she generally contemplates the sign and *los pálidos*, she also looks inward at her mirrored reflection. The pallid ones, in turn, huddle to stay warm and watch L. Iluminada (while she convulses, smashes her head, burns her hand, masturbates and collapses). The novel also describes the process of filming this voyeuristic spectacle. The cameras, then, film men watching L. Iluminada's narcissistic performance. Elsewhere, someone describes having scrutinized the film footage of L. Iluminada's fall. Ultimately the reader "watches" this entire matrix of reticulating gazes. This situation suggests a series of questions about the technical, aesthetic and ideological foundations of film making and, by extension, discourse.

The question presents itself as to whether or not the montage that comprises *Lumpérica* effectively inflects the pressure of voyeurism. The technique of montage alone does not necessarily reorient the gaze. Baudrillard observes that fragmentation can ultimately only reinscribe a central code: "Montage and codification demand, in effect, that the receiver construe and decode by observing the procedure whereby the work was assembled. The reading of the message is then only a perpetual examination of the code" (*Simulations* 121). If montage merely rearranges a male code, how can a text break out of the phallogocentric "groove"? The problem of the gaze in film converges with the problem of critical distance in language. As Helena Michie writes, "Feminist writers necessarily live and write at the center of a paradox; they are using patriarchal language to destroy patriarchy and the language it produces" (130). On one level *Lumpérica*'s "perpetual examination of the code" leads to a recognition of the manner in which the code functions. But Eltit does more than examine the code, she deconstructs it. Superimposing montage and performance, Eltit creates and employs a special kind of "body language." By fragmenting performance and performing montage, Eltit clears space within the paradox of discursive representation.

In *Lumpérica*, the narrative montage revolves around L. Iluminada's body, a nonidealized feminine figure, placed at the center of a plaza, a film and a novel. Her relationship to language constitutes the core of *Lumpérica*. Significantly, her language and thought patterns, as well as the novel itself, correspond to a distinctly scrambled code:

> Con la palma de la mano entre sus labios dice—tengo sed—y son
> sus mismos labios los que la hieren con sus movimientos. Pero en-
> tonces con la boca pegada a su mano comienza el sentido inverso

de su frase. Desconstruye la frase, de palabra en palabra, de sílaba
en sílaba, de letra en letra, de sonidos. Torciendo su fonética.
Alterando la modulación en extranjero idioma se convierte ... Ha
desorganizdo el lenguaje. (36)

This *situation*, a broken woman at the center of a chaotic code, recalls
an observation by Teresa de Lauretis concerning woman's place in
representation: "The position of woman in language and in cinema is
one of noncoherence; she finds herself only in a void of meaning, the
empty space between the signs" (8). In *Lumpérica*, the plaza—a void of
meaning, an empty space between signs—corresponds to L. Iluminada's
position of noncoherence in language and cinema, as well as society at
large. An analysis of the novel, then, should take into account the crucial significance of L. Iluminada's situation—the plaza—both structurally and contextually.

THE PLAZA AS FRAME: THE
MARGIN AS CENTER

While the narrative focus perpetually re-presents L. Iluminada from bag
lady to actress to pure textual inscription, her spectacle remains confined within an unnamed square in Santiago. The first and last chapters,
portraying a realistic image of the plaza, frame the passages of narrative
experimentation. In developing a chain of varying viewpoints, *Lumpérica* highlights a silent presence within the dimensions of the public
square. What, then, is the textual significance of mute, inarticulate
bodies within the spatial and metaphorical construct of the plaza?[18]
Bakhtin's theory of "grotesque realism" specifically highlights the
role of the body within the space of the public square. Bakhtin theorizes
the (medieval) plaza as the locus of popular theater where the employ-
ment of grotesque language leads to the destabilization and subversion
of political and social hierarchies. Although *Lumpérica* by no means
produces the carnivalesque laughter that Bakhtin associates with
Rabelais, the physical deterioration of L. Iluminada and the pallid ones
constitutes a modern permutation of grotesque realism. L. Iluminada's
festering body oozes into the world of the plaza much as Bakhtin
describes the grotesque body in contact with its environment:

> It is not a closed, completed unit; it is unfinished, outgrows itself,
> transgresses its own limits. The stress is laid on those parts of the
> body that are open to the outside world ... the emphasis is on the

apertures or the convexities ... the open mouth, the genital or-
gans, the breasts ... The body discloses its essence as a principle
of growth which exceeds its own limits only in copulation, preg-
nancy, childbirth, the throes of death, eating, drinking, or defeca-
tion. This is the ever unfinished, ever creating body. (Bakhtin 26)

Not only does *Lumpérica* focus on L. Iluminada's physical openings,
"Se vierte por los convencionales orificios" (172), but the protagonist
repeatedly opens and reopens her body: "Estrella su cabeza contra el
árbol ... indaga [la herida] con sus uñas" (19). In the Ensayo General
she progressively gashes open her skin. Elsewhere, she peels off the
scab, "retira la costra" of recently closed wounds (186). L. Iluminada, an
open body in an open plaza, exposes herself to the public gaze.

The plaza functions as a social vacuum, attracting Santiago's mis-
fits and transients who have nowhere else to go. These homeless
"desarrapados" seek warmth "inside" the public square at night. *Los
pálidos* return, "para permanecer allí con el cuerpo distendido" (28).
Attracted by the light, they shiver in the plaza with no protection from
the cold:

Porque permanecer tanto tiempo expuesto al frío y rigidez hace que
el cuerpo se agarrote.
diseminados como esculturas—intensamente pálidos—en la plaza
se estremecen las rodillas—duelen las orejas—escasea aire en los
pulmones. (28)

Their bodies, like the plaza, are unredeemingly open to the cold. Archi-
tecturally, the plaza corresponds to an open box. While *los pálidos* stare
at L. Iluminada, cameras, the narrator and the reader peer inside the
plaza, watching the lives of Santiago's homeless.[19]

At the same time, a first-person woman narrator looks at, touches
and enters the body of her narrative double: "Y mi cara de madona
mirando su cara de madona ... y toca interior su lengua profana ... toca
su pecho de madona y lo moja ... toca sus piernas de madona caliente...
y mis manos de madona abren sus piernas de madona y la lamen" (28–
30). The text later recasts this scene of lesbian intercourse in section
6.2 from the perspective of the originally passive woman:

Escribió:
como la más rajada de las madonas le presté mi cuerpo tirada en la
plaza para que me lo lamiera. (123)

This sexual intercourse, the physical spreading of her legs, leads to a feeling expressed metaphorically as openness: "me voy descascarando madona ... me abro" (128). She feels as if she is coming out of her body, leaving the skin that encapsulates her. Emotionally, then, whether the intercourse is understood as real or imaginary, physical or virtual, the character escapes the confines of her body. Physically, on the other hand, L. Iluminada remains perpetually framed within the plaza's quadrangle throughout the Santiago curfew. As María Inés Lagos writes, "su actuación ... se da en un lugar, Santiago, y en una plaza pública durante las horas del toque de queda en un país que sufre un estado de sitio" (136). Open both to the elements and to the public eye, the urban plaza represents a paradoxically closed space.

Raymond Leslie Williams characterizes *Lumpérica*'s plaza as a distinctly postmodern space: "The public plaza of Santiago de Chile in *Lumpérica* is a postmodern world of Jean Baudrillard, where human beings have the same exchange value as merchandise, 'as commercial products' and 'as merchandise of uncertain value'" (54). *Lumpérica* indeed explores the notion of "exchange value" of human beings, although this notion hardly constitutes a new "postmodern" condition. For Williams, the novel's meta-textual fragmentation evokes Baudrillard's hyperreal: "As the scenes in the novel are filmed and discussed, those conversations recall Baudrillard's admonition that 'there is no longer any medium in the literal sense; it is now intangible, diffuse and diffracted in the real, and it can no longer even be said that the latter is distorted by it'" (54). I would argue against this interpretation. Despite *Lumpérica*'s narrative distortion, the overall effect obliges a recognition of reality rather than nonreferential Baudrillardian hyperreality: "Porque sí el frío era real" (41). Although the novel represents a vertigo of images via a myriad of media and perspectives, the drab concrete plaza remains central. Rather than eliminating referents, the text pushes Santiago's marginal "others," the *lumpen*, conspicuously into the frame of a quotidian urban center.

LOS GRAFITIS DE LA PLAZA:
REINSCRIBING THE PUBLIC SQUARE

The sociological importance of plazas in Latin American culture goes hand in hand with the establishment of national and civic patrimony. García Canclini describes the plaza as a public stage where hegemony conditions (and represents) the official version of national identity:

> Se colocan en una plaza, un territiorio público que no es de nadie
> en particular pero es de "todos," de un conjunto social claramente
> delimitado, los que habitan el barrio, la ciudad o la nación. El
> territorio de la plaza ... se vuelve ceremonial por el hecho de
> contener los símbolos de la identidad, objetos y recuerdos de los
> mejores héroes y batallas, algo que ya no existe pero es guardado
> porque alude al origen y la esencia. Allí se conserva el modelo de la
> identidad, la versión *auténtica*. (emphasis original, 178)

Plazas not only showcase institutional representations of history in the
form of monuments and civic ceremonies, but they are also often sites
of protest gatherings from varied, even opposing, viewpoints. Monuments and plaza walls become transformed into public palimpsests
when inscribed with graffiti texts and murals. Graffiti, writes García
Canclini, "es un modo marginal, desinstitucionalizado, efímero, de
asumir las nuevas relaciones entre lo privado y lo público, entre la vida
cotidiana y la política" (316).

Lumpérica constitutes a graffiti-like reinscription of the national
plaza. The social space of the public square coincides with a narrative
plane: "Este lumperío escribe y borra imaginario, se reparte las palabras, los fragmentos de letras, borran sus supuestos errores, ensayan sus
caligrafías, endilagan el pulso, acceden a la imprenta" (116). The section, "Los Grafitis de la Plaza," typologizes page by page eleven different uses for writing: "La escritura como proclama ... como desatino ...
como ficción ... sentencia ... refrote ... evasión ... objetivo ... iluminación ... burla ... abandono" and "erosión" (123–33). Continually
altering the context, *Lumpérica* explores the progressive accumulation
of multiple meanings. At the foot of each page, lines of text appear as
would graffiti texts at the base of a plaza wall. The sentences or sentence fragments convey the sexual and poetic ambiguity characteristic of
actual graffiti.

L. Iluminada chalks graffiti on the floor of the plaza (in Chapter
5.3). The words she writes, "dónde vas," resonate differently depending
on who encounters her question. Is the protagonist asking herself, in-
trospectively questioning the direction of her life? Or does her question
address pedestrians, or *los pálidos*, passing through the plaza? Within
Lumpérica's self-reflexive, meta-textual context, the text's implied
author poses the literary equivalent, "Quo Vadis" (96). While writing
the novel, the implied author simultaneously analyzes herself, her
protagonist and ultimately her text-in-progress. On another level the

question speaks to *Lumpérica*'s pedestrian, the reader. Where are you going with this text? Finally, in the sociopolitical context, this graffiti pointedly addresses all of contemporary Chile: Where are you going now? To summarize, the graffiti text "sprays" outward, simultaneously constituting a number of diverging and interrelated messages. This performative urban literature does not merely dissolve but rather intervenes—reinscribing the city as text. The question still presents itself as to how this episode of urban inscription relates to the novel textually and how it figures in Eltit's political intervention.

INTERROGATING THE PLAZA: RE-PRESENTING REPRESENTATION

The graffiti, "dónde vas," also echoes *Lumpérica*'s enigmatic scenes of interrogation. Chapter 2, consisting of an absurd enquiry, probes the utility of a public plaza: "Me preguntó:—¿cuál es la utilidad de la plaza pública?" (45). The point of view alternates, irredeemably blurring the distinction between fictional character, narrator and author. At the chapter's onset a first-person narrator responds to questions. Suddenly, at the bottom of the first page, the narration switches to a third-person dialogue between *el interrogador* and *el interrogado*. The very point of the examination essentially disappears. Initially the interrogation focuses on the plaza, eliciting a detailed and never sufficient description:

> Es un cuadrado ... su piso es de cemento, más específicamente baldosas grises con un diseño en el mismo color. Hay árboles muy altos y antiguos y césped. A su alrededor se disponen los bancos; algunos de piedra y otros de madera. (47)

The topic of the interrogation changes abruptly, however, from the use-value of a plaza to "la caída de L. Iluminada" (55).

From here the focus scatters, creating an even more confused sense of narrative vertigo. The fourth scene compounds textual possibilities by overlapping "la proyección de dos escenas simultáneas" (54): "Tal vez una podría fundirse en la otra y así es el hombre (cualquiera) el que estuviera a punto de caer en la plaza ... sería a ella tal vez a la que interrogaban ... Si ella interrogara en cambio, de confusos asuntos habría tratado" (55). Far from clarifying the correct order of events, the text multiplies the confusion exponentially. The reader becomes trapped in a series of confounding questions. Who fell? Who interrogates? Who answers? And who, if anyone, witnessed this "event" (which may or may not have taken place)?[20]

Interrogation functions as a leitmotif that recurs thematically throughout *Lumpérica*. Contextually, the power dynamic between *el interrogador* and *el interrogado* evokes an encounter with the (secret) police in post-coup Chile:[21] "Alguien ya no estará allí, unos cuantos nombres serán borrados del kardex y el kardex destruido y la plaza dejará de ser importante. Vuelve a ser la decoración de la ciudad" (56). The *interrogador* demands obedience, forcing the *interrogado* to describe the plaza again and again: "Tenía que seguir el juego ... La obediencia era lo que correspondía" (48). The situation in the plaza alludes to the tenuous condition of contemporary reality under dictatorship. People simply disappear, their names erased. The public plaza becomes a superficial facade, a decoration, remodeled by those who *represent* the nation.

This scene of interrogation links the notions of political, technological and ideological representation. In the context of film, "cutting," corresponds to a reorganization of reality, framing specific perspectives, *tomas*, and re-presenting them in *cuadros*. In the editing process, cutting film both reduces and interrupts the original footage. Reconstructive splicing later results in a "produced" narrative. In Chapter 7, the cross examination regarding "la caída de L. Iluminada" eventually becomes an argument about the film. A dissatisfied director interrogates someone (an actor? a technician?) insisting that he restate, over and over, the sequence of events. From as early as Chapter 1 the novel and film repeatedly stop and restart, always subject to revision: "Supieron desde siempre que la escena sería rehecha" (41). This endeavor of cinematic reproduction, "rehacer la escena, reproducir ese original" (144), evokes the discursive manipulation of political representation and hegemony. The Pinochet regime, accordingly, strives to re-present Chile, recasting the film, as it were, and projecting an image of political order.

In time the interrogation uncovers a planned rebellion within the film. The *interrogado* confesses his guilt, attempting to derail the *mise en scène* by impeding L. Iluminada's fall and convincing her to abandon the script: "Le dije: si caes ahora no habrá posibilidad de rehacer este entarimado. Le dije: borra lo escrito ... esta caída es fragmentaria, tu parlamento está balbuceante. Retoma la voz, corrige la caligrafía" (147). The mutiny fails however when the planned subversion gets cut from the film:

Dio la voz de corte, pararon las máquinas justo cuando la muchacha mudaba la voz para decir por enésima vez '¿dónde vas?', que no lo dijo en realidad, sino con seguridad en mi oído dijo 'es tiempo

perdido me redujeron a cuadros y yo misma a letra y esos mismos a
acciones. (148)

The director, in other words, refuses the protagonist the right to represent herself. In this case then, the authority figure controls the image of
the public plaza. *Lumpérica* nevertheless re-presents the representation of (and in) the
public square again and again, projecting a montage of variously
cropped and overlapping images. Unlike political discourse, the novel
underscores its own representational apparatus, interrogating the notion
of representation at the same time as it continually re-presents the
image of L. Iluminada. This strategy approximates the Brechtian technique of destroying mimetic illusion. For Brecht, theatrical alienation
effects should expose the mechanical and structural apparatus that
constitute theater:

> There is a point in showing the lighting apparatus openly, as it is
> one of the means of preventing an unwanted element of illusion;
> ... If we light the actors and their performance in such a way that
> the lights themselves are within the spectator's field of vision we
> destroy part of his illusion of being present at a spontaneous,
> transitory, authentic, unrehearsed event. (Brecht 141)

The reader does not observe L. Iluminada unmediated in the plaza but
rather tracks the halting movement of cameras, *pálidos*, and onlookers
while they, in turn, reconfigure her image. Each time the reader settles
into one of *Lumpérica*'s modes of representation, narrative alienation
effects break his or her temporary identification.

In spite of these Brechtian *coups de théâtre*, *Lumpérica* effectuates a
subtly different performance. The spectacle takes place in a Santiago
plaza rather than a theater or simulated filmset: "La plaza será lo único
no ficticio de todo este invento" (25). By highlighting the divergent
images of L. Iluminada and *los pálidos* between different representational media, the novel generates a circular interrogation of representation in
the full sense of the word.[22] Images of L. Iluminada fuse indistinguish-
ably with her interminably re-presented body. Whereas Brechtian alienation effects foreground the simulation of theater, *Lumpérica*'s film conflates reality and performance. Unlike Brechtian theater, *Lumpérica*'s
reader perpetually wonders if L. Iluminada represents a spontaneous or
rehearsed spectacle. In lieu of contemplating the performance from a

secure critical distance, *Lumpérica* implicates the reader within the representation and interrogation of L. Iluminada.[23]

The episode of interrogation proves ultimately to be a scene in the same film it examines: "Anuncian en escena al interrogador y al interrogado" (147). In other words, it is a self-reflexive film within a self-reflexive novel. Early in this chapter I suggested that *Lumpérica* represents the process of reading and language. Interrogation, furthermore, corresponds to a subsequent link in *Lumpérica*'s signifying chain. The reader, analyzing the novel's respective interrogations, interrogates the text. By examining L. Iluminada under the light, the interrogation investigates the plaza, her situation and the scene in the film. *Lumpérica*, consequently, explores its own representational foundations and at the same time implicitly interrogates the reader about the situation in Chile.

Critical "interrogations" of *Lumpérica* lengthen the chain by examining the novel and previous analyses of it in the context of critical theory. It is specifically tempting to describe *Lumpérica* as a literary example of several feminist theories, particularly those regarding the body and its relation to subject formation. Critics have frequently cited *Lumpérica*'s spectacle as a process of feminine corporeal scripting that is analogous to Hélène Cixous's manifesto, "writing the body."[24] The passages of lesbian intercourse have led others to draw parallels with Monique Wittig's deconstruction of sexuality and Judith Butler's notion of "performative gender."[25] This same tendency—to "explain" *Lumpérica* by ascribing Eltit's work to poststructuralist theoretical paradigms— arises with respect to Eltit's discursive agency. L. Iluminada's eroticism and her condition of physical decadence, for example, recall Kristeva's notion of the "abject."[26] These observations, in many ways viable, help elucidate the respective theories. As a literary example, *Lumpérica* can provide textual body to theoretical treatises. At the same time, nevertheless, employing *Lumpérica* as a novelistic example of theory tends to oversimplify Eltit's poetics and *Lumpérica*'s narrative complexity.

An extended analysis of *Lumpérica*'s eighth chapter, "Ensayo General," underscores the transtextual interface between Eltit's corporeal and narrative bodies. In the Ensayo General (155–67) a narrator's body literally becomes text, inscribed by the blade of a knife in a series of six self-immolating incisions. Although nearly every critic briefly mentions the Ensayo, the series of textual *cortes* has yet to be analyzed in detail. The same critical omission exists with respect to Eltit's real-life performance of self-mutilation.[27] Significantly, a photo of Eltit's arms (see Figure 2-1), introduces the Ensayo, implying a concatenate continuity between the novel and Eltit's "art action." Although this reading of a continuum by no means implies an equal sign equating *L. Iluminada*, Diamela Eltit and the novel's implied author,[28] the Ensayo General constitutes the textual nexus linking Eltit's scarification, her novel and the video *Maipu*.

In my reading of the Ensayo General I attempt to flesh out how the chapter performs narratively, how it functions within the context of *Lumpérica*, and how this passage correlates to a crucial section of Eltit's overall performance. Explicating the Ensayo reveals an assemblage of different variations of incision. This systematic manipulation of mutilation leads to an understanding of how Eltit's performance responds to the problem of critical distance. Before concluding, I discuss Eltit's inscription in relation to Roland Barthes's theory of textual body, "Le plaisir du texte." Although Eltit's text superficially resembles Barthes's narrative body of *coupures* and *jouissance*, this skin-deep correlation masks a profoundly divergent political agenda. First, however, a critical "dissection" of the Ensayo General will reveal an internal reflection, or *mise en abyme*, of *Lumpérica*'s general representation.

THE ENSAYO GENERAL:
NARRATIVE MUT-IL-ATION

Eugenia Brito correctly posits a relationship between the incisions and *Lumpérica*'s syntactical and narrative fragmentation: "La rotura de la piel coincide con la rotura—la ruptura—de la sintaxis y con la ruptura de un sentido único" (172). Eltit shreds language—pulling words apart into syllables, substituting mathematical and orthographic symbols, varying the typeset, altering syntax and substituting words from slang, underground and indigenous vocabularies. Nevertheless, while she tears language apart this mutilation results in a reconstituted, poetic language that releases the myriad shards of meaning contained within words.[29]

The Ensayo General begins with three one-line verses (E.G. 1, 2 and 3), each of which occupies an entire page. These enigmatic fragments (preceding the series of epidermal incisions) represent a passage of narrative laceration. While tearing words apart, the text paradoxically liberates and mutates a multiplicity of images. The first page:

Muge/r/apa y su mano se nutre final-mente el verde des-ata y maya
se erige y vac/a-nal su forma. (152)

Figure 2-1. Diamela Eltit's self-mutilated arms from *Lumpérica*.
(Photograph courtesy of Lotty Rosenfeld.)

poses a problem in determining who is the subject. Based on the conclusion of the preceding chapter, "Se encenderá la luz de la plaza. Seguirá el espectáculo" (148), the text infers L. Iluminada as the subject. Yet the Ensayo highlights the polyvalent multiplicity inherent in language. Multiple meanings resonate between the connotations of poetically charged vocabulary, as well as between privileged and hyphenated syllables. The phrase, like the novel, cannot be translated into a unified logical sentence structure. It projects, on the other hand, a wide spectrum of images that relate to the novel's central scene. L. Iluminada (mujer rapada) alternately ties and unties (des-ata) the lewd (verde, bacanal [vac/a-nal]) narrative "forma," *Lumpérica*. A hybrid figure (woman/animal: vac/a-nal su forma, se nutre ... el verde), her mind wanders in the vacant plaza. Illiterate, she moans and mews (muge, maya), faints (des-maya) and then erects herself (se erige), feeling pleasure in unleashed (des-ata, a-nal) animalistic hedonism.

E.G. 2, equally enigmatic, continues to compound images with multiple meanings. Again the text initially evokes L. Iluminada as subject:

> Anal'iza la trama=dura de la piel: la mano prende y la fobia
> es/garra. (153)

On one level, this page suggests the figure of L. Iluminada in the plaza. *Lumpérica*, from the beginning, presents the protagonist examining her weatherworn face in a mirror: "Se devuelve sobre su propio rostro, incesantemente recamada, aunque ya no relumbre como antaño cuando era contemplada con luz natural" (9). While sitting in the plaza, L. Iluminada traces the contours of her body, rehearsing the lines that she will literally inscribe as text in the coming pages: "Se toca la piel en el mismo momento en que se curva más aún sobre el pasto, hasta que la cabeza cae sobre la tierra reblandecida" (12–13). Her hand (la mano prende) superimposes images emanating from the verb *prender*, meaning "to grasp," "adorn," and "catch fire." At the end of Chapter 7 she grips the chalk with which she writes on the plaza floor: "Tiene tiza entre los dedos" (148). In Chapter 1.4 she deliberately burns her hand in the fire: "Frente a la fogata acerca su mano, adelanta su mano sobre las llamas y la deja caer encima" (35). Finally, toward the end of the novel, after cutting off her hair, L. Iluminada embellishes her appearance with a necklace: "Guardó las tijeras ... Sacó un collar de pedrerías. Se lo puso alrededor del cuello" (207).

While the narrative fragmentation of these lines implies a series of imbricated images, reading the Ensayo produces a hermeneutic sensation akin to L. Iluminada's disorientation. As I observed earlier, L. Iluminada (at the center of an experimental film in a fragmented novel) is cognitively, psychologically and linguistically confused:

> Ella deja oír restos de lenguaje, retazos de signos. Socavada por tierra y pasto ... Se observa a sí misma, como si su nombre le otorgara rasgos diferentes. (13)

This confusion, which the novel reiterates hermeneutically, is a crisis of narrative. Notice how Jean-François Lyotard's description of a crisis of meta-narrative could be recontextualized to describe *Lumpérica*: "The narrative function is losing its functors, its great hero ... its great goal. It is being dispersed in clouds of narrative language elements" (xxiv). *Lumpérica*'s perplexing narrative fragmentation reproduces L. Iluminada's unclear awareness of herself as subject.[30] The Ensayo General "hacks up" *Lumpérica*'s already fragmented subject.

The Ensayo's (con)fusion of images and ruptured narrative significantly increases the text's projection by implying a multiple series of simultaneous subjects. Whereas "Anal'iza la trama=dura de la piel" infers L. Iluminada, the phrase also evokes *Lumpérica*'s implied and historical authors. While L. Iluminada examines her image in a mirror, Diamela Eltit performs an analogous repetition. She gazes at her narrative reflections—her implied author (diamela eltit), who in turn contemplates L. Iluminada. At the same time, Eltit turns her gaze outward to the shattered mirror of contemporary Chile,[31] analyzing the shredded fabric of Chilean society. Reading the *luminoso, Lumpérica* and the situation in Chile, this series of female images raises a symbolic flag of mutilated skin ("iza la trama=dura de la piel"). Finally, this Borgesian chain of authors and mirror images reflects back to the reader who analyzes the difficult "cut-up" narrative.[32]

Mutilation, then, constitutes yet another process in *Lumpérica*'s perpetual re-presentation of representation. E.G. 1, 2 and 3 distort, mutilate and mutate the image of L. Iluminada in the plaza. The resulting textual ambiguity produces a (con)fusion of subjects—L. Iluminada, diamela eltit, Diamela Eltit and the reader—on parallel narrative planes. This passage of linguistic laceration gives way to an apparently *linear* section in which the narrative clearly describes a series of epidermal incisions. As I have mentioned before, Eltit subjected herself to an analogous episode of mutilation. Reading her corporeal effacement will underscore the multimedia and transtextual continuity of her performance. First, however, a close examination of the narrative incisions will exemplify the consistency of Eltit's expression.

READING INCISIONS: REHEARSING AN
IN-SCRIPTING PERFORMANCE

How does one read a cut body as text? Much as L. Iluminada teaches us how to read between the *luminoso*'s signs, the Ensayo General presents narrative directions for how to read *Lumpérica*'s fragmented performance. The corpus of the Ensayo clearly draws parallels between physical incisions and writing as textual in-scription. The text orients the first cut on her left arm and presents it as a mark, or *sign*: "Horizontal sentido acusa la primera línea o corte del brazo izquierdo. Es solamente marca, signo o escritura que va a separar la mano que se libera mediante la línea que la antecede" (155). Breaking the corporeal unity, the line marks a boundary that bisects her arm. Applying the structuralist conception of language—meaning derives from difference—the cut-body-as-text would be read by comparing the respective sections on each side of the incision.

The second gash acquires significance through comparison with its predecessor, "Es manifiestamente más débil ... está regido por el primero del brazo" (156). Reading the body allows for several divergent forms of conceptualizing the text. One could highlight the actual incisions as *signs* or, alternatively, measure the skin between the lines. The essay's implied author interprets the third incision in relation to the pattern previously established: "Está fallado al interrumpir en una línea oblicua el sentido horizontal de las líneas anteriores ... mirada en conjunto con las otras—acusa una errata o bien el intento por cambiar de recorrido" (157). This "error," or change of direction, recapitulates the experience of reading *Lumpérica*. As soon as one begins to follow a narrative line (L. Iluminada in the plaza, a film of her, an interrogation, an evaluation of the film and so forth) the novel interrupts its progression and changes direction.

Following the third "line" the text severs the narrative series of incisions, shifting to a meta-textual analysis of the preceding pages. This self-reflexive "cut," splitting the Ensayo General by delaying the progression of epidermal scoring, recalls the interrupted film shoot from the previous chapter: "Dio la voz de corte, pararon las máquinas" (148).

Within this interval of frozen narrative the text interrogates the first three slices individually and in relation to one another: "El primer corte, si es aislado, es el ensayo general. ¿Es realmente un corte? Sí porque rompe con una superficie dada ... El corte es el límite. Entonces ¿cuál es la frontera? ¿el corte mismo? No, es apenas la señal" (158). The Ensayo General, then, probes the cutaneous incisions of its exposition with (cross-cut) meta-narrative *cortes*.

The following page begins parenthetically, hence separating the series of epidermal and narrative lacerations orthographically. This new narrative *corte*, "(En relación al corte de la fotografía)" (159), widens the meta-textual implications of the Ensayo General. Whereas the preceding section reads and analyzes the narrative in-scription, the text now examines a photographic reproduction (in other words, a representation) of the incisions *sub judice*. This section specifically examines a photograph of Eltit's lacerations (included in the original edition) in the context of photography (such as in framing the image or cropping the print).[33] This photograph of lacerated skin renders a two-dimensional, flattened image: "Se lo aplana en el rigor de una nueva superficie" (159). Viewing the photograph, the reader's eye cuts open the surface image, "rota por el ojo que corta allí su mirada" (159), much as a reader cuts through the text. The eye's hermeneutic potential remains limited, nevertheless, to linear interpretation: "El ojo que lo lee ... se encarcela en una lectura lineal" (159).

Accumulating questions and returning to the sequence of epidermal slashing, the text problematizes a linear reading by inverting the chronology. The Ensayo "chops up" and precariously reconfigures the narrative order of incisions that it had previously established. The reader no longer knows where to enter the series, because "el tercer corte podría haber sido el primer corte que se hizo" (160). The complications compound progressively with the remaining incisions. The fourth slice, itself physically interrupted "por un fragmento de piel," evokes two (logically divided) hypotheses related to both time and depth:

(a) La línea fue realizada en más de una etapa.
(b) La hoja que efectuó el corte se levantó levemente. (162)

In the fifth cut, the text introduces burn to create a new surface variation: "Se inscribe sobre (o bajo) la epidermis quemada, que se ha vuelto a ciencia cierta barro, barrosa, barroca, en su tramado" (163). The text continues to superimpose epidermal mutilations until a final sixth incision becomes subsumed and expelled by the burnt flesh (now blistered and showing a raised scab and the traces of singed hairs; 163–6).

The Ensayo General, in summary, consists of an open series of epidermal, narrative, temporal, logical and visual *cortes*. The text obstructs the individual incisions with skin fragments and then splits the narrative sequence, thereby reading, analyzing and dividing itself. Finally, on the last page of the Ensayo General, the focus moves backward to encompass the entire subject, who poses in the plaza gripping the knife: "Hace frío, y tal vez sólo por eso tiende su pose en la plaza ... Los dedos de su mano derecha sostienen la pequeña y afilada hoja. Sin mirarse la acerca hasta su cuero" (167). Significantly, as she raises the knife to her skin on the *last* page of the "Ensayo" (meaning "test," "essay" and "rehearsal") she has yet to inflict any incisions: "Se va a iniciar el Ensayo General" (167). Chronologically, then, by juxtaposing the last cut cyclically to the first, the Ensayo rehearses a circular performance of in-scription.

As in Barthes's *texte scriptible*, "il n'a pas de commencement; il est réversible; on y accède par plusieurs entrées dont aucune ne peut être à coup sûr déclarée principale" (*S/Z* 12). This cyclical pattern repeats concentrically (textually and meta-textually as well as structurally and thematically) throughout the novel. The fictional time line, beginning at nightfall and ending in the morning, represents a "slice of life" in terms of a temporal cycle. The interrogation scenes, rehearsed repeatedly, "como una escena circular ensayada una multiplicidad de veces" (141), re-state the events perpetually re-produced in the film. *Lumpérica* itself is an open series of *cortes* that perpetually revises itself, reconfiguring the image of L. Iluminada in the plaza. Even the last scene leads into the novel's opening. Written to be re-read, *Lumpérica* plausibly "begins" at the novel's end, Chapter 10, when L. Iluminada cuts off her hair, and it continues to the following dusk (Chapter 1.1) when she burns and cuts her skin.[34] This cycle of *mutilation–inscription* can be traced throughout the novel's editorial history as well. The photograph of Eltit's arms was cut from the second edition. Furthermore, when the second edition did not sell well, the press shredded or chopped up the unsold copies. Planeta has since published a third edition (1998) and reincorporated the photograph.

The Ensayo General marks the convergence of culture and discourse via a metaphor of an inscriptive performance. García Canclini explains culture in terms of representation: "Toda cultura es ... producto de una puesta en escena, en la que se elige y se adapta lo que se va a representar

... Las representaciones culturales ... son siempre re-presentaciones, teatro" (187). Hegemony, in other words, is inscribed through a cultural performance that simultaneously edits out subaltern discourses. The Ensayo General underscores the process of dominant cultural inscription on the stage of the public plaza and throughout society at large.[35]

This circular chicken-and-egg continuity linking incision, inscription and representation also holds true between Eltit's real-life action and L. Iluminada's spectacle. From a biographical and historical perspective, Eltit's action precedes the publication of *Lumpérica*. Her self-mutilation, then, corresponds to a pre-textual in-scription that initiates and motivates her novelistic representation. As she writes in the Ensayo General, "Lo verídico de los primeros cinco cortes más las quemaduras es pensarlos, por ejemplo, como pose y pretextos" (165). Although the novel and video constitute subsequent texts that record, document and re-present Eltit's action, this chronology can be inverted. In the video *Maipu*, Eltit displays her recently burnt and slashed arms while reading from *Lumpérica*'s manuscript. Accordingly, the fictional episode of incisions prefigures the author's self-immolation. Eltit's performance, in other words, rehearses the scene of in-scription narratively delineated in *Lumpérica*'s Ensayo General. Before considering the expression and implications of Eltit's overall performance, nevertheless, it is crucial to "read" the articulation of Eltit's scarified body-as-text.

(RE)ARTICULATING THE DISCURSIVE BODY

In her essay, "Las retóricas del cuerpo," Nelly Richard interprets Eltit's self-mutilation as a political protest predicated on the exercise of personal sacrifice: "Esas prácticas de mortificación corporeal ... se inscriben en la tradición primitiva de los sacrificios comunitarios que ritualizan la violencia como una manera de exorcizarla" (*Margins* 142). Accordingly, sacrifice derives from the paradigm of Christianity whereby self-inflicted pain unites individual experience with a collective identity and suffering: "Como si, al analogizarse las marcas del deterioro autoinflingido en el cuerpo del artista con las marcas de padecimiento inscritas en el cuerpo nacional, el dolor y su sujeto se colectivizaran en una misma cicatriz" (142). For Richard, Eltit symbolically assumes the violence of the Chilean dictatorship by gashing and burning her body.[36]

This reading of a mutilated national body constitutes a coherent national allegory representing the violation of the military coup. Nevertheless, while this *embodiment* of the political context is valid, it merely traces Eltit's largest and most general metaphor. Furthermore, this mechanism of corporeal rhetoric denounces the military siege of Chile via a strategy analogous to the same allegorical discourse that the military government manipulated. If from the fascist perspective the coup was necessary to save the mother *patria* from evil communist infection, a self-sacrificing mutilation only projects the inverse—a national body that has been raped.

Reading *Lumpérica* as a national allegory, while essentially correct, ignores the performative component of Eltit's (re)articulation of the discursive body. *Lumpérica* does not merely represent the violence of neo-fascism symbolically. In addition, the novel systematically reads and deconstructs the discursive and representational violence that precedes and legitimates oppression. Rather than countering the hegemonic discourse by replacing the fascist allegory with another allegory, Eltit displaces the former and proceeds to efface her own narrative allegory.[37]

Lumpérica deconstructs, re-presents and subsequently self-de(con)-structs. By carving her skin as text Eltit's performance embodies her awareness of the poststructuralist paradigm, in which the binary concept of critical distance proves paradoxical. She can no more get outside of language or discourse than she can escape her body. Eltit represents a wounded body as she simultaneously mutilates the discursive and representational texts—official discourses, her novel and her body. She slashes herself in protest while also affirming the power to re-write (and represent) her own body. (Re)inscribing herself as text, Eltit constitutes a transtextual performance—she seizes control of her body and represents a multimedia series of corporeal, literary and visual texts.

The only critic noting the transtextual continuum linking Eltit's action, *Lumpérica* and *Maipu* is Nelly Richard in a study describing genre crossing as a trend among CADA artists. Richard describes *Lumpérica* as a novel that represents a narrative performance while actualizing another, external, performance:

> "Lumpérica" (1983) recopila en su interior las instancias en las que deja de ser libro para existir como performance, o en las que se funde en una triple exterioridad: *biográfica* (el sujeto-mujer protagoniza un trabajo de estigmatización corporeal mientras lee parte de la novela de la que es autora), *social* (el burdel donde ella lee como escenario de explotación sexual) e *interproductiva* (el arte, el cine o el video, como "otros" de la literatura). (*Margins*, emphasis original, 147)

Lumpérica, in this regard, goes beyond the traditional boundaries of a novel. Representing L. Iluminada's performance, *Lumpérica* constitutes one crucial phase in Eltit's overall performance. "Reading" the video *Maipu*, furthermore, helps bring the full extension of Eltit's perform-ance into focus. *Maipu* documents Eltit's performance at the same time that it embodies L. Iluminada's fictional spectacle.

FROM 'LUMPÉRICA' TO 'MAIPU' AND BEYOND: TRACING THE PROJECTION OF ELTIT'S PERFORMANCE

> A critical ... reading of the text, of all the texts of a culture, in-states the awareness of that contradiction and the knowledge of its terms; it thus changes the representation into a performance which exceeds the text.
>
> —Teresa De Lauretis

In *Maipu,* Eltit reads *Lumpérica*'s Chapter 4.4, "De su proyecto de olvido." Focusing on minute details of her body, the narrator compares herself to her unnamed twin: "Las uñas de sus pies son a mis uñas gemelas" (87). Meta-textually, the passage suggests a parallel between "diamela eltit" (90) and her fictional character/*gemela*, L. Iluminada. The author re-presents herself narratively, depicting her textual body in minute physical details: "Cada uno de sus dedos es cubierto por múl-tiples granulaciones, intransables líneas" (89). Ultimately, both of these bodies constitute symmetrical texts bearing parallel lines of inscription: "Sus brazos son a los míos gemelos en su simetría ... Muestran en la transparencia de la piel el trazado venoso que los circunda" (89). The passage then conflates three corporeal subjects—narrator, protagonist and author.

"De su proyecto de olvido," nevertheless, like *Lumpérica* in gen-eral, ambiguously implies a number of simultaneously plausible sub-jects. It is far from clear who narrates the passage and to whom she compares her body. The confusion created by overlapping subjects recalls Barthes's deconstruction of (hermeneutic) grammar, "La lecture, l'oubli," in *S/Z*:

> *Je lis le texte.* Cette énonciation ... (sujet, verbe, complément) n'est pas toujours vraie. Plus le texte est pluriel et moins il est écrit avant que je le lise; je ne lui fais pas subir une opération

prédicative ... appelée *lecture,* et *je* n'est pas un sujet innocent ...
Ce "moi" qui s'approche du texte est déjà lui-même une pluralité
d'autres textes, de codes infinis, ou plus exactement : perdus (dont
l'origine se perd). (emphasis original, 16)

For Barthes the process of reading (writerly) texts transcends the grammatical hierarchy implied between reader, writer and text. Eltit as well
subverts grammatical structure, conflating subject(s), verb(s) and
object(s). Eltit represents narrative pandemonium—a (con)fusion of
images and words, of *lumpen* and América, of bodies and texts, of
authors, protagonists, readers, films, interrogations, spectacles, performers and performances *ad infinitum. Lumpérica* superimposes this
kaleidoscopic projection onto the screen of the public plaza:

Nombres sobre nombres con las piernas enlazadas se aproximan
en traducciones, en fragmentos de palabras, en mezclas de vocablos, en sonidos, en títulos de films. Las palabras se escriben
sobre los cuerpos. Convulsiones con las uñas sobre la piel: el
deseo abre surcos. (12)

On the surface, then, Eltit's orgy of bodies, signs and language evokes
what Barthes, in *Le plaisir du texte,* refers to as *jouissance.*

For Barthes, a *texte de jouissance* imposes a multifaceted and, at
times, difficult relationship with the reader: "celui qui met en état de
perte, celui qui déconforte (peut-être jusqu'à un certain ennui), fait
vaciller les assises historiques, culturelles, psychologiques, du lecteur,
la consistance de ses goûts, de ses valeurs et de ses souvenirs, met en
crise son rapport au langage" (25–6). Not only does Eltit's experimental
narrative require the intellectually engaged reading that Barthes
cultivates, but *Lumpérica* incarnates similar corporeal and hedonistic
metaphors as Barthes's theory: "Le texte a une forme humaine ... mais
de notre corp érotique" (Barthes 30). A close reading of *Lumpérica*
reveals an endless series of production, cleavage and reproduction of an
erotic textual body. As Barthes writes, "Le plaisir en pièces; la langue
en pièces; la culture en pièces" (82).

Nevertheless, in spite of the correlation between corporeal and literary metaphors, Eltit's novel does not fit neatly into Barthes's aesthetic
mold. Andreas Huyssen points out that Barthes's distinction between
jouissance and *plaisir* "reintroduces, through the back door, the same
high culture/low culture divide ... which were constitutive of classical

modernism" (Huyssen 42–3). Although Eltit's (neo-avant-garde) novel hazards sophisticated literary experimentation, she attempts (perhaps ingenuously) to subvert the hierarchy of cultural elitism. As Huyssen observes, for Barthes "there are the lower pleasures for the rabble, i.e., mass culture, and then there is the *nouvelle cuisine* of the pleasure of the text, of *jouissance*" (emphasis original, 42). Eltit, conversely, represents a different version of textual *jouissance*, that, unlike Barthes, regards society's margins as the locus of a significant "culture."[38] Barthes's *literary* theory ignores political contradiction, reveling instead in the cultured joy of high art: "The euphoric American appropriation of Barthes' *jouissance* is predicated on ignoring such problems and on enjoying, not unlike the 1984 yuppies, the pleasures of writerly connoisseurism and textual gentrification" (43). For Eltit art, culture, politics and discourse intertwine inextricably within the incestuous *jouissance* of the *lumpen*.

Significantly, Eltit's performance of *Lumpérica*'s manuscript takes place in a brothel (located on Maipu Street in Santiago). By reading in a space where women's flesh is routinely rented, Eltit implies a parallel between literary production and prostitution. By publishing *Lumpérica*, Eltit sells both a narrative body, L. Iluminada, and her own textual/sexual body.[39] As she writes in *Lumpérica*, "el luminoso anuncia que se venden cuerpos. Sí, cuerpos se venden en la plaza" (13). Eltit's reading evokes images of L. Iluminada, while at the same time addressing an audience of prostitutes attending her performance. The last line of the chapter, "Su alma es a la mía gemela" (90), for example, might be translated as either "Her soul [L. Iluminada's] is the twin of my soul," or "Your soul [the audience's] is the twin of my soul," due to the ambiguity of the subject pronoun *su* in Spanish.[40] Consider also the novel's title, *Lumpérica*, which conflates three terms, *lumpen* (underground), *perica* (Chilean slang for a prostitute) and *América*.

Historically, as Luce Irigaray writes, women correspond to passive objects that are circulated among men for pleasure and reproduction: "Woman is traditionally a use-value for man, an exchange value among men; in other words, a commodity ... *Women are marked* phallically by their fathers, husbands, procurers. And *this branding determines their value* in sexual commerce" (emphasis added, 31). *Lumpérica*, accordingly, is sold on the literary market, where its commodity value is configured by the consensus of critics. And yet by marking herself, by inscribing her own body as text, Eltit critically underscores the traditional dynamic of woman as commodity. Although she cannot completely invert the market principle, she calls attention to the obscene exploitation inherent in the gender economy. Her performance in *Maipu*, consequently, situates the brothel as a locus of narrative. She explicitly inserts herself (and her text) within the narrative–sexual market economy. "Aunque no es nada novedoso," she writes in *Lumpérica*, "el luminoso anuncia que se venden cuerpos" (13). Further, she addresses prostitutes, who are traditionally the goods sold, not the sellers or critics. This gesture recontextualizes both *Lumpérica* and prostitution, highlighting an act of literature within the covert space of the brothel.

Eltit's conflation of literature and prostitution thus works simultaneously in two directions. If marketing a novel corresponds to selling one's body, prostitution, conversely, sells fiction. Prostitutes create and exchange fictional fantasy for payment. Feigning physical desire in exchange for money, prostitutes perform in a world of fiction. As the text specifies, "en esos años se dividió entre la ficción y la ficción de sus oficios" (83). *Lumpérica* not only exposes reality through fiction but markedly underscores the constant play of fiction in reality. "Reading" *Maipu*, furthermore, indicates a signifying chain of texts, images and performances in perpetual flux between reality and fiction.

Maipu reveals an extraordinary sequence of interconnected *mises en abyme* that constitute the continuum of Eltit's multimedia performance. The video text explicitly foregrounds Eltit's arms, focusing on her skin literally in-scribed as text. As Peter Brooks writes in *Body Work: Objects of Desire in Modern Narrative*, the process of corporeal inscription indicates a transformation of the body into a literary text that can be interpreted: "The bodily mark is in some manner a 'character,' a hieroglyph, a sign that can eventually, at the right moment of the narrative, be read" (22). Eltit, a woman/text, sits in front of a camera reading *Lumpérica*. Significantly, *Maipu* presents Eltit in the process of reading her work-in-progress. The video, accordingly, documents a temporary stage in *Lumpérica*'s textual evolution. Several times the camera focuses over her shoulder, revealing her typed manuscript replete with handwritten corrections. Eltit, a woman/text, sits reading (on camera) *Lumpérica*-in-progress. The definitive *Lumpérica*, in turn, represents (and re-presents) L. Iluminada, a woman/text, who sits reading the *luminoso* while performing on camera.

The meta-textual relationship that defines these representations of representations can also reverse direction. *Lumpérica*'s manuscript appears as content in *Maipu*, comprising both audio and video image. *Lumpérica*, conversely, displays a video still from *Maipu*—a double projection of Eltit's face—on the cover (of the original edition). *Projection* works as the lynchpin of Eltit's double-edged critique. While the successive images of incision-becoming-script retreat farther and farther into fictional representations, Eltit's act of self-mutilation, the novel and the video spiral outward to protest all-too-real social, political and discursive violations. The political reality she opposes, in fact, authorizes and constructs a violent fiction.

Chilean neo-fascism projected its own fictional representation of an ideal woman—the Madonna—and placed her prominently upon a pedestal.[41] Susana Santos catalogues the stereotype created by the "discurso pinochetista" for Chilean woman as an ideology in which "woman" appears not as a historical person or subject but rather as an idealized object:

> Es una esencia permanente e inalterable, pertenece a una naturaleza no biológica sino social, sometida a leyes inmutables. Es considerada objeto de la historia, no sujeto. Es espíritu, no cuerpo. Pertenece a un orden axiológico, determinado por el Poder. (8)

Diamela Eltit's *Lumpérica* knocks this ideological sculpture off of the pedestal and places her inverse image center stage in the public plaza. Eltit displaces the mythical Madonna and replaces her with L. Iluminada (and *los pálidos*). And yet Eltit not only mutilates the fictional woman, but she furthermore effaces the pedestal—the discourse—that supports the Madonna image. As Julio Ortega writes, Eltit's text goes beyond a mere inversion of the power hierarchy: "Reemplazar el patriarcado con el matriarcado solo confirma las jerarquías. Se trata, por lo tanto, de poner en crisis el sistema mismo de representación ... Desconstruir el discurso de la representación para construir el habla de un sujeto femenino plural" (54). Eltit's narrative shredding constitutes a neo-avant-garde performance, both deconstructive of narrative, and narratively poetic. Eltit radically re-presents narrative to articulate a critique that mutilates the fascist image of national, cultural and political unity.

Let us now return to my initial question of whether or not Eltit establishes critical distance. I have been arguing that she generates a multimedia and transtextual *performance* that re-presents the allegorical figures and the representational projections of dominant discourse. Furthermore, I emphasize that rather than merely displacing and replacing the official discourse with a subaltern representation, Eltit paradoxically effaces and deconstructs her own counterdiscourse. *Lumpérica*'s self-reflexive awareness demonstrates that both hegemonic and counter-hegemonic representations are products of infinite repetitions of signifying displacements. How, then, within this signifying quagmire is it possible to measure critical distance?

Rather than establishing *distance*, Eltit (con)fuses her critique with(in) the system of representational discourse. Presupposing the irresolvable aporia that no text can get outside of language and that no countercultural critique escapes from its host culture, Eltit marks off an internal space that can be visualized metaphorically as a performance within the frame of a public square—internal, precisely because of her awareness that both she and her narrative are represented (but not silenced) by the images, laws, representations and realities of an infinitely complex hegemonic matrix. The performance dynamic, constituting a dialogue between spectator and performer, instates an active process of communication that exceeds monological pronouncement. An audience gathering around a performer delineates a circle whose circumference both separates the performer from the surrounding city and at the same time attracts more spectators to view and interpret the performance. Eltit does not explain her position but rather writes, reads and *performs* narrative. The hermeticism of her performance, consequently, reflects an agenda that avoids and denies authoritarian predication.[42] Instead of "informing" her public, Eltit vies to provoke thought and action.[43]

Eltit's performance cannot be succinctly explained. Rather than a concise meaning, a frame-by-frame analysis of *Lumpérica* produces a montage of overlapping images. I am aware, however, that even while stressing *Lumpérica*'s polyvalency, my reading traces a continuous line through Eltit's intentionally cut-up narrative. The line I propose, nevertheless, spirals and frays in such a way as to annul beginning and end. Rather than closing the text, interpreting *Lumpérica* as a key episode in Eltit's *performance* expands the textual corpus from a fragmented novel to an open series of corporeal, literary and visual episodes. Reading this performance reveals not only what the text says but also how it performs narratively, socially and politically.

Eugenia Brito writes that the publication of *Lumpérica* inaugurates a resurgence of "resistance literature" in Chile:

> No es casual que justamente fuera a partir de esta novela que la literatura de la Resistencia viera aparecer a la ciudad y sus habitantes en el espacio literario abierto por D.E. Posteriormente a la apari-

ción de Lumpérica, su primera novela, la ciudad va a circular más
libremente en la literatura chilena. (167)

Eltit's performance, then, carves an opening within the hegemony of
post-coup Chile. The ensemble of Eltit's texts functions, both individually and intertextually, within the context of her literary, artistic and
political action. Much as each episode of *Lumpérica* contributes to L.
Iluminada's *mise en scène*, each of Eltit's "texts" plays a protagonizing
role in the representation of a performance that exceeds the text. Cutting
through and across narrative, images, discourse and flesh, Eltit realizes a
performance that in turn performs critically, clearing a space for critical
performance and politically trenchant critique.

LOS VIGILANTES: *WATCHING POWER PLAY*

Because *Lumpérica* contributed to the articulation of a literature of resistance and the Chilean political system has moved toward a democracy
because of that resistance, it is significant to consider how Eltit's
writing has evolved during the transition to democracy. Eltit's recent
novel, *Los vigilantes* (1994), reiterates her interest in exploring the
margins of society, the political implications of language and the
manner in which discourse marks and determines disparities of power.
As in her other works, she conjugates this text as a (con)fusion of signs
that cannot be reduced to any single or definitive meaning. Magdalena
Maíz-Peña emphasizes the manner in which the novel's fragmented
"textual hybridity" leads to a multiplication of potential meanings:

> Es una conjunción de fragmentos, montaje de voces y pulsiones,
> mezcla de texturas, de saltos semánticos y sintagmas quebrados, de
> silogismos narrativos mutilados y en transformación que colocan
> al lector en la intersubjetividad de una realidad carente de significa-
> do fijo, delimitado, jerárquico. (33)

In spite of this unfixed and open-ended narrative, a close analysis of the
text reveals a coherent structure, a plot, and a subtle political critique.
The novel is structured as a triptych, in which two chapters of a
mentally disabled child's stream of consciousness frame a collection of
letters written by his mother.[44] *Los vigilantes* provides a glimpse
inside the minds and lives of a dysfunctional family on the verge of
disintegration. The novel is an exercise of voyeurism: The reader

observes the mother and child while the mother and child observe the neighbors, the child's father and the father's mother. These, in turn, are themselves in the process of spying on the lives of mother and child. This obsessive observation of a family's private space goes on to transcend the confines of a particular family. A close textual reading of *Los vigilantes* underscores the manner in which Eltit's novel represents contemporary "democratic" Chile as a transparent "seeing machine," much like Michel Foucault's concept of a panoptic society in which individuals are implicated in the processes of societal control. My contention is that *Los vigilantes* can be read as a metaphor evoking the network of social relations shaping contemporary Chile. In essence, *Los vigilantes* represents and observes the matrix of panoptic power relations affecting Chile during the transition to democracy.

If power is the central preoccupation of *Los vigilantes*, language certainly constitutes its medium and framework. Since her early experiments with linguistic shredding in *Lumpérica*, Eltit has interrogated the manipulation of language and the transparent consequences of official (hegemonic) discourse. Contemporary feminist critics often refer to the paradox of language when discussing the difficulty of articulating feminist critique. How can women write feminine or feminist texts, they ask, when language itself is a patriarchal structure? Gabriela Mistral, on the other hand, expresses a very different, women-centered, viewpoint. For Mistral, Sara Castro-Klarén explains, language begins with the mother as she teaches her child to name the items and things of the world.[45] *Los vigilantes*, a novel in which the central characters are a mother and her child, is an exploration of language, writing and power. My point is not to argue for an inherently feminine or masculine structure of language but rather to highlight the manner in which Eltit's novel situates reading and writing at the center of a struggle for power between mother and father that is staged on the body of their son. The child embodies a pre-verbal form, a "larva" (13). His actions, games, appearance and health are arbitrary signs that do not carry fixed meanings. The adults surrounding this child attempt to invest his signs with meaning. "Tu hijo se ha convertido en un pretexto" (52) writes the mother. Here she asserts that the child serves as a pretext for the mother-in-law's intervention in their lives. At the same time this pre-verbal child represents a pre-text on a meta-textual level. The child-larva and the conflictive meanings that emerge from the signs of his behavior, appearance and body constitute the textual and conceptual frame of *Los vigilantes*.

The second and central chapter of the novel is composed of a series of letters written by the mother to the father of her child. Although the reader has access to only one side of this epistolary dialogue, it becomes clear that we are witnessing an uneven power struggle. In the first few letters, their disagreement centers around the child's education, his expulsion from school and when (or if) he will re-enroll. The tension builds as she responds to more and more accusations of alleged negligence and misconduct that will ultimately deny her custody of the child. After losing the trial, the woman refuses to cooperate. She flees with her child, abandoning her house in the city—a controlled space of law and order—and moves outside to the streets as a homeless *desamparada*. Ironically, outside of her house she remains somewhat less exposed to the public gaze.

The title, *Los vigilantes*, echoes throughout the novel. The mother complains in her letters of haunting invasions of privacy and personal space. Eltit's lyrical prose evokes the expanding invasion of the public into the private with alliteration and specular repetition. "Mi vecina me vigila y vigila a tu hijo," she writes, "se dedica únicamente a espiar todos mis movimientos" (29). In subsequent letters she insists that other neighbors also spy and that the ubiquitous surveillance penetrates the city streets: "La vigilancia ahora se extiende y cerca la ciudad" (32). She complains frequently of surprise inspections by the father's mother. As the threat of the court case nears, the tone of her letters varies. Whereas she threatens to kill her child's father in one letter (45–7), she begs for forgiveness in the next (48–50). Desperate to avoid *un juicio* that will separate her from the child, she answers his accusations with a range of strategic responses that, when considered together, form a pattern of repetition. Initially she denies his claims; subsequently, she admits some truth, insisting, nevertheless, that he has misunderstood the gravity, intent and details of her actions. This cycle of denial, confession and plea bargaining raises some doubts as to the accountability of the narrator's word. At the same time the reader understands that this mother–letter writer is losing a desperate struggle for custody and power.

The father, an absent figure throughout the novel, maintains an invisible presence of constant and apparently menacing surveillance. Though we never see him nor read his words, this father is ever-present—in his absence he paradoxically occupies the center of the city and the novel. Like the guard in the central tower of the Panopticon, this father sees without being seen. Notice that *Los vigilantes*'s father-mother conflict involves each of the major elements of what Foucault calls a panoptic disciplinary society. Although conceived initially as a model prison, Bentham himself wrote that the Panopticon correlates equally well to the design of hospitals, insane asylums and schools. According to Foucault, panopticism serves to position individuals within their place in society so as to avoid contagion, to educate, to discipline, to sort out confusion and to guarantee social order. Indeed *Los vigilantes* presents education, protection from contagion, discipline, mental health and social order as the major themes motivating the dispute between the mother and father figures. Whereas their early domestic disagreements center around "una correcta educación" for their child (33), her contact with homeless *desamparados* raises the related issues of public health and civic order. The boy, consequently, must be watched, observed and examined by a physician (92).

In the (hegemonic) goal of "el orden contra la indisciplina" (110) the neighbors have passed laws against aiding the homeless. Via the perpetual exercise of never-ending vigilance the neighbors attempt to maintain social and civic order: "Persiguen una ciudad inmaculada ... Han decidido volverse los guardianes de las calles" (64–5). By highlighting the themes of education, civility, health and order, *Los vigilantes* underscores the network that links them together institutionally and socially. "Is it surprising," Foucault asks, "that prisons resemble factories, schools, barracks, hospitals, which all resemble prisons?" (228). Each of these institutions strives for social order through panoptic principles of continual vigilance, seeing, and the constant threat of being seen. The world of *Los vigilantes* has become a giant seeing machine that functions independently and impersonally, through and with its own momentum: "La vigilancia ahora se extiende y cerca la ciudad. Esta vigilancia que auspician los vecinos para implantar las leyes, que aseguran, pondrán freno a la decadencia que se advierte" (32). As Foucault conceives of panoptic society, "It has become a transparent building in which the exercise of power may be supervised by society as a whole" (207). In the absence of a dominant authority figure overseeing his subjects, the society of *Los vigilantes* functions as a mechanism of self-supervision.

Los vigilantes does not specify when or where the action takes place. The mother/letter writer imagines her court case as an event outside of history, "cuya concurrencia va a marcar el arbitrario y maligno signo de los tiempos" (100). Maíz-Peña describes the narrative as a novel enacting both social and historical (con)fusion: "*Los vigilantes* se vuelve signo de épocas, puestas en escena, dramatizaciones de pre y postmodernidades, de presentes y pasados históricos e histéricos y deformaciones sociales, políticas y culturales de terrores contemporáneos del colonialismo, dictadura, y catástrofe ecológica amenazantes" (33). Although certain aspects of the novel resonate with the repression of a dictatorship—"En las calles," writes Eltit, "se ha instalado el gobierno de la parte prohibida de lo público" (53)—it seems to function more as a pseudodemocratic legal network of surveillance. Power is not exercised here through interrogations by the secret police as in *Lumpérica* (1983), or by the military in the violent *redadas* of Eltit's second novel, *Por la patria* (1986), but rather functions through neighborhood networks of surveillance. As Jean Franco writes, "this society works through the internalization of regulations on the part of citizens who act as vigilantes" ("Afterword" 234). The process, as Eltit evokes it in *Los vigilantes*, is one not of imposed authoritarian discipline but internalized cooperation. Ever watchful, the neighbors perpetually gather information that can be presented in court in an effort to maintain a semblance of civic order. Foucault's description of a panoptically controlled society specifies the democratic nature of the institution: "The disciplinary mechanism will be democratically controlled, since it will be constantly accessible ... [It] enables everyone to come and observe any of the observers" (207). Eltit presents the Santiago of *Los vigilantes* as a self-perpetuating panoptic seeing machine. Always subject to potential surveillance the neighbors in Eltit's novel become the subjects of their own incarceration: always watched, always watching.

   Though my reading explicitly focuses on the dynamic of social control in the novel, images of order/disorder recur on a number of related literary and linguistic levels. Narrated through the mind of a child who cannot speak, the first and third chapters comprise thoroughly (con)fused fragments of language, logic, syntax and skin: "Mamá no está tranquila, lo noto en su pantorrilla engranujada. Tiene muchos pedacitos de piel desordenados. Desordenados. Los dedos que tengo están enojados con su desorden" (13). Reading through the (con)fusion of images, nevertheless, the reader perceives the presence of a subject, albeit an indecipherable subject, who thinks and reads in a language all his or her own. This pre-verbal child observes his mother in the process of writing the letters that will comprise the center of the novel: "Ahora mamá está inclinada, escribiendo. Inclinada, mamá se empieza a fundir con la página. A fundir" (16). Watching his mother while the world observes them, the child reads his mother's thoughts. As she contemplates her words on the page, the child sees his mother/writer becoming one with the text. Although he cannot speak or express himself linguistically, the child engages in an enigmatic game with his *vasijas*. His mother repeatedly attempts to glean some kind of meaning from his cups; she attempts to *read* them as if the child were manipulating an unknown code: "Me propone acertijos que yo debo resolver. Sé que hay una clave, una leyenda, un rito, una puesta en escena, una provocación en cada una de las ordenaciones" (92). Her effort to interpret the child's cup game evokes an embedded *mise en abyme* of *Los vigilantes*. The narrator/letter writer attempts to read the logic of her child's prelinguistic game while the reader attempts to read the novel—to read simultaneously the mother's reading of the cup game, the child's thoughts and her readings of the father's letters. The child describes his mother's posture: "Ahora mamá está inclinada, escribiendo. Inclinada" (16). She describes his cup game in language that recalls his reading of her relationship to her writing: "Tu hijo *se inclina* ahora sobre las vasijas" (emphasis added, 87). She spends considerable time, furthermore, attempting to read the (child's) father's letters (which the reader never directly sees). In the case of these implied letters she describes their coded intent as manifestly transparent: "Entiendo la clave de tus juegos con mayor precisión que las adivinanzas que me plantea tu hijo. Porque es evidente que tú dictas una ordenación en la que yo soy la única pieza" (93). Text, in Eltit's novel, constitutes a coded encounter between reader and writer that implies two different processes of order: ordering the signs in the construction of the text, on the one hand, and subsequently, the imposition of an interpretive order onto and with this text on the other.

The significance of language and writing in *Los vigilantes* cannot be overestimated. The mother realizes that her writing will be used against her, that the words that she writes to express her innermost feelings will be used as proof in the trial: "Las palabras que te escribo pueden llegar a ser catalogadas como anárquicas, una agrupación furiosa asegurará que son ininteligibles" (109–110). The question presents itself as to who will catalogue her words. Franco points out that the recipient of the letters represents an abstract power figure: "The addressee may be the child's father, or a guardian figure but he is also a more abstract entity—the name-of-the-father, or the divine" (234). This question of the absent, power-wielding father plays a crucial role in the novel.

Obviously, the theme of the absent father is not unusual; it has been ubiquitous in contemporary Spanish American literature at least since Rulfo's *Pedro Páramo*. In the Chilean context, nevertheless, the paradoxical presence of an absent father bears concrete political implications. During the dictatorship, Pinochet explicitly adopted a (neo)fascist authoritarian rhetoric wherein he presented himself as the "father" of the people. Though absent from his role of dictatorial father today, the general who secured himself a position of Senator for Life continues to exercise considerable power in Chile. As of March 1998, retired General Pinochet remains very much present in the Senate, the Constitution (which he had rewritten long before stepping down from the presidency) and the neo-liberal economic policies begun during his regime that continue to rule Chile. Note the subtitle to Marco Antonio de la Parra's *Carta abierta a Pinochet: Monólogo de la clase media chilena con su padre*. De la Parra explicitly describes Pinochet as a power-wielding father, paradoxically absent and omnipresent in Chilean politics as well as the Chilean psyche: "Ustedes han vencido ... Tienen derecho a contar la historia. Nosotros ... al monólogo con el padre ausente. O el padre omnipresente, que no contesta cuando le hablan, al que da miedo hablarle" (26). This image of Pinochet-as-father is reminiscent of the father and his position in *Los vigilantes*. According to this reading, Eltit's novel (and De la Parra, four years later) put a new register on the image of the absent father. Rather than describing a family in need of a man, the situation here would be a case of an abusive father who won't go away.

I do not mean to definitively identify, and hence limit, the role of the father in *Los vigilantes* with Pinochet, though he certainly represents many of the same ideas. In his "Mensaje a la mujer chilena" speech of April 1973, Pinochet referred to his government as the "autoridad *vigilante*," charged with the responsibility to oversee the nation's honor and moral integrity, and to permanently stamp out the threat of international communism (emphasis added, 16). In her reading of Pinochet's "Mensaje a la mujer" speech, Mary Louise Pratt observes the manner in which Pinochet assigns women the traditional role and educational responsibility of motherhood:

> Women are told that, following the traditions of "the West" (*el occidente*), their "mission as women and mothers" has been and remains to defend and transmit spiritual values ... educate and instill consciousness and conscience, and serve as repositories of national traditions. (152)

In *Los vigilantes* some of Pinochet's privileged vocabulary surfaces in the mother's responses to the letters of this absent father: "Dices que ... hemos olvidado los modales de Occidente" (71). Power has indeed become diffused in the transition toward a democratic Chile, but it remains closely tied to the hands (literal and political) of the dictatorship's absent father.[46]

When I presented an earlier version of this analysis at a conference, one colleague responded that my depiction of contemporary Chile seemed "exaggerated." He had recently returned from Cuba, where in his experience "everyone always feels watched." "But not Chile," he insisted. I have no basis to comment on his contrast with Cuba, which is irrelevant to my current study, but will stand by the metaphor for Chile. The recent installation of cameras in downtown Santiago is a case in point. In order to control *delincuencia*, Carabineros employ a highly sophisticated computerized observation center that allows for 24-hour surveillance. This dynamic of constant observation is not limited to police enforcement, however. According to Tomás Moulian, in *Chile Actual: Anatomía de un mito*, observation constitutes a key component in the contemporary enthusiasm for shopping malls: "Vigilancia ... es muy importante porque satisface la neurosis paranoica del Chile Actual, representa la garantía de estar siempre observados por un Gran Ojo" (113). Seeing and being seen in a safe environment provides a stage on which to enact the neo-liberal consumerism that characterizes present-day Chile. A brief description of the political situation, furthermore, may help to underscore the condition of *confinement* that informs Eltit's narrative depiction of panopticism in contemporary Chile.

The central thesis of Moulian's recent analysis, *Chile Actual: Anatomía de un mito*, presents the current image of democratic Chile as a "myth." Chile has undergone not a "transition" to democracy, a process that would imply progress, but rather in Moulian's terminology, "transformism." For Moulian, the democratic image of contemporary Chile was prepared during and by the dictatorship to obtain consensus and to legitimate the basic structures of the regime's politics. "Llamo transformismo," Moulian writes, "al largo proceso de preparación durante la dictadura, de una salida de la dictadura, destinada a permitir la continuidad de sus estructuras básicas bajo otros ropajes políticos, las vestimentas democráticas" (145). Moulian sustains that the Chilean legal, political and economic systems remain trapped within the Constitution, "una jaula de hierro," which the regime imposed in 1980 (49–56). This Constitution, which the *Concertación* agreed to after finalizing negotiations for the transition to democracy in 1989, guarantees the presence of nonelected "designated" senators from the Armed Forces, and specifically a position as *senador vitalicio* for Pinochet. A legal "headlock" proves even more restricting than the symbolically charged presence of the Armed Forces in the government. Unable to obtain a quorum to change the Constitution, the Chilean legal system and society remain essentially *caged*. Eltit's novel, *Los vigilantes*, takes place in this type of "protected democracy" wherein the application of the law enacts a foregone conclusion.

As the child's mother well knows, her letters will be read, catalogued and judged in a court of law where they will be used to represent her as an unfit mother. This description of her anarchic writing, furthermore, also evokes clear parallels with the novel itself. Doubtless some critics will dismiss *Los vigilantes* as an anarchic, unintelligible text just as they have done with each of Eltit's previous works. But in spite of the novel's confusing ambiguity, I argue that a close reading of this ambiguity can lead us to a significant, though not foregone, conclusion. While reading the second chapter of *Los vigilantes* one tends to empathize with the mother. It appears that the absent father figure and the ever-spying neighbors violate the private life of the mother and her child. She seems to be a woman of integrity whose mistake—she welcomed homeless people into her home—bears witness to her upstanding character. Her self-contradictions and admissions of falsity, however, do cast some doubt on this reading. At one point she claims that her parents are long dead (57); in the next letter she admits they live but explains that for her they have been long dead (60). She insists repeatedly that she cares diligently for their child, until the final chapter when we learn that she has abandoned the house, become homeless and, for all practical purposes, has turned into a nonfunctional child. No longer writing, the task of explanation now falls back to her son: "Mamá ahora no escribe porque busca confundirse con la noche ... Mamá ahora no habla y se mece en una esquina ... Mamá ya casi no tiene pensamientos. Solo tiene la baba y su risa" (121–6). At this point we witness a complete role reversal with the child, who now, out of necessity, must care for his mother. Chapter 3, "BRRRR," represents an inversion of the first chapter "BAAAAM." Here, the child has not only assumed the role of caring for his now nonverbal mother, but at one point forces her to swallow her own breast milk:

Extraigo las últimas, las últimas, las últimas gotas de leche del
pecho de mamá y pongo mi boca en su boca. En su boca. Mamá
siente su leche en la boca y quiere escupirla, pero yo le cierro la
boca con todas las fuerzas que tengo. Que tengo. La obligo a tragar
su leche. Su leche. (127)

Observing this nonfunctional mother wandering aimlessly through
the streets, the reader may question initial assumptions of her condition
as innocent victim. Perhaps the father's accusations of negligence were
somewhat warranted? Perhaps she was indeed an incompetent mother,
unfit to care for their child? At the same time one might argue that the
father drove this woman out of her house, broke her and pushed her into
the streets. Franco correctly observes that the novel stages, instead of
resolving, crises of multiple possibilities: "Eltit's method is to stage
two possibilities—either Woman reacts to the rules that she cannot
alter, or she is outside rational thought. The novel brings both these
possibilities into crisis. Eltit is not in the business of suggesting solu-
tions" ("Afterword" 235). The point of *Los vigilantes*, I would agree, is
not to choose sides but rather to contemplate and investigate the matrix
of power. "Quise trabajar una ambigüedad," Eltit herself responds in an
interview: "Los discursos no son definitivos. Yo aquí estoy jugando
mucho con los códigos. Son códigos de sobrevivencia. Juego con el
sistema" ("Interrogando" 297). (Con)fusing the signs of civility and
power, Eltit forces the reader to enter the *juicio* of signification. *Los
vigilantes* represents the contemporary social system as an imperfect
system of signs, a (con)fusion of signs that, though arbitrary in terms
of meaning, remains subject to the monological imposition of order
that emerges from within the panoptic mechanism. Foucault argues that
individuals exist inextricably inside of a play of power that manifests
itself as a conflation of signs:

The play of signs defines the anchorages of power; it is not that
the beautiful totality of the individual is amputated, repressed, altered by our social order, it is rather that the individual is carefully
fabricated in it ... We are neither in the amphitheatre, nor on the
stage, but in the panoptic machine, invested by its effects of
power, which we bring to ourselves since we are part of its mechanism. (217)

Rather than choosing sides, then, Eltit's novel represents the ambiguity of the system itself. In his description of *Los vigilantes* as a novel of "counterpoints," José Luis Samaniego comments that Eltit demands active participation of her reader: "Es posible hablar de un contrapunto entre autor y lector, pues el primero propone al segundo un ejercicio pensante, de cooperación activa, en el desciframiento de su discurso" (204). It is important to emphasize that this counterpoint between the author and the reader bears serious political consequences. *Los vigilantes* does not merely present the reader with a gimmicky hermeneutic game. Eltit evokes an active reader in order to underscore the complicitous role that the reader plays in this text specifically and in the larger (panoptic) social "text" of contemporary politics.

The father figure, addressed always in the novel as "tú," has no name. Toward the end of the chapter, when the mother acknowledges that she has lost the judgment, she writes that she no longer knows who the father is: "¿quién eres? ¿en qué vecino te simulas? ... ¿Desde qué dependencia oficial has emitido tus ordenanzas?" (115). Ultimately, Eltit forces the reader to occupy the position of authority, to interpret the letters and to impose the law of signification and order on the novel. *Tú*, then, in the case of *Los vigilantes*, corresponds to a multiple entity. *Tú* signifies the father as well as you and me, all of us—*los vigilantes*—watching and being watched, somewhere in the middle of the seeing machine.

NOTES

1. To date Diamela Eltit has published six novels: *Lumpérica* (1983), *Por la patria* (1986), *El cuarto mundo* (1988), *Vaca sagrada* (1991), *Los vigilantes* (1994), and *Los trabajadores de la muerte* (1998). *Los vigilantes* was awarded the Chilean prize Premio José Nuez for best novel in 1995.

In addition she facilitated a "testimonial," *El padre mío* (1989), transcribing (and prologuing) the words of a schizophrenic street person. Her other recent book, *El infarto del alma* (1994), is a collaboration with the photographer Paz Errázuriz.

She was awarded a Guggenheim grant for literature in 1985 and a grant from the Social Science Research Council in 1988. In the political sphere she was appointed cultural attaché for the Chilean Embassy in Mexico during the administration of Chilean President Patricio Aylwin, 1990–94. The most comprehensive bibliography of work about Eltit appears in Juan

Carlos Lértora's *Una poética de literatura menor: La narrativa de Diamela Eltit* (1993).

2. I should note that Eltit's videos (produced in collaboration with Lotty Rosenfeld) are unavailable commercially and have never been distributed. When I asked Eltit for a copy, promising that I would not redistribute them, she assured me that the videos were merely *ensayos* of limited interest: "¿a quién pueden interesar esas cosas?, sin contar que son trabajos de una máxima precariedad, ni siquiera son piezas audiovisuales formales, más bien ensayos en los que deposité parte de mi locura" (fax to the author, Oct. 27, 1993). *Maipu* is not a carefully crafted work of art but rather is a videographic document that registers a key episode in Eltit's political and literary performance. Eltit's choice of the term "ensayo," furthermore, underscores the pertinence of considering her performance actions together with the "Ensayo General" of *Lumpérica* (which I propose in this chapter).

3. On the role of gender in the Pinochet coup, see Sonia Montecino's *Madres y huachos: Alegorías del mestizaje chileno*. Montecino *partially* inverts the image of women's passivity with respect to the coup. In her chapter on "maternal politics," Montecino describes how right-wing women took to the streets (before the coup), clattering cookware and protesting what they perceived as the communist rape of the Chilean *matria* (motherland). While this political intervention implicates these women in the rise of Chilean (neo)fascism, Montecino points out that these women situated themselves within the patriarchal discourse as mothers, calling on male soldiers to restore a traditional state of order (103–10).

4. In her article "Remapping Culture," Franco recognizes some feminist agency in Eltit's work: "It is too easy to dismiss as 'elitist' middle-class women writers who have chosen to write difficult or self-reflexive prose, since frequently (as in the case of Diamela Eltit and Cristina Peri-Rossi) they address questions of women's sexuality or the definition of aesthetic desire and pleasure, which generally have been represented in masculine terms. On the other hand, to consider their testimonials as major alternatives to the prevailing literary institution is problematic" (183).

5. All quotations from *Lumpérica* are cited parenthetically with the pagination from the 1991 edition of Editorial Planeta Chilena.

6. The video of the police beating of Rodney King projected images that demystified the democratic illusion of law and order. The initial acquittal of the police after scrutinizing the video in court manifests the nearly total control hegemony exercises (to the point of reconfiguring clear visual images). This slippage between reality, images and the law underscores the problem of law enforcement as an act of interpretation. In "Force and Sig-

nification" Derrida posits that there is no Book, or Law, only books and laws. Laws, like all texts, are subject to (and enforced by) a biased act of interpretation.

7. Besides Eltit, the original members of CADA included the poet Raúl Zurita, the visual artists Lotty Rosenfeld and Juan Castillo and the sociologist Fernando Balcells. Nelly Richard's *Margins and Institutions: Art in Chile Since 1973* is the best source for information (and analysis) of CADA interventions.

8. Raquel Olea, in "El cuerpo-mujer," notes that traditional critics from the Left in Chile actually boycotted experimental literature, dismissing it as elitist (83–4).

9. In an article in *boundary 2*, "Postmodernism, Postleftism, Neo-Avant-Gardism: The Case of Chile's *Revista de Crítica Cultural*," Vidal excoriates the journal under Richard's editorship. Arguing that articles in the *Revista* "fuse the political and the aesthetic to the extreme that the latter completely replaces the former" (220), Vidal suggests that the "postmodernist avant-garde" in Chile suffers from a "posttraumatic stress disorder" that precludes them from presenting "real alternatives" and results in their displacing the "real origin of the violence" for "macrotheoretical" questions of aesthetics (224–5). In her "Reply to Vidal," Richard explains her journal's theoretical perspective. She reads Vidal's attack, furthermore, in terms of inversion: "He projects onto the *Revista* his own traumatic phantasmagoria of loss and suffering" from "his exile in a North American university" (230).

10. Georg Gugelberger and Michael Kearney, for example, assert that testimonial literature "directly *militates against* the increasing postmodern concerns that realism and representation are dead" (emphasis added, 11). George Yúdice relegates nonlinear "postmodern" narrative to the repressive realm of hegemony. In his article "Testimonio and Postmodernism," Yúdice argues that Derridian deconstruction and poststructuralist theory as practiced by Spivak, Foucault and Kristeva "only recuperates the other as absence, the *is not* against which the subject of discourse *is*" (emphasis original, 22). For a consideration of the relationship between the issue of human rights and the deconstruction of the subject see the collection of Oxford Amnesty Lectures, *Freedom and Interpretation*, edited by Barbara Johnson.

11. I am by no means denying the importance of testimonial "literature" as a genre that gives voice to subaltern "others." What I am taking issue with is the uncritical dismissal equating nonlinear, fragmented narrative with frivolous (postmodern) pastiche.

12. Juan Carlos Lértora, in his essay, "Diamela Eltit: Hacia una poética

de literatura menor," interprets Eltit's narrative in terms that approximate a "testimonial" agenda: "La base ideológica de toda esta escritura se sustenta en una profunda, genuina solidaridad con esos seres desamparados que no tienen voz en América Latina" (34).

13. In an interview with Julio Ortega, Eltit describes the sociopolitical context informing her first novel: "*Lumpérica* fue escrita enteramente bajo los tiempos más rígidos de la dictadura, incluso en esos años, los libros chilenos debían pasar por una oficina de censura para su publicación" (230).

14. Roland Barthes, in *S/Z*, contrasts the productive interpretation of "reading" a *texte scriptible* to the comparatively closed representation implied by a *texte lisible*: "l'enjeu du travail littéraire ... c'est de faire du lecteur, non plus un consommateur, mais un producteur du texte" (10). I am using Barthes's term, "writerly," to emphasize the open-endedness of *Lumpérica* without adopting his evaluative connotation that this aesthetic is superior to the "readerly" texts of mass culture. Eltit, in fact, underscores the paradoxically cultural aspects of the *lumpen*. I specifically address this issue later in this chapter. For a critique of Barthes's modernist bias see Andreas Huyssen's article "Mapping the Postmodern," pages 39–47.

15. In her prologue to *El padre mío*, Eltit describes her impressions of Santiago's street population in theatrical terms: "Era posible acotar la dramaticidad que las figuras del vagabundaje portaban. Esta tensión dramática se encarnaba materialmente en sus figuras desplegadas en las calles, plazas y rincones de la ciudad" (12).

16. These various commentaries on pages 15, 17, 23, 24, 26, 37, 38 and 40 are organized into discrete sections, each of which is preceded with a bold-typed title.

17. I do not mean to imply that Mulvey ingenuously posits aesthetic manipulation as a means to overturn dominant culture. The essay I allude to, "Visual Pleasure and Narrative Cinema," responds to the legacy of Hollywood cinema, which remained only marginally challenged at the time she was writing. In a later essay, "Film, Feminism and the Avant-Garde," Mulvey refines and elaborates her theory. While she persists in saying that "realist or illusionist aesthetics ... cannot satisfy the complex shifts feminist imagery desires" she also admits that there is still "pleasure" in the "bare bones of the cinematic process" (119). She furthermore cautions against an exclusively aesthetic feminist cinema: "Women cannot be satisfied with an aesthetics that restricts countercinema to work on form alone. Feminism is bound to its politics" (124).

18. Elizabeth Grosz, in her essay "Bodies-Cities," briefly traces the conceptual paradigms with which Western thought has historically classi-

fied the relationship between the body and the city. Grosz's interpretation posits an intersubjective (non-Cartesian) "interface" in which bodies and cities shape, represent and reinscribe each other. In my view *Lumpérica* constitutes a singular example of a lopsided interface between bodies and the space of Santiago during dictatorship.

19. In the prologue to *El padre mío*, Eltit refers to the marginalized world of the *lumpen* as the inverted image of the city. She visualizes the street people as sculptures, creating, in Spanish, the play on words "it is culture": "En esta perspectiva me era posible establecer nociones que permitían percibir algunos argumentos culturales propios, desde la alteridad que asumían sus cuerpos errantes en la ciudad. Es-Cultura, pensé. Esculturas diseminadas en los bordes negando la interioridad arquitectónica, tomando, en cambio, las fachadas, a partir de constituirse ellos mismos en puros ornamentos, en fachadas después de un cataclismo" (12–13).

20. Within the historical context of post-coup Chile, this could be interpreted as a parody of the government briefings that, paradoxically, reported leftist activities without formerly admitting that opposition to the government existed.

21. Sara Castro-Klarén, in her article "Escritura y cuerpo en *Lumpérica*," sees this display of authoritarian power as the key to *Lumpérica*'s "riddle." For Castro-Klarén, *Lumpérica* represents L. Iluminada's experience of a nocturnal torture session. I would argue that torture constitutes one of many plausible interpretations of *Lumpérica*. In *Por la patria*, on the other hand, certain passages clearly allude to physical and psychological torture.

22. Maria Inés Lagos, in "Reflexiones sobre la representación del sujeto en dos textos de Diamela Eltit: *Lumpérica* y *El cuarto mundo*," coherently analyzes Eltit's representation of fragmented subjects in the context of feminist and psychoanalytic theory. While Lagos emphasizes Eltit's representation of subjectivity, I underscore the continuum between literary, cinematic, discursive and political re-presentation that traverses Eltit's performance.

23. Film critic Steven Shaviro, in *The Cinematic Body*, describes postmodern film (specifically Fassbinder's *Querelle*) in terms that apply well to Eltit. Shaviro writes, "The modernist critical paradigm regards involvement or fascination as a state of ideological mystification, and employs the alienation effect as a tool to undo this state. Postmodernism, in contrast, views the very claim to demystification with suspicion ... Instead, it regards both involvement and alienation as particular subject positions or modes of implication. *Querelle*, then [and I will add *Lumpérica* here], does not deploy alienation against identification, but [rather] treats them alike as effects of

the cinematic apparatus ... In contrast to the Brechtian paradigm ... the alienation effect does not free the audience from involvement in the spectacle, but itself functions as a new mode of complicity" (163–4).

24. María Inés Lagos observes that L. Iluminada, like Cixous, affirms her right to own and enjoy her body: "La protagonista de *Lumpérica* recupera en esa noche ... su derecho a su propio cuerpo, a gozar de él, y a moverse con libertad" (134). Guillermo García Corales, as well, writes that L. Iluminada attempts to "recuperar el territorio corporal que se le ha confiscado" (117). In a footnote García Corales adds that Cixous "consideraría este tipo de situación en diálogo con la llamada 'escritura del cuerpo' que confronta al discurso autoritario partiarcal" (124).

25. Lagos emphasizes the fragmented sexual identity of Eltit's feminine subjects: "En las obras de Eltit hay una clara voluntad de representar individuos sexuados, fragmentados y cambiantes, cuya corporalidad—manifestada especialmente en su sexualidad—cuestiona los roles sexuales vigentes" (129–30). Lagos offers Judith Butler's *Gender Trouble* and Monique Wittig's "The Straight Mind" as theoretical paradigms that evoke the instability and sexual fluidity of Eltit's subjects. In addition, Lagos understands Eltit's fragmented narrative as an example of Elaine Showalter's metaphor of narrative "quilting" (133).

26. Raquel Olea writes, "El gesto de autoerotismo y la provocación que se ejerce por lo abyecto como objeto caído ... es radicalmente un excluido de lo social, según señala Julia Kristeva" ("El cuerpo-mujer" 90). Julio Ortega and Fernando Moreno T. employ Kristeva's abjection respectively in their readings of *Por la patria* and *Vaca sagrada*.

27. The cover of Juan Carlos Lértora's book, *Una poética de literatura menor: La narrativa de Diamela Eltit*, reproduces a work by the artist Gonzalo Díaz. Díaz's design displays a video still of Eltit's face and a superimposed red outline of an arm marked with incisions. The back cover of the book shows the wounded female torso connected to the arm. The torso is cut across the breast by a ruler, evoking a measure for film editing. Curiously, none of the excellent essays in the book (by ten different critics) closely analyzes the "Ensayo General," Eltit's self-mutilation or the video/performance *Maipu*.

Eltit briefly discusses her performance art in her interview with Ana María Foxley, "Me interesa todo aquello que esté a contrapelo del poder." See also Nelly Richard's *Margins and Institutions*.

28. Also significant is the inclusion of the author's name in lower case, "diamela eltit," toward the end of Chapter 4.4 (90). Eltit discusses this detail in the interview with Sonia Riquelme, "Narrativa chilena joven:

Diamela Eltit y su novela *Lumpérica*": "El acto de escribir tiene que ver con la libertad ... Como sujeto, autora de una novela, tengo la libertad de inmiscuirme ... Tengo que aclarar de todos modos que esa cercanía entre 'diamela eltit' y 'L. Iluminada' es otras veces una distancia infinita entre el personaje y yo misma" (50).

29. The historical avant-garde, of course, employed this technique long before Eltit. In Chilean tradition, Vicente Huidobro's masterful long poem, "Altazor," stands as a classical instance of poetic expression through linguistic de(con)struction.

In an essay based on Bakhtin, "Word, Desire and Novel," Julia Kristeva describes the "poetic word" in terminology that applies coherently to Eltit's narrative: "The poetic word, polyvalent and multi-determined, adheres to a logic exceeding that of codified discourse and fully comes into being only in the margins of recognized culture" (37).

30. Sara Castro-Klarén explores the lack of a subject in her article, "Del recuerdo y el olvido: El sujeto en *Breve Carcel* y *Lumpérica*": "*Lumpérica* no es una escritura en que el sujeto, idéntico a sí mismo se postula como centro de significado ... Cada vez que el sujeto intenta postularse ya sea como imagen ... o como palabra ... ni la persona ni el sujeto llegan a decirse. Quedan en fragmento de una presencia ausente" (202–3).

31. For a study applying the Lacanian mirror as an analogous stage in the formation of (an always already fragmented) Chilean cultural identity, see José Joaquín Brunner's "Un espejo trizado."

32. For brevity's sake, I proceed directly to the corporeal section of the Ensayo General. E.G. 3 constitutes a similar narrative *montage* in which Eltit simultaneously stretches and fuses poetic words, thus superimposing and multiplying images: "Muge/r'onda corporal Brahma su ma la mano que la denuncia & brama" (154). Here again the subject evokes a hybrid, woman/animal, who moans ("Muge ... & brama") and wanders ("r'onda"). Her body, "corporal Brahma," connotes both an enlightened deity (Iluminada) and a breed of cattle. The language surrounding her hand, "su ma la mano," combines "su mano" from E.G. 1 (152) with "la mano" of E.G. 2 (153). Recombining syllables, one might read "suma la mano" or "su mala mano," or even, "ahma su mala mano."

33. Critics have cited the photograph as a nexus linking the novel with its biographical (extra-literary) context. Julio Ortega, in his essay "Diamela Eltit y el imaginario de la virtualidad," interprets the "Ensayo General" in the related processes of reading and writing: "Intenta describir (leer) la fotografía de una mujer (¿la autora en plan de lectora?, ¿la novela auto-gráfica?)" (65–6). María Inés Lagos, in "Reflexiones sobre la representación del

sujeto en dos textos de Diamela Eltit: *Lumpérica* y *Cuarto mundo*," pushes the idea farther: "Por una parte la metaficción crea conciencia del carácter construido del tejido literario, pero por otro, la buscada relación con la realidad histórica, a través de la fotografía y la inclusión del nombre de la autora ... plantea la relación entre texto y experiencia" (135).

34. Thematically as well, *Lumpérica* evokes the reproductive cycles of women and the universal need for sleep, food and light (itself a cycle) among society's nonproductive sector.

35. Gilles Deleuze and Félix Guattari in *Anti-Oedipus: Capitalism and Schizophrenia*, employ the metaphor of corporeal "inscription" to describe the interrelatedness of culture, violence, language and writing:

> Cruelty is the movement of culture that is realized in bodies and inscribed on them, belaboring them ... The sign is a position of desire; but the first signs are the territorial signs that plant their flags in bodies. And if one wants to call this inscription in naked flesh 'writing,' then it must be said that speech in fact presupposes writing, and that it is this cruel system of inscribed signs that renders man capable of language, and gives him a memory of the spoken word. (145)

36. In this essay Richard analyzes Eltit's mortifications together with those performed by Eltit's former partner, Raúl Zurita.

37. The question of allegory brings to mind Fredric Jameson's controversial assertion that all Third World literature necessarily evokes national allegory. His thesis is extremely problematic, especially due to his insistence on *all* and the ambiguity apparent in the label "Third World literature."

Jameson has written more recently, nevertheless, about new, open, allegory as opposed to static symbolic allegory. In *Postmodernism or the Logic of Late Capitalism* Jameson specifies: "[Postmodern] allegorical interpretation is ... first and foremost an interpretive operation which begins by acknowledging the impossibility of interpretation in the older sense" (167–8). My reading of *Lumpérica*, then, coincides with Jameson's *new* allegory.

38. In the interview with Juan Andrés Piña, Eltit describes *El padre mío* as an effort to challenge the dichotomy, high culture–*lumpen*: "Publiqué el libro *El padre mío* porque me pareció interesante reproducir esta voz de la calle, en un medio chileno muy sacralizante e idólatra con lo 'literario.' Poner esa voz marginal en un libro me parecía importante, hasta diría subvertor" (239). She also expresses her aversion toward melodramatic literature

that romanticizes the victimization of the lower classes: "Habitualmente cuando se escribe sobre estas realidades marginales se hace desde una mirada compasiva, llorona, burguesa en definitiva, donde el autor está conmovido por la pobreza ... Detesto esa visión de ciertas novelas que compadecen a los 'pobrecitos' y donde se está a punto de regalar la ropa usada" (240).

39. Eltit explicitly returns to this fusion of writing and prostitution at the conclusion of her third novel, *El cuarto mundo*. In the penultimate sentence "diamela eltit" (lower case) gives birth to her daughter. The novel concludes by pronouncing that *la niña sudaca* (pejorative term for a South American girl) "will be sold on the market" (128). For a discussion of this scene, see Lagos's essay, "Reflexiones sobre la representación del sujeto en dos textos de Diamela Eltit: *Lumpérica y Cuarto mundo*."

40. In the interview with Juan Andrés Piña, Eltit explains that the majority of people who attended this reading lived or worked in the area: "Asistieron no más de ocho personas ligadas al mundo de la cultura, y el resto del público eran del lugar: prostituas, borrachos y travestis" (234).

41. The meta-discursive origins of the ideal-woman-as-Madonna clearly derive from Roman Catholic ideology. In the secular sphere, the military government sponsored the formation of volunteer women's organizations whose stated objectives aimed to support the dictatorship's neo-liberal policies as well as the moral values of family and patriotism. Comprised in large part by wives of government officials, the hierarchical structure of these organizations paralleled that of the government. (General Pinochet's wife served as president of the Secretaría Nacional de la Mujer and the Centros de Madres [CEMA-CHILE]). Upper-class housewives also participated in various color-coded organizations, *Damas de colores*, which carried out highly visible acts of charity. For a catalogue and analysis of women's organizations in Chile in the twentieth century (including groups that opposed the dictatorship as well as those sanctioned by the government) see María de la Luz Silva Donoso's *La participación política de la mujer en Chile: Las organizaciones de mujeres*.

42. Derrida demonstrates in "Force and Signification" and "White Mythology" that violence is inherent in predication and that discursive violence always precedes physical violence. Similarly, Aijaz Ahmad in "Jameson's Rhetoric of Otherness and the 'National Allegory,'" observes the ideological collusion of "description" and the violence of colonial discourse:

> "Description" is never ideologically or cognitively neutral ... to "describe" is to specify a locus of meaning, to construct an object

of knowledge, and to produce a knowledge that shall be bound by
that act of descriptive construction. "Description" has been central, for example, in the colonial discourse. It was by assembling a
monstrous machinery of descriptions—of our bodies, our speech-
acts, our habitats, our conflicts and desires, our politics, our
socialities and sexualities—in fields as various as ethnology, fiction, photography, linguistics, political science—that the colonial discourse was able to classify and ideologically master the
colonial subject, enabling itself to transform the descriptively
verifiable multiplicity and difference into the ideologically felt
hierarchy of value. (6)

43. In the interview with Juan Andrés Piña, Eltit explains her intentions in terms of effecting a cultural transformation: "Me interesaba
transformar ese espacio de tráfico carnal por algunos minutos, en un tráfico
cultural ... Me importó, como gesto, leer esos trozos de la novela. No me
interesaba montar un espectáculo para que la gente lo apreciara o lo
despreciara, sino que engranar o desengranar pensamientos" (234).

44. The novel does not specify the exact nature of the child's condition. Jean Franco writes, "The child whose monologues open and close the
novel is certainly 'abnormal'. He has a dissonant laugh, bangs his head
against the wall, and plays incomprehensible games" (234). Eltit mentions
that she was thinking of Faulkner's *The Sound and the Fury* and Beckett's
Molloy while writing *Los vigilantes* (personal interview, 19 March 1996).

45. See Castro-Klarén's discussion of Mistral and the power of the
"mother tongue" in her introduction to *Women's Writing in Latin America:
An Anthology*, eds. Sara Castro-Klarén, Sylvia Molloy and Beatriz Sarlo
(Boulder: Westview P, 1991), 9–10.

46. In earlier work Eltit has underscored the oppression of the discourse
of the father figure in Chilean politics. In *El padre mío* (1989), for example,
she presents the words of a mentally ill street-dweller, known as *el padre
mío*, whose rantings challenge the legitimacy of authoritarian discourse.
For a discussion of Pinochet's "Mensaje a la mujer chilena" speech and
Eltit's *El padre mío* and *Lumpérica* see Mary Louise Pratt's article, "Overwriting Pinochet: Undoing the Culture of Fear in Chile" (1996), 151–63.

CHAPTER 3

Alejandro Jodorowsky:
Reiterating Chaos, Rattling the Cage of Representation

> To arrive is just an illusion.
>
> —Guillermo Gómez-Peña

Although many artists have experimented with multiple media and genres, Alejandro Jodorowsky's creative corpus spans an extraordinary range of expressive formats. Through mime, film, comics, theater and novels, Jodorowsky narrates an initiatic search for self in a world gone haywire. On the surface, Jodorowsky's works appear vastly different from one another. *El loro de siete lenguas* (1991) forms an expansive counter-epic, satirizing Chile of the 1950s with black humor and slapstick. *Las ansias carnívoras de la nada* (1991), by contrast, condenses a confusing series of oneiric and hallucinatory experiences within a short narrative that is devoid of any historical or even logical anchor. *Donde mejor canta un pájaro* (1992) evokes an aesthetic of magical realism, tracing and fictionalizing Jodorowsky's genealogical tree from turn-of-the-century Russia through the Jewish migration to Argentina and leading, ultimately, to the author's biological conception in Chile. Jodorowsky's early theater, *Teatro pánico* (1965), stages dramas of existential stagnation in the tradition of the theater of the absurd. *L'Incal* (1981–1989), a six-volume comic book of science fiction adventures, juxtaposes episodes of intergalactic warfare with the internal struggle of a detective-protagonist-fool figure. Jodorowsky's most recent books, *Sombras al mediodía* (1995) and *Canciones, metapoemas y un arte de pensar* (1997), present *microcuentos*, poems and songs that foreground and parody the quest for meaning in "New Age" existence.

In spite of the many differences, each of Jodorowsky's works constitutes a metaphysical foray into the confusion of space and subjectivity. Jodorowsky's art, in other words, perpetually explores psychic conundrums that revolve around "place" and "identity." Who am I? Where am I? Where do I come from? Where am I going? These questions, recurring throughout Jodorowsky's *oeuvre*, resonate with the disorientation associated with postmodernism.

Instead of constructing a linear narrative, Jodorowsky emphasizes flagrantly grotesque and violent cycles. Reading his diverse corpus of texts together, nevertheless, reveals a recursive symmetry on both thematic and structural levels. Though I take into account Jodorowsky's work in film and pantomime, my analyses focus on his recently published novels, *El loro de siete lenguas* and *Las ansias carnívoras de la nada*, his play for theater, *El túnel se come por la boca* and the best-selling graphic novel, *L'Incal* (1981–1988), which he produced in collaboration with the graphic artist Jean Giraud, known as Moebius.[1] In this chapter I analyze the discursive function of chaos in Jodorowsky's writing within the context of contemporary postmodern "confusion."

Theoretical models of postmodernism, ranging from Baudrillard's "hyperreal of electronic simulation" to Lyotard's "crisis of Grand Narratives" and Jameson's "logic of late capitalism," postulate an atomizing fragmentation of the traditional notions of space and subjectivity. Theories of postmodernity not only posit a fracturing of the subject in terms of psychic identity, but furthermore inhere a distortion, if not dissolution, of traditional spatial, temporal and political configurations.

Why do images of disorientation (referring to a myriad of different phenomena) appear ubiquitously in so much postmodern theory? I do not mean to equate the theories of Baudrillard, Lyotard and Jameson but rather I mean to underscore the pervasiveness of confusion in all three paradigms. In *Chaos Bound*, N. Kathryn Hayles highlights a paradoxical order inherent to contemporary chaos. Whereas today's geopolitical coordinates defining "body," "language" and "nation" continue to shift between ambiguous unmappable fields, electronic communication media effectively organize economic power into transnational networks. Hayles conjectures that "disorder has become a focal point for contemporary literary theories because it offers the possibility of escaping from what are increasingly perceived as coercive structures of order" (265). Contemporary information technology marshals an unprecedented degree of potentially totalitarian global order.

ALLEGORICAL ALLEGORY: MOVING
TOWARD THE ORIGIN

Disoriented and fragmented subjects wandering in amorphous voids characterize the Jodorowskian quest for meaning. In spite of the salient differences, all four works elaborate pronouncedly circular narratives. All of these texts actualize and allegorize dramatic and spiritual quests. In *El túnel* a couple seeks the light at the end of a circular tunnel. In *Las ansias carnívoras de la nada* three characters traverse Chile looking for their lost memory. In *L'Incal* nearly everyone searches for a small crystal-like object, the "incal," which carries within it infinite power. *El loro de siete lenguas* enacts a search for Truth, Paradise and the "original language."

Throughout his career, Jodorowsky repeatedly reconstructs narrative *quests for an origin*. His bizarre, grotesque and ultraviolent searches nearly always precipitate ironic epiphanies. In his film, *The Holy Mountain*, a group of seekers undergo rites of purification before ascending the mountain in search of a group of masters. At the summit, these "masters" turn out to be mannequins.

Mystically, this allegory implies that the search itself corresponds to a misguided endeavor—wild-goose chases, overlooking the forest for the trees, the *quête du soi* for the quest for the Grail. After unmasking the mannequins on the mountain, Jodorowsky (an actor in his own movie) orders the technicians to pull back the cameras. The conclusion reveals the machinery behind the filmed illusion. Not only are the masters dummies but the viewer discovers that the scene took place on a simulated filmset, far below the actual summit. Through the lens of a camera we see cameras filming the scene. Although related, this gesture of aesthetic distancing is not exactly a cinematic version of the Brechtian alienation effect. By breaking the illusion of spectacle, Jodorowsky also implies that behind each illusion lies an infinite series of invisible illusions. As he concludes in *The Holy Mountain*, "we are images, dreams, photographs." For the mystic Jodorowsky, life itself is a continuum of illusions. His quests for an origin lead to the realization that the "origin" corresponds to another copy, or simulacrum, in a perpetual series of embedded facsimiles.

Although this mystic predisposition shapes Jodorowsky's expression, his writing also implies significant narrative consequences. In her book, *Megalopolis*, Celeste Olalquiaga relies on Walter Benjamin's notion of allegory to describe the transformational changes implicit in the postmodern condition. Allegory, writes Olalquiaga, "represents a continuous *movement toward an unattainable origin*, a movement marked by the awareness of a loss that it attempts to compensate with a baroque saturation *and the obsessive reiteration of fragmented memories*" (emphasis added, xx–xxi). It is precisely this kind of movement that Jodorowsky portrays in his cinematic, theatrical and narrative quests. Narrating continuous quests toward an unattainable origin, Jodorowsky allegorizes allegory. Jodorowsky's futile quest-narratives reinscribe the function and process of modern allegory. Jodorowsky's writing, in other words, re-members the indefinite deferral of narrative in and of itself.

Even Jodorowsky's biographical history exemplifies a search that is at one moment a quest and another a denial of a stable origin. Jodorowsky describes his childhood as a time of persecution, beginning a lifetime of alienation:

> Les enfants ne m'acceptaient pas parce que j'étais "Russe" ...
> Le jeunes gens ne m'ont pas accepté parce que j'étais "juif" ...
> Les Français ne m'ont pas accepté parce que j'étais "Chilien" ...
> Les Mexicains ne m'ont pas accepté parce que j'étais "Français" ...
> Les Américains pensent que je suis "Mexicain."
> (quoted in Larouche 16)

In 1953, at the age of 24, he emigrated from his native Chile to France, where he sought the legacy of the historical avant-garde.[2] Upon abandoning Chile, Jodorowsky literally burned his photographs, the testimonial artifacts of his personal history, and cut all ties with his family. Relocating himself in Paris, Jodorowsky performed with (and wrote for) the world-renowned mime Marcel Marceau. He also made contact with André Breton's *cercle surréaliste*, which he dismissed as a reductive, closed and conservative literary "circle." In 1962 Fernando Arrabal, Roland Topor and Jodorowsky founded their own "movement," *le mouvement panique*, refusing the rules, limitations and hierarchy that they associated with Surrealism.[3] After fourteen years, Jodorowsky moved to Mexico, where he staged "happenings" (*efímeros*), directed more than a hundred theatrical plays and made the films *Fando y Lis*, *El Topo* and *La montaña sagrada*.[4] In 1975, he returned to Paris, where he now prolifically writes film scripts, graphic novels, novels and short stories.

QUESTS FOR AN ORIGINAL COPY

To introduce this inquiry of the Jodorowskian quest narrative, I would like to relate an anecdote from my own (re)search. After reading the French edition of the *Incal*, I attempted to acquire the series in Spanish. After considerable time, worry and long-distance phone calls, a friend in Spain bought the series for me, and (fearing the reliability of the postal service) shipped me the comics by international courier. I received a phone call twenty-four hours after he mailed them in which I was informed that my "documents" (six comic books) had cleared customs. When the package arrived I inspected my long-awaited Spanish version of the *Incal*. The use of *vosotros*, the verb *coger* and typical peninsular slang immediately confirmed that the Spanish copy of the *Incal* was indeed "Spanish"—a Chilean author's graphic novel, copied and translated to Castilian Spanish from French! Ironically, this Castilian translation enjoys distribution throughout Latin America.[5]

This chain of translation brings to mind the poststructuralist critique of determinant meaning in language. My research ethic was to analyze an "original" version of the text. And yet as Derrida painstakingly demonstrates in *De la grammatologie*, no amount of research can isolate a true *origin*, even in (nontranslated) "pure" language. Signs do not signify an original referent, "meaning," but rather they signify other signs (signifiers), themselves projecting and signifying the signs or traces of other previous signs. Even if one were to "bracket" off the infinite *différance* of language, the collaborative production process between Moebius and Jodorowsky further problematizes the notion of an original *Incal* text. Where, in other words, does the *Incal* "text" begin?

Structurally, a reader might be tempted to separate Moebius's graphic designs from Jodorowsky's written scenario. Nevertheless, while Moebius's drawings graphically illustrate the *Incal*'s text, a reader's interpretation derives from interaction between the graphic and literary images. Hermeneutically, one could argue that the written text actually *illustrates* Moebius's drawings, because the eye contemplates the pictures before reading the words. Roland Barthes, in his essay "The Photographic Message," proposed this kind of inverted view of illustration, text and image in his analysis of newspaper photographs. Rather than separating Jodorowsky's and Moebius's respective contributions, the *Incal* comic constitutes a collective collaboration, wherein each artist illustrates the other's images. Essentially, an *original* or autonomous text does not exist.

The *Incal*, then, can be visualized as a graphic and textual dialogue that twists together the images (both graphic and narrative) of Moebius and Jodorowsky. It is significant to note as well that Jodorowsky did not initially "write" the script but rather recounted (and mimed) his ideas to Moebius, who sketched while listening to the scenario. In interviews Jodorowsky explains that the concept for the *Incal* occurred to him in a dream. Moebius recorded their conversation on tape for later referral. Subsequently, the two collaborators discussed and jointly altered the plot. After Moebius had finished his drawings they worked together to establish the textual dialogues.[6]

It would be reductionist, nevertheless, to index Jodorowsky's dream, or even the collaborative dialogues, with Moebius as the "origin" of the *Incal*. To the contrary, the *Incal* appears on the crest of an expansive intertextual chain. Jodorowsky and Moebius first began collaborating on a never-finished film project of Jodorowsky's. They (and others hired by Jodorowsky) worked for more than two years and spent two million dollars toward a film version of Frank Herbert's novel, *Dune*. After the financial backers recanted support, the project was aborted.[7] In interviews Jodorowsky and Moebius describe the *Incal* as a creative response to the emotional crisis that resulted from the failure of the *Dune* project.[8] A paradoxically nonexistent film, then, constitutes the *Incal*'s most immediate intertext.[9]

It should be clear now that the *Incal* corresponds to a unique conglomeration of narrative re-presentations. A collaborative comic deriving from a never-made film of a best-selling science fiction novel, the *Incal* propagates a continuum of images from an extensive internarrative palimpsest. Although my analysis mainly discusses the *Incal*'s direct legacy in Jodorowsky's subsequent work, a controversial trace of the *Incal* remains present in film industry technique. At the time of Jodorowsky's *Dune* project, the use of hand-drawn storyboards was not a prevalent aspect of film making. The influence of Jodorowsky's *Dune* and the *Incal*, then, is in part technical and methodological innovation. The current trend of films made from comic books (*The Crow*, *The Shadow* and *Mask*, for example) bears witness to the significance of the storyboard–comic connection. [10] This consideration of the evolution of the *Incal* marks the convergence of history, narrative, language and modern allegory. Couldn't each of these systems be visualized as "a continuous movement toward an unattainable origin" (Olalquiaga xx–xxi)? In this chapter I analyze Jodorowsky's allegorical *mise en scène* of narrative both within and across his *ouevre*. I argue that the relationship of his various works to each other reiterates the motion narrated by each text. First, however, I would like to trace the commercial projection of Jodorowsky's serialized comics, which branch out from the *Incal* to form an expansive trajectory of intertextual re-production.

SERIALIZATION: DETHRONING THE ORIGINAL

Presently, two new series of comic books have evolved from the *Incal* story. This adapted serialization reiterates the internal momentum of comic book adventures, which are always "to be continued" in the following volume. Now however, rather than merely progressing from one album to the next, readers continue from one narrative series to another. Interestingly, the six installments of the *Incal* (published between 1981 and 1988) represent a circular adventure that begins and ends with the image of a detective, John Difool, falling from a bridge (see Figure 3-1). Difool descends, ascends and later re-descends through layers of a well-shaped urban construction, *la cité puits*. He wanders up and down from subterranean tunnels (inhabited by genetic mutants) to the bottom of the acid lake (concealing subversive guerrilla groups) through the *anneau rouge* (the center of prostitution and drug use) to the higher levels (reserved for the aristocracy) to the vast expanses of the galaxy (including planets inhabited by a species of warfaring bird hybrids, called "Bergs"). Difool eventually arrives at a spiritual high point where he obtains a vision of the Creator, only to ultimately fall back down through each of the levels to his nadir in the *cité puits*.

The "closed" circularity of the *Incal* poses an interesting logistical problem of narrative development. Because the *Incal* portrays Difool locked into a cycle of perpetual repetition, the series remains narratively "closed" to further development. How, then, can the story continue after its completion as a graphic novel? In 1989 Jodorowsky and Moebius published an eight-page subplot that purportedly takes place temporally within the *Incal*'s cycle. This "chapter" constitutes a quintessential meta-text that emulates the structure of a Chinese box to contribute additional information to the *Adventures of John Difool*. Deep in the heart of his inviolable "Méta-bunker," the Méta-baron's robot (Tonto, who loves his master for his robotic ear) tells another robot the story of the Méta-Baron's initiation as a Meta-Warrior (during which the Meta-Baron received his robotic ear). Within the robot's story, the Méta-Baron himself relates his own history to a woman named Animah. The robot's story concludes with the explanation of how the Méta-Baron

Figure 3-1. John Difool falling, from Jodorowsky and Moebius's *Incal*.
(Courtesy of Les Humanoïdes Associés SA, Geneva.)

became the guardian of an androgynous infant. The child is destined to continue in the path of the Méta-Baron, to become the next Meta-Warrior. This new (meta)chapter ironically appears at the conclusion of an analytical book written about the *Incal*, Jean Annestay's *Les Mystères de l'incal* (58–66).

Significantly, this meta-chapter of narrative flashback branches off to another story. Jodorowsky now writes another series of comics, *La Caste des Méta-Barons*, with the Spanish artist Juan Gimenez. In this series, Gimenez and Jodorowsky expand and develop the genealogical history of the Méta-Baron. In the first fourteen pages of the first volume, *Othon le Trisaïeul* (1992), Gimenez literally redraws Moebius's version of the (meta)chapter described above. Although the dialogues, plot, characters and setting are identical repetitions of Moebius's "original," Gimenez renders the illustrations in a vastly more complex style. Rather than copying Moebius's clearline, cartoon aesthetic, Gimenez heightens the depth and color tones, creating a more complex, or "realistic," image.

In 1995 Jodorowsky published the last of another six-volume series, *Avant L'incal*, with the Yugoslavian artist Zoran Janjetov. As the title suggests, *Avant L'incal* represents the *Incal*'s protagonist, John Difool, before the now classic novel's diegetic "beginning." In contrast to Gimenez's work, Janjetov's drawing clearly attempts to *imitate* the atmosphere of Moebius's original *Incal*. The story takes place in the same high-tech dystopian urban city where dejected members of the lower classes continually throw themselves off the bridge, "Suicide Alley." Janjetov accurately *copies* location and setting from specific Moebius drawings. At times he depicts a young John Difool in situations that chronologically pre-figure episodes of the original *Incal*. Janjetov's last panel is a nearly identical copy of Moebius's rendition of John Difool's original fall. This repetitive aesthetic heightens the coherence between *Avant L'incal* and the *Incal*. Jodorowsky's comic books seem to branch and fork endlessly, like a graphic Byzantine novel with limitless possibilities. The overall effect, furthermore, serially subverts the authority of the original *Incal*.

Following an Adornian line of thought, one might label the proliferation of *Incal* spin-off series as an example of the culture industry squeezing a narrative for maximum profit.[11] Jodorowsky's commercial success is indisputable. His scenarios sell hundreds of thousands of comics and are translated into eleven languages. In spite of its best-seller status, nevertheless, the *Incal* occupies a unique position with respect to the entertainment industry. The *Incal* emerged as a counter-response to the Hollywood film industry's quelching of the film version of *Dune*. In an interview in *L'Année de la bande dessinée: 1981–1982*, Jodorowsky explicitly describes the comic book medium as an outlet for circumnavigating the censorship of multinational corporations:

> Aujourd'hui, si je veux faire un film, je dois passer par mille censures. Il n'y a pas encore de multinationales de la B.D. Ça commence à se faire, ça se fera, mais pour l'instant on est toujours dans l'Age d'Or parce qu'on peut se produire en liberté. Ça ne va pas durer beaucoup. Après, il faudra inventer un autre art. Les créateurs de B.D. sont les artistes les plus libres au monde. Ils ont encore la possibilitée de l'individualité. (201–2)

On one level, then, Jodorowsky positions himself as an underground artist, an individual who opposes the market-driven manipulation of the culture industry. At the same time, nevertheless, the expansive serialization of *Incal* spin-offs exploits the marketing techniques central to culture industry commodification.

What, then, are the political consequences of this tension? In and of itself, Jodorowsky's practice of extending and reusing aspects of the *Incal* is neither significant nor unusual. Nevertheless, the extent to which he explicitly thematizes the concepts of commodification and repetition in both his comics and his (nongraphic) novels implies a potentially subversive angle to his appropriation of popular culture.

Jodorowsky's re-rendering of already published material brings to mind the postmodern problem of copy and original. Not only do Jodorowsky's series of comics proliferate a continuum of copies, and spin-offs, but the narratives themselves explicitly (and repeatedly) address the issues of "appearance" versus "reality" in the contexts of electronic technology and political power. Walter Benjamin's essay, "The Work of Art in the Age of Mechanical Reproduction," forecasted a political potential for industrially (re)produced art forms:

> The instant the criterion of authenticity ceases to be applicable to artistic production, the total function of art is reversed. Instead of being based on ritual, it begins to be based on another practice—politics. (224)

Mass production, in other words, erodes the elitist notion of artistic purity associated with high modernism. In hindsight, of course, Benjamin's appreciation for mechanically reproduced art sounds utopian. I am by no means suggesting that Jodorowsky comprehensively obliterates hegemony. I *am* saying that he problematizes the discourses of authenticity and representation. Barry Smart's assessment of Benjamin aptly describes Jodorowsky's serial agenda: "The original loses its authority ... The very notion of an original begins to become problematic as techniques of (re)production develop" (112). Jodorowsky repeatedly evokes the world of postindustrial reproduction within the mechanically reproduced genres of comics and film.

My contention is that Jodorowsky takes advantage of culture industry techniques in marketing strategy at the same time that he critiques the system at large. Merely situating him as either hegemonic or counterhegemonic grossly oversimplifies his dialectical relationship with industrial culture. Jodorowsky's comics engage in a complex relationship with market capitalism. They manifest a self-reflexive awareness of their complicity with the hegemonic marketing techniques, which they are simultaneously critiquing. I return to the *Incal* at a later point in this chapter to analyze Jodorowsky's critique of the mass media's (hegemonic) manipulation of images. First, however, I would like to analyze the deconstruction of authenticity via *literary* images in Jodorowsky's (nongraphic) writing.

(CON)FUSING THE INSIDE AND THE OUTSIDE

From his early writing Jodorowsky renders images of spatial, psychic, temporal and metaphysical disorientation. In his play, *El túnel se come por la boca*, Jodorowsky stages the futile quest of a couple who endlessly search to escape from a circular tunnel.[12] "Signs" have lost all coherence with physical topography and point uselessly in all directions: "Flechas de metal, oxidadas y nuevas, con letras de distintas épocas y en diversos idiomas, indican hacia todas direcciones: '¡Salida!'" (23). This confusion, which is at the same time temporal, linguistic and spatial, allegorically evokes existential angst. As the chorus explains, the search for an exit corresponds to a quest for light: "El túnel en sí es una gruta: Nosotros lo llamamos 'pasaje' porque marchamos incesantemente buscando una luz que nos indique el camino" (25). The drama allegorizes the desire for orientation in life, a direction in which to proceed, a way out of the darkness of the cave.[13]

Obviously, *El túnel*'s circular structure impedes the characters from making forward *progress*.[14] This frozen narrative recalls situations of ludic stagnation characteristic to the theater of the absurd, for example, Beckett's "En attendant Godot." At the same time, nevertheless, Jodorowsky's rendition of an absurd life with "No Exit" evokes a spiritual form of existential *engagement*. Although life itself may be devoid of sense, for Jodorowsky, it is up to us to create or "make" sense. Whatever meaning we construct may not correspond to truth (as would neo-Platonic reason) but still provides a meaningful orientation.

Early in the play a man and a women stage an absurd dance of self-imprisonment: "Sostienen un marco con siete barrotes, el hombre de un lado; la mujer del otro ... El primero sostiene los barrotes 1 y 4; la otra, los barrotes 4 y 7" (31). The two *prisoners*, A and B, alternately beg each other for freedom:

> A: ¡Estoy prisionero, sálvame, por favor!
> B: No. El prisionero soy yo ...
> A: No juegue conmigo: estoy detrás de los barrotes.
> B: Burla cruel. Estos barrotes están ante mí. (31)

This episode theatrically deconstructs the binary relationship separating inside from outside. Their lack of perspective relegates both A and B to the status of prisoner. As Derrida would say, "the outside *is* the inside." The world cannot be divided into simple binary oppositions, neither existentially in terms of who is "free" nor linguistically. Derrida places the word *is* "under erasure," emphasizing that the linguistic description is both unavoidable and inexact. We cannot get outside of language in order to describe reality. For Jodorowsky, everyone is a character, trapped within the "text." The problem compounds dimensionally when three other identical couples enter the scene: "Se juntan formando una celda cuadrada con las cuatro rejas" (31). Even when a choreographed reversal inverts the cell—"Los cuatro que estaban dentro giran y quedan fuera. Los otros están ahora en el interior" (32)—all involved insist that they are imprisoned inside the bars.

Jodorowsky's allegorical dramas convey the philosophy that our confinements derive from self-imposed limitations. He literally embodies this concept in *La jaula*, a pantomime routine that Jodorowsky wrote for Marcel Marceau.[15] In this now classic performance the mime discovers himself imprisoned inside a glass box. When the mime manages to escape from his cubic enclosure he finds himself trapped inside another larger box. Here, as in *El túnel se come por la boca*, Jodorowsky represents an eternally imprisoned character. Analyzing the routine's *mise en scène* in addition to the plot reveals a double coded narrative. Whereas *La jaula* presents a spectacle of a man in a cage, the *act* of pantomime both narrates the story and builds the cage. With the gestures of his own body the mime literally constructs the very cage that confines him. Allegorically, the cage exists as a mental construct and depends completely on its prisoner's collusion. For Jodorowsky, we are imprisoned in our bodies because we consent to the illusion of our bodies as cages.

At the same time, in *La jaula* the cage illusion arises from a transparent *narrative* construct. Although the mime performs in silence, his representation of confinement enacts the all-encompassing and inescapable extensions of language. Jodorowsky's written text prevails unseen behind the pantomimed cage, much as language remains invisible within thought, even within thought about language per se. In *La jaula*, then, the mime embodies the predicament of a writer. In all of his texts Jodorowsky shapes illusions out of words, moving, through narrative, beyond the limitations of the quotidian world. And like the mime in his "jaula," Jodorowsky proceeds to sequentially break through the cages. He remains, nonetheless, perpetually confined to the transparent prisonhouse of language.

EL LORO DE SIETE LENGUAS: REITERATING THE QUEST OF LANGUAGE

Jodorowsky's first novel, *El loro de siete lenguas*, depicts the body as if it were an open cage. Here bodies constitute transmutable, nonhermetic dwelling places. The novel humorously describes the spirits of dead characters seizing control of living bodies and channeling their voices, personalities and even memories through them at inopportune moments. This "slippage" of inside versus outside challenges the spatial and temporal coordinates of reality. The flesh of a woman character remains impervious to corruption in death. At the other extreme the dictator's body literally rots off his bones in life. Life and death are not isolated conditions but rather coexist within each other.

The plot of *El loro de siete lenguas* represents a quest in which a bacchanalian group of friends, "los compañeros de la papa florida," pursues the truth.[16] The name of this collective represents a humorous *mise en abyme* for their journey. "*La papa*," in Chilean slang, is a humorous term used to designate the truth or essence of something. At the novel's conclusion, seven seekers who have survived an apocalyptic earthquake successfully arrive at "el Paraíso perdido" where they find the remnants of "el Lenguaje Original" preserved by animals (340). Their quest, then, becomes one of learning and acquiring this language.

At the center of this paradise, an ancient human-sized parrot cease-lessly repeats what survives of the divine "Lengua Madre." These students of life and truth make progress in their original language lessons: "Parece ser que pudieron hilvanar algunas frases" (340). According to legend, they reconstruct Chile: "Pensaron profundamente en su larga patria, Chile, y le dieron vida" (340). *El loro de siete lenguas* presents a narrative of search, apocalypse and narrative re-Creation.

Described as such, this millenarian episode of post-apocalyptic Creation seems to reinstall order, much as an epic narrative traditionally restores order after social upheaval. The novel, nevertheless, reveals an ironic void at the core of a hollow simulacrum. Rather than discovering the original language, the seekers merely encounter a bird unconscious-ly parroting bits and scraps of the language: "Vieron a un loro indefenso … que incesantemente, sin ninguna comprensión, repetía los vocablos del hombre original" (340). If Jodorowsky's narrative describes a quest toward the origin, it paradoxically articulates the Foucauldian dictum that "in modern thought, such an origin is no longer conceivable" (*The Order of Things* 329). As Foucault writes, when one attempts to articulate the essence of language, "all he ever finds is the previously un-folded possibility of language" (330). The "original language" they pursue at the epilogue of *El loro de siete lenguas* is more a fragmented representation than the real thing. They discover vowels, not words; potential speech, not language.

This episode comprises the novel's epilogue, which furthermore situates the scene as a *leyenda* (340). A story, in other words, reproduc-ing (without precision, perhaps allegorically) an event that reputedly occurred once upon a time. A legend of an encounter with copied shards of language hardly constitutes a stable and orderly return to the origin. In Foucault's words, "origin is by no means the beginning … Origin … is much more the way in which man articulates himself upon the already-begun of labour, life, and language" (330). Returning to the origin, the characters discover a fragmented representation of language, the system that enables representation itself.

Within Paradise lies a core of chaos. *El loro de siete lenguas* decon-structs virtually all semblances of order whether biological, temporal, psychological, political or narrative. Throughout the novel's three hun-dred forty-six pages, no individual character stands out as protagonist or hero. The lives of some thirty characters spiral throughout the plot(s), disappearing, re-emerging and intersecting in bizarre combinations. This sprawling narrative weaves together the fragmented life stories of a myriad of individuals (many of whom embody an assortment of multiple personalities). This is not to say that the text is disorganized. The respective stories progress in segments, cyclically narrating one of the novel's many story lines, breaking to another and then resuming with previously left-off threads. At the end of the novel, the various strands twist together in the form of a circle. *El loro de siete lenguas*, accordingly, superimposes an aesthetic framework of narrative chaos over a carefully conceived structure. Given this dynamic of *controlled irregularity*, the paradigm of "chaos theory" functions as a suggestive approach to both Jodorowsky's work and narrative in general.

CHAOS AND NARRATIVE: A NONLINEAR PARADIGM

I am by no means equating paradigms of science and literature. It is not that nonlinear science can explain a novel, but rather that chaos theory can be used as the basis for analogies that elucidate Jodorowsky's narrative agenda. Although the epistemological distance between science and literature might appear forbiddingly vast, keep in mind that chaos theory's most formidable accomplishment has been to bridge the gap between seemingly unrelated disciplines. Researchers from fields spanning physics, biology, chemistry and mathematics have identified parallel structures—"recursive symmetry"—relating the dynamics of systems as diverse as dripping faucets, the eye movements of schizophrenics, the weather and the stock market.[17] Ultimately, nonetheless, my reading underscores a significant difference between the scientific notion of chaos and narrative.

Temporarily bracketing the differences distinguishing mathematics and language, I would like to compare the dynamics of chaotic narrative to nonlinear equations. It is crucial to recognize that the scientific use of the term "chaos" conveys a different meaning than the word's vernacular connotation. Within a scientific context, chaos represents only virtual randomness. An equation becomes chaotic when the results of a given formula become nonpredictable. Chaos theory has shown, however, that a subsequent analysis reveals a kind of deep structure, or order, that can be observed when the system is compared with other occurrences of chaos. As I mention above, Jodorowsky's *El loro de siete lenguas* appears chaotic, but a close reading reveals a carefully coordinated structure. The act of producing narrative consists of a structuring process, which, no matter how fragmented, always constitutes a certain degree of pre-established order. What N. Kathryn Hayles calls "orderly disorder," then, might describe any narrative system.

Hayles compares mathematician Mitchell Feigenbaum's work on nonlinear (iterative) equations to language. What is interesting about these equations is that they inevitably reach a point at which the results become nonlinear, chaotic and unpredictable despite the consistent repetition of a regular function. ("To iterate a function means to use the output of one calculation as input for the next, each time performing the operation called for by the function" [Hayles 153]). Feigenbaum concluded that since the functions are iterative, the chaos can only enter the system from aberrant "initial conditions" (Hayles 183). In other words, "iteration produces chaos because it magnifies and brings into view these initial uncertainties" (Hayles 183).

Is it possible to compare a novel to a nonlinear equation? One might object that language and mathematical equations are not iterative in exactly the same way, that mathematical iteration is more regular than the repetition that constitutes narrative.[18] And yet while the regularity of periodicity varies, the two systems remain analogous on multiple levels. Compare linguistic codes, themselves constituted by periodically repeating signs, to a nonlinear equation. Iterate the code (the function of repeated letters, words and grammatical structures) to form sentences, paragraphs, then chapters and ultimately a novel. This novel, like the chaotic output of a nonlinear equation, results in an indeterminate text.

The same analogy can be made on the level of narrative. Metaphors, images and themes (themselves built from the code) undergo iteration in order to construct a cohesive narrative.[19] Hayles underscores the similarities between Derridean deconstruction and chaos theory: "Because all texts are necessarily constructed through iteration (that is, through the incremental repetition of words in slightly displaced contexts), indeterminacy inheres in writing's very essence" (181). And if narrative itself is constructed from the continuation of an iterative code, the act of reading also corresponds to another (indeterminate) reproduction of this ongoing sequence of repetition. Consider the manner in which James Gleick describes the process of analyzing a nonlinear equation: "Analyzing the behavior of a nonlinear equation ... is like walking through a maze whose walls rearrange themselves with each step you take" (24). Substituting the word "text" for "nonlinear equation," Gleick's metaphor applies aptly to the hermeneutic process.

Although the validity of this analogy is not specific to "nonlinear narrative," the application of chaos theory to the writing of Jodorowsky is particularly appropriate for several reasons. Not only is narrative iterative in and of itself, but Jodorowsky repeatedly *reiterates* explicitly iterative codes. As Umberto Eco has pointed out, popular literature such as westerns, detective stories and superhero comics are inherently redundant structures in which the reader expects recognizable repetitions. Jodorowsky's work gravitates toward these genres of repetitive popular narrative. His film *El Topo* derives from the "spaghetti western" tradition. His comics, the *Incal* and *Avant l'incal,* juxtapose a detective motif with a story of mystic initiation. His most recent film, *Santa Sangre,* emerges from the tradition of horror films.

In spite of his predilection for working with the genres of popular culture, Jodorowsky's aberrant texts do not merely perpetuate traditional conventions. Jodorowsky's *Incal* cyclically subverts iterative patterns. (I will expand on this point later in this chapter). Jodorowsky paradoxically breaks the iterative code of these repetitive genres while at the same time reiterating an obsessive search and deconstruction of an authoritative original. In this sense the repetitions occurring over the course of his career construct (intertextually) a "narrative" of chaos. To understand this construction, I would first like to trace the evolution of chaos in Jodorowsky's first novel.

SIETE LENGUAS IN SEARCH OF A CHARACTER: A CASE OF INITIAL INDETERMINACY

If *El loro de siete lenguas* constructs a chaotic narrative, the elements of chaos come into play from the text's inception. The story begins *in medias res* when a group of literary friends decide to trick their pedantic friend, La Rosita, by "inventing" a philosopher: "Decidieron crear un filósofo italiano. Resultó Carlo Poncini, nacido en Arezzo en 1893 y desaparecido misteriosamente en Roma en 1931. Fabricaron una biografía" (9). La Rosita proves their supposed invention fact by showing them an article about Poncini in a journal. Subsequently, through a strange coincidence, the group finds out that Poncini currently lives in the south. Note also that rearranging the letters of his name, Carlo Poncini, (coincidentally?) produces the partial phrase, "no par coinci." Their search to find the philosopher rearticulates *El loro*'s multiple quest motif: "Ya el grupo tenía una finalidad: ir a rescatar al filósofo olvidado" (150–1). When they finally encounter Poncini, a character named Zum "reads" Poncini's history by reading his palm (273–4). Poncini, the object of their quest (whose hand ultimately becomes a text), had arrived in the south on a quest of his own, which began while he was reading: "Leyó que ... de mujer a mujer se pasaban los restos de un lenguaje sagrado, quizás el más antiguo del planeta ... Abandonó todo y vino al sur del mundo" (274).

The novel delineates a circular plot: A fictional narrative, *El loro de siete lenguas*, represents a group of writers who create a character, Carlo Poncini. When they seek and find this character they learn that Poncini himself is on a quest for (the sacred) language. They survive an apocalypse, find the remnants of language and re-create Chile. Their fictional creation, accordingly, drew his writers to the origin. A character gives his creators (themselves characters) the potential to create.

TAROT: A CARTOMANCIC METAQUEST

El loro de siete lenguas superimposes even more quest allegories than those I have just described. Upon opening the novel, one immediately notices that the text of the prologue wraps around images of cards from the Marseille tarot (see Figure 3-2).[20] These images are by no means gratuitous adornment. Tarot—a system of images whose interpretation purportedly provides a path toward the pursuit of truth and understanding—constitutes a meta-text that informs and shapes the Jodorowskian quest. Cartomancic interrogation entails a "seeker" who asks a question and a "reader" who interprets the archetypal symbols displayed on the chosen cards. This process recalls the hermeneutic convergence of reading and writing. To read tarot is to articulate an interpretation of iconographic images. Reading the images, consequently, results in the construction of a narrative.

Tarot constitutes a *mise en abyme* that overlaps with *El loro*'s quest to create a meaningful text. The epigraph's cyclical scene of re-Creation translates another tarot card, Le Monde (which appears on the last page of the epigraph [see Figure 3-3]), into narrative: "Pensaron profundamente en su larga patria, Chile, y le dieron vida. Los cuatro mil doscientos kilómetros de la tierra larga se elevaron en el aire como una serpiente que unió cabeza y cola. Ese círculo vivo, con todos los ciudadanos convertidos en ángeles de ideales ardientes" (340). *El loro de siete lenguas*, then, comprises Jodorowsky's reading and rewriting of tarot images.

Ningún personaje es real, ningún sitio es verdadero, cualquier parecido es coincidencia. Hablamos de un Chile que no es Chile. Describimos un Universo paralelo. Entre los años cuarenta y cincuenta, en alguna de las infinitas gamas de mundos, existió un país tan largo que semejaba una torre. En sus alturas habíamos construido un paraíso en forma de corona. Cuando estalló la tormenta y fuimos alcanzados por el rayo, caímos al suelo para vernos obligados a marchar sobre las manos, buscando a tientas los blancos fragmentos del alimento divino, al que ingenuamente habíamos llamado Poesía...

Figure 3-2. Tarot images and accompanying prologue from *El loro de Siete lenguas*. (Courtesy of Dolmen Ediciones.)

Figure 3-3. Tarot image, Le Monde. (Courtesy of Dolmen Ediciones.)

The novel's prologue, "Cayendo de la casa de Dios," renders an allegorical image of Chile that both interprets and illustrates the card titled La Maison Dieu (which appears on page 7 of the novel [see Figure 3-4]): "Existió un país tan largo que semejaba una torre. En sus alturas habíamos construido un paraíso en forma de corona" (6). As one continues to read the prologue, the text expands the card's iconographic design into a story: "Cuando estalló ... caímos al suelo para vernos obligados a marchar sobre las manos, buscando a tientas los blancos fragmentos del alimento divino, al que ingenuamente habíamos llamado Poesía" (6). Reading the card, the prologue translates the tarot's iconographic symbolism into an allegorical narrative. Significantly, this narrative itself follows the lines of a legendary quest.

Although the prologue conjugates the search for "blancos fragmentos del alimento divino, al que ingenuamente habíamos llamado Poesía" (6), in an allegorical mode, the plot of *El loro de siete lenguas* depicts a literal pursuit of literature and poetic fame. The novel dramatizes this through the adventures of two poets, Juan Neruña and Nepomuceno Viñas, in an absurd enmeshment of intertextuality, plagiarism and politics. Needless to say, these characters emerge as caricatures of Chile's "Poeta nacional," Pablo Neruda and "anti-poet" Nicanor Parra. The diegetic see-saw of copy and imitation within the text extends to extra diegetic historical "origins." Don Nepomuceno Viñas, the elitist *director General de la Sociedad de Poetas*, begins a journey prefigured by tarot in the novel's prologue after an incident of public humiliation: "Cuando ... recibió la patada ... comenzó a caer de la torre al barro" (87, see Figure 3-4). A self-indulgent obsession propels Viñas's quest. Searching for fame, Viñas seeks to be pursued—to become, through poetry, a public enemy: "vengador de una clase oprimida, terror del régimen traicionero" (88–9).[21]

The Tower card cannot be limited to Viñas, however, as the novel portrays an entire gamut of seekers in pursuit of various objectives. The dictator-president, Gegé Vihuela, mercilessly pursues leftists for treason. Again Jodorowsky makes use of onomastic play to parody a historical figure, in this case Gabriel Gonzalez Videla, the president of Chile from 1946 to 1952. To Viñas's chagrin, nevertheless, President Vihuela labels Viñas's rival poet, Juan Neruña, as the public enemy: "Grandes titulares anunciaban la persecución del poeta y senador del P.C. Juan Neruña" (89). Neruña instantaneously becomes the hunted "people's poet," thus assuming the public image that Viñas jealously covets. Nepomuceno Viñas, meanwhile, refuses to concede defeat: "¡Injusticia!

Figure 3-4. Tarot image, La Maison Dieu
(Courtesy of Dolmen Ediciones.)

¿Por qué darle publicidad a él y no a mí? ¿Acaso mi poesía no vale más que la suya?" (89). Viñas quixotically invites a companion to flee nonetheless, in the hope that one day he will be pursued: "Comencemos a huir desde ahora. Algún día, si insistimos, terminarán por perseguirnos" (89). His unfollowed flight toward pursuit ironically becomes a fulfilled prophecy.

Jodorowsky's carnivalesque entanglement of poetry and politics underscores the common denominator of *representation* in history, literature, theater and government. In Chilean history, poets (from Vicente Huidobro and Pablo de Rokha to Pablo Neruda) have traditionally represented the political Left. In *Las ansias carnívoras de la nada*, Jodorowsky conflates the discourses of Neruda and Pinochet—the dictator always speaks in lyrical poetry. Jodorowsky's literature satirically unmasks the "fiction" hidden beneath the veneer of political discourse. Language, in other words, whether literary or political, constitutes a performance with serious consequences.

Theatrical performances, especially circus shows, recur throughout *El loro de siete lenguas*. Jodorowsky's fascination with circus imagery derives in part from personal experience (his father worked in the circus, where he hung by his hair), and the Bakhtinian carnival paradigm provides theoretical insight as to the role of the circus in Jodorowsky's narrative poetics. Bakhtin emphasizes the anarchic nature of carnivals, observing that they surpass and corrode spatial and political boundaries. Carnival constitutes a polyvalent (con)fusion of signs that, like language, evades monological control. According to Bakhtin's theory, "carnivalistic laughter ... is directed toward ... a shift of authorities and truths, a shift of word orders" (127). In Jodorowsky's circus, analogously, "el Poder y la risa *se confunden*" (emphasis added, 145). Even the dichotomy between performers on stage and spectators in the audience dissolves: "Carnival is not a spectacle seen by the people; they live in it ... There is no other life outside it" (Bakhtin 7). In *El loro de siete lenguas, los compañeros* form a circus after escaping from a military massacre. They do not temporarily wear clown costumes—they actually *become* clowns: "Vivirían disfrazados de payasos las veinticuatro horas del día" (91).

In Jodorowsky's manifesto "Hacia el 'efímero pánico': O ¡Sacar al teatro del teatro" (*Teatro pánico*), he describes contemporary society in terms of a three-ring circus: "Nuestra actual civilización es un CIRCO donde los personajes se dividen en augustos, payasos y público. El hombre pánico es el payaso; el ciudadano que sólo afirma una idea y busca una única solución a cada problema y cree 'ser', es el augusto; la inmensa masa mirona e inerte es el público" (13). He and his Panic Movement collaborators attempted a (neo)avant-garde revolution during the 1960s that intruded into the quotidian social sphere with unstructured carnivalesque "happenings"—*efímeros*. By "taking the theater out of the theater," Jodorowsky aimed to infuse the everyday world with a hedonistic atmosphere of carnival, thus shattering the hegemony of traditional representation. His manifesto describes the passive spectator as capable of evolving to the *payaso* state of consciousness: "Todo público es un augusto en potencia y todo augusto puede evolucionar en payaso porque el mundo es pánico ... El espectador ... va ascendiendo hasta llegar al payaso, hombre pánico total que goza panorámicamente de la mezcalona del circo, que ve a la universal fiesta pánica y se sumerge en ella" (13).

El loro de siete lenguas actualizes this ascension to become an enlightened clown. The *compañeros* follow the example of the novel's eternal jester figure, Piripipí, who wore his clown face continuously for more than fifty years: "Hacía más de medio siglo que no se quitaba el maquillaje" (112). Rather than a decorative costume, Piripipí's clown suit and makeup are the signs of his essence: "Ponerle otro traje no era cambiarle el disfraz, sino disfrazarlo, como también era disfrazarlo quitarle la pintura y darle un aspecto normal" (112).

The clown figure represents an enlightened state of awareness that fuses the illusion of truth with the truth of illusion. In *El loro*, the full-time clowns abandon "la ilusión de ser personas para convertirse en personajes" (91). Piripipí transcends individual limits, becoming a collective archetype, a *face*, in other words, of subversive dissent. When the "original" clown commits suicide, another character (Von Hammer) dons his makeup and continues the role. Elsewhere, in the concentration camp at Pisagua, some four hundred political prisoners all assume the insoluble makeup-face of Piripipí (187). Still later, Juan Neruña appears as Piripipí (281). Finally, after losing his bid for dictator, General Lagarreta disappears behind the face of the clown (333). That each of these individuals wears the face of Piripipí is by no means a homogenizing gesture. Inherently polyvalent, the clown face and costume explicitly juxtapose a spectrum of colors, patterns and painted emotional signs.

The performance given by the *Gran circo de la Papa Florida Gran* conveys this sense of irreducible plurality. One clown pretends to drown in a steel tub while the others discuss the situation from philosophical and technical angles:

> Un toni ahogándose mientras alrededor suyo otros payasos discutí-
> an interminablemente acerca de los métodos de salvarlo, sin estirar
> una mano para sacarlo del agua. La situación duraba lo que la resis-
> tencia del "indigno" público. (91)

Consisting "únicamente de payasos" (85), the circus lacks any structure or hierarchy of performers. At a later performance, the division between spectators and performers completely disappears. Performing without an audience, the entire group dives into the tub of water and screams for help (138).

In the crucial tenth chapter, Jodorowsky weaves a double perform-ance of political representation into the act. President Vihuela attempts to harness the circus as an instrument of political propaganda. Specifi-cally, Vihuela tries to organize the chaotic free-for-all into a straight-forward narrative of political discourse: "Todo había sido preparado y cronometrado por sus agentes de propaganda" (143). While the clowns discuss whether and how to save their drowning colleague, Vihuela steps forward and offers his hand: "Yo, Gegé Vihuela, Presidente de la Nación, en nombre del pueblo extiendo mi mano hacia ti, oh payaso heroico, para que te unas en la lucha contra el enemigo común, el comunismo" (143).

This slapstick circus of "Los loros humanos," nevertheless, refuses any and every notion of social, political and logical order. La Rosita, a *dead* homosexual *compañero*, takes control of the rescued clown's body and irreverently parodies the presidential discourse. They silence La Rosita's indiscretion by plugging his mouth with a felt carrot and the "perorata fue tomada como chiste" (144). The president precedes with his programmed performance, yelling "¡Gegé con el circo!" (144) when Nepomuceno Viñas enters the scene. The ensuing showdown pits poetry against politics. Viñas, the president of the Society of Poets, attempts to seize the notoriety he covets by publicly humiliating the president of Chile:

> Los actores iban a responder en coro "¡Los payasos con Vihuela!"
> cuando Nepomuceno Viñas, que no había participado en el acto,
> portando un pastel cremoso, llegó coronado de laureles y vestido

con su toga de Presidente de la Sociedad de Poetas. Vociferando su
Y que duerma Epsilón, aplastó la torta en la cara del atónito Presidente. (144)

Analyzing the circus, then, highlights a convergence of uncontrollable,
polyvalent signs. Like a Bakhtinian carnival, the clowns' act resists any
conclusive conclusion. Their spectacle, "una función sin comienzo ni
fin" (91), does not progress in the sense of a pre-plotted narrative but
rather evolves toward indeterminate, nonpredictable chaos. The president's propaganda agents, on the other hand, attempted to limit the
circus to a definitive monological message. Finally realizing the in-
tractable nature of the circus, Vihuela takes refuge in the chaotic indeterminacies of parody: "Bravo, toni. Tú y yo nos hemos unido. ¡El Poder
y la risa se confunden! ¡Qué genial imitación del traidor Neruña!" (145).
    President Vihuela clowns his way out of the predicament by pub-
licly decorating Viñas as "Antipoeta Nacional" (145). That evening
President Vihuela directs his own theatrical simulation:

> Un grupo de soldados vestidos de obreros, a los gritos de "¡Abajo
> Vihuela, arriba Tito!" "¡Mueran los payasos!" "¡Viva la guerra!"
> lanzaron bombas Molotov y acribillaron los carromatos. Inmedi-
> atamente llegó otro camión cargado de periodistas ... Pronto el
> país leería indignado que un grupo de arteros comunistas, enviados
> por el fugitivo Juan Neruña, había atacado y asesinado a los hu-
> mildes y patriotas payasos del circo "Los loros humanos." (146)

Vihuela stages a sham performance of terrorism *against himself* in order
to destroy the circus. In this scene, as in other similar passages, Jodorowsky's novel parodies actual *performances* of true military repression.
In Latin America, government-endorsed death squads have been known
to simulate *acts* of guerrilla terrorism in order to legitimize subsequent
military repression. Critic Frank Graziano discusses the scripting of
feigned subversion in the Argentine "dirty war": "Pseudoterroist acts
were staged by the military and then duly neutralized as though they
were real in order to perpetuate the illusion of revolutionary threat (and
of competent action eliminating it) that generated whatever legitimacy
the Junta could claim" (65). Theatrical conceits, then, give the military
a validating pretext for violence. *El loro de siete lenguas* re-presents this
political manipulation of representation.

From the brief extracts given here it is obvious that *El loro de siete lenguas* generates an extremely anarchic or chaotic narrative. And yet while the novel might initially appear heavy-handed, Jodorowsky buries an intricate structure of interrelated quests beneath the surface. The prologue, for example, graphically foreshadows the development of the multiple quests. When Piripipí commits suicide—setting fire to himself and standing on his head—he too emulates the fall prefigured by the tarot's Maison Dieu card (see Figure 3-4): "El fuego empezó a consumirlo: Piripipí se arrodilló, colocó sus palmas en las brasas ardientes y luego apoyó la coronilla" (147). The card's burning tower, furthermore, evokes the destruction of the circus. Subsequently, the *compañeros* begin their quest anew, searching for Carlo Poncini among the Indians in the South. Nepomuceno Viñas, in turn, begins living his poetic dream: "Esta vez lo buscaban de verdad. Era un fugitivo político" (147).

(MIS)TAKEN IDENTITIES: (CON)FUSING THE COPY OF A COPY WITH A COPY

Viñas's life as a dissident poet owes itself to an extraordinary series of falsified identities. Intending to punish Juan Neruña, President Vihuela discovers that he cannot remember what the poet looks like. Photographs of Neruña do not exist: "Se había dado a la Poesía, quería ser él la Poesía y la Poesía no tenía cuerpo humano" (192). It is significant that Neruña had formerly worked as the president's secretary of propaganda (141). He abandoned the writing of linear propaganda in the pursuit of poetry. Here again, the text reiterates the allegorical search from the prologue: "Cuando estalló la tormenta ... caímos al suelo ... buscando a tientas ... Poesía" (6).

The president's goal, to seek out and annihilate the elusive Neruña, is in essence yet another narrative quest. Neruña seeks poetry, Viñas seeks poetic fame, and Vihuela searches for the poet Neruña. Unable to pursue an invisible man, Vihuela vies for a practical alternative and assigns Neruña a new face. The president publishes a wanted poster of Nepomuceno Viñas's face (which he remembers from the cake incident) with the name of Juan Neruña, public enemy number one (192).

This substitution of faces, like an irregularity entered into an equation, results in magnified chaos later. After coincidentally seeing the poster, a group of striking coal miners mistakes Viñas for Neruña.

They immediately herald him as "La voz del pueblo," praise him publicly and beseech him to recite his poem *Canto al Minero*. When Viñas
finds himself incapable of opening his mouth, his friend, El cojo
Valdivia, saves the situation by lying. He announces that the mountain
air damaged "Neruña's" throat and that the bard cannot speak. The crowd
accepts Valdivia's offer to recite Neruña's poem for him, which he had
purportedly memorized. Valdivia's lie is in essence a fictional narrative—he amplifies the misrepresentation disseminated by the poster.

The parrot-shaped secretary of *La sociedad de poetas chilenas* improvises a poem, imitating Juan Neruña's style:

> Y los versos con ritmos y matices idénticos a los de Juan Neruña
> fueron emergiendo para formar un canto que denunciaba el sufri
> miento del pueblo, la explotación, la traición de Vihuela, la venta
> del país a las Compañías extranjeras, para luego aportar la espe
> ranza con un llamado a la unión obrera. (202)

Nepomuceno Viñas chimes in with the last three verses and receives a
standing ovation. Valdivia's imitation of Neruña, coupled with President Vihuela's poster, converts Nepomucino Viñas into the "people's
poet" on the spot.

This ongoing relationship of *El loro Valdivia* improvising imitations of Neruña for Nepomuceno Viñas, who recites the concluding
verses, dramatically fuels the workers' revolution. When the false
Neruña's fame as the people's poet grows to gigantic proportions,
Viñas's life becomes endangered. Emotionally too weak to confront the
danger, Viñas refuses to step before the crowd. El cojo Valdivia then
disguises himself as Nepomuceno Viñas and appears before the mass of
workers:

> Valdivia recitaba imitando la voz de Juan Neruña ... No, pero ...
> *imitando la voz de Nepomuceno Viñas cuando imitaba a Neruña* ...
> El cojo Valdivia, sin cojear, estirado como lápiz ... con el cráneo
> rapado en el que se elevaban tres mechones, vestido con su traje, se
> hacía pasar por él, por Juan Neruña ... Y *la imitación era perfecta*.
> (emphasis added, 250)

Ultimately this chain of imitation comes full circle. The "real" Juan
Neruña confronts Nepomuceno Viñas and compliments the imposter's
poetry: "Las odas que improvisa son lo mejor que he escrito. Usted ha

llevado el estilo Neruña a su perfección" (280). It was Valdivia, nevertheless, who imitated Neruña. Viñas accordingly parrots *el loro's* improvisations. Thus the copy of the copy surpasses the original.

This chain of poetic imitation can be compared to a chaotic equation that magnifies initial indeterminacies. Viñas's (mis)taken face catalyzes social disorder, upsetting the prevailing economic and power structures with the chaos of a workers' revolution. Reading "backwards" through the series of iterative mimicry leads ultimately to an uncertain "origin," Juan Neruña. The poet Neruña is in fact infinitely indeterminate. We find out later that he was literally born without a face. His vocation as a writer, furthermore, situates him somewhere in the middle of the iterative continuum—writers do not create language but rather rearticulate an always already iterative code.

The plot of *El loro de siete lenguas*, accordingly, approximates a poststructuralist allegory of language itself. Derridean grammatology posits a paradoxically absent nonorigin, a "trace," at the *always already signifying* souree of language: "The trace is not only the disappearance of origin ... it means that the origin did not even disappear, that it was never constituted except reciprocally by a nonorigin, the trace, which thus becomes the origin of the origin ... Yet we know that ... if all begins with the trace, there is above all no originary trace" (Derrida 60). Jodorowsky's novel depicts quests for fame, poetry and, ultimately, the "original" language. And yet each apparent origin corresponds to another copy of a copy. There is no origin.

This metaphor of writer-as-parrot who reiterates an already iterating series extends beyond Jodorowsky's novel into the realm of "real" literature. Before the story begins, the prologue reminds the reader of the novel's purely fictional format: "Ningún personaje es real, ningún sitio es verdadero, cualquier parecido es coincidencia. Hablamos de un Chile que no es Chile. Describimos un Universo paralelo" (6). In spite of this parody of publisher disclaimers, nevertheless, Jodorowsky explicitly elaborates noncoincidental similarities with historical individuals, names and events.

This slippage between illusion (or fiction) and reality figures prominently throughout *El loro de siete lenguas*.[22] The diegetic Neruña and Viñas, for example, constitute immediately recognizable parodies of Pablo Neruda and Nicanor Parra. The novel's plot fictionally animates the literary rivalry between Parra and Neruda alongside the political conflict between Neruda and Gonzalez Videla. Neruda (as part of the *Partido Comunista*) originally worked and wrote poems for Gonzalez Videla's candidacy. After becoming president, Gonzalez Videla declared the Communist Party illegal and sent Neruda into exile. Parra, years later, was accused of supporting the Pinochet dictatorship. These historical referents also perpetuate intertextual sequences of literary imitation. Neruda's name, for example, was a *nome de plume* (his given name was Neftalí Reyes Basualto) that the bard copied from the Czechoslovakian poet Jan Neruda. Viñas's role of antipoet in *El loro de siete lenguas* evokes the book that Parra published in 1954, *Poemas y antipoemas*, which rejected the Nerudian tradition of poetry. In his essay, "Antipoesía y poesía conversacional en Hispanoamérica" (*Para una teoría de la literatura hispanomericana*), Roberto Fernández Retamar describes Nicanor Parra's *antipoesía* in terms of his rivalry with Pablo Neruda: "Con repecto a Parra ... se trata de la poesía *anti-Neruda*. Eso quiere decir que no se entiende del todo la función de la poesía de Parra si no se está algo familiarizado con la poesía caudalosa, copiosa, pretenciosa, de Pablo Neruda" (145). And yet while Jodorowsky clearly references the competition between Parra and Neruda, this rivalry does not precisely reflect the origin of Jodorowsky's characters. Years before Parra, Vicente Huidobro (another of Jodorowsky's major influences) had already referred to himself as "antipoeta" (in his poem *Altazor* [1936]).

Jodorowsky, then, re-presents poets who repeatedly represent their world through language while entering into a political struggle for power. Neruda, of course, rendered his experiences of exile and clandestine hiding into poetry in his *Canto general*. He explicitly refers to González Videla as "el traidor de Chile" and "una rata," who rose up on "los hombros del pueblo" (234). It is clear that Jodorowsky parodies the historical personages together with their writing. Neruda's poem, "La tierra se llama Juan," becomes "¡La Patria se llama Juan!" in *El loro de siete lenguas*. In Neruda's poem, Juan is an allegory for the oppressed mestizo worker. In Jodorowsky's novel, the workers shout the phrase in praise of Juan Neruña.

The novel's opening epigraph—"Reconozco una sola verdad: la verdad de la ilusión" (9)—epitomizes Jodorowsky's world view. For the writer Jodorowsky, life and fiction are inextricably knotted, both in political rhetoric and practice, within a (con)fusion of literary signs. Conflating the voices of Neruda and Parra as a *loro de siete lenguas*, Jodorowsky satirizes the concept of a people's poet who speaks in the name of the *pueblo*. He reaffirms the creative value of literature, denying the (Chilean Communist Party's) manipulation of literature as a political tool.

CONFUSING THE CHAOS OF BABEL

What does this cynical play between copy and original, as well as performance, illusion, literature and reality signify politically? If the world is merely a narrative hodgepodge—a carnival of copies of copies without any original—is there a subject in this text? Is there a subject in Jodorowsky's (con)fusion of signs? Where do we as readers figure in Jodorowsky's proliferating series of images? By underscoring a void at the center of his narrative quests, Jodorowsky prepares a space for the reader. Seekers must become their own heroes. Rather than seeking out "representatives," Jodorowsky's narratives endorse an agenda of self-empowerment. Playing the role of protagonist, the reader-seeker must become the subject of his or her own life.

Jodorowsky's discourse traces a seamless loop that paradoxically celebrates and annihilates individual autonomy. In his third novel, *Donde mejor canta un pájaro*, the character Teresa survives yet another military performance–massacre. Later in the novel, after suffering a mental breakdown, Teresa begins shooting at the legs of everyone in uniform: "Dejó cojos a un policía, dos soldados, un mozo de café, una liceana, un heladero, tres muchachos vestidos de futbolistas, un huaso, una enfermera y un Viejo Pacuero ... vendiendo maní confitado" (247). Exalting "difference," Teresa wages war against human herd behavior: "¡Abajo la igualdad! ¡Viva la diferencia!" (247). Her rampage intensifies when she concludes that order transcends the external signs of clothes: "Cuando decidió que los cuerpos humanos, por tener igual constitución, cabeza, tronco y extremidades, eran uniformes, *se armó el caos*" (emphasis added, 247).

Jodorowsky, like his character Teresa, wreaks havoc out of order. He stretches conventions, literary as well as societal, subverting forms of propriety and structure. The conspicuous lack of a protagonist in *El loro* manifests the author's predilection for multiplicity and diversity rather than order. Augusto Boal, in *Teatro de oprimido*, delineates the history of the theatrical roles of protagonists and tragic heroes in political terms:

> When Thespis *invented* the protagonist, he immediately "aristocratized" the theater, which existed before in its popular forms of mass manifestations, parades, feasts, etc. ... The tragic hero, who later begins to carry on a dialogue not only with the chorus but also with his peers ... appears when the State begins to utilize the

theater for the political purpose of coercion of the people. (emphasis original, 33)

As an *Enfant terrible*, Jodorowsky repeatedly violates taboos, reveling in episodes of gory, perverse and sadistic hedonism. As he writes in *El loro de siete lenguas*, "Desde ahora todas las leyes podían ser transgredidas" (166).

Jodorowsky's celebration of individuality and difference underscores the isomorphic symmetry common to the human condition. This tendency parallels a paradigm shift noted by Hayles that follows the transition from a "focus on individual particles or units" to the recursive symmetry of chaotic fields (169). According to Hayles, "the fundamental assumption of chaos theory, by contrast [to Newtonian paradigms], is that the individual unit does not matter" (170). In chaos theory, as in Jodorowskian philosophy, ultimate relevance belongs on the level of the system.

Jodorowsky's character Teresa evokes an image of the world as an endless continuum of images, much like Baudrillardian hyperreality where signs and referents have terminally imploded:

> Somos unos impostores, en este mundo que no es auténtico, donde no hay nada verdadero y lo real es un espejismo. Uniformes por todos lados, copias de copias de copias, cada traje, cada cuerpo, cada alma, es un disfraz. La superficie está en todas partes y el centro en ninguna. (248)

Jodorowsky both asserts and deconstructs the notions of difference and individuality. On the one hand he narrates a heterogeneous world in which the notion of normality does not exist. At the same time, however, Jodorowsky stops short of exalting the (modernist) supremacy or elitism of the individual subject. Ultimately, Jodorowsky denies the existence of individual authority.

Although not overtly political, Jodorowsky's narrative agenda celebrates the subversive multiplicity of language. The quest begins with the Tower (of Babel) card and concludes (in the epilogue) by reading another tarot image, Le Monde (341). Like nearly all of Jodorowsky's works, the novel ends by completing a circle: "Pensaron profundamente en su larga patria, Chile, y le dieron vida. Los cuatro mil doscientos kilómetros de la tierra larga se elevaron en el aire como una serpiente que unió cabeza y cola" (340). Rather than concluding with a unified vision, nevertheless, Jodorowsky scatters unity, representing a *perpetually already re-presenting loro de siete lenguas*. Like the "creator" of Borges's "Ruinas circulares," the novel demonstrates that a subject's perceived identity derives from a continuum of always already represented characters. Deconstructing monological representation, Jodorowsky's (con)fusion of literature and politics celebrates polyvalency (multilingualism as literary Babel). As René Jara writes, novels do not "represent" reality but rather subvert the reductive notion of representation: "Las palabras hablan *en lenguas* y dicen, confusa y atropelladamente a veces, que las representaciones no son verdades" (emphasis original, 52–3). Jodorowsky, then, invokes *un loro de siete lenguas*, not limiting the multiplicity of language to order but rather reiterating the polyvalence of chaos.[23]

L'INCAL: REITERATING ITERATION

Whereas *El loro de siete lenguas* constructs an elaborate historical narrative based on mistaken identities, plagiarism and imitation during the 1940s and 1950s, the *Incal* projects into the future, graphically evoking a carnivalesque hyperreal universe predicated on simulation. The *Incal* presents a technologically advanced world scattered with electronically reproduced images. The detective-protagonist, John Difool, becomes embroiled in his adventure when a young-looking woman hires him to accompany her to "l'anneau rouge" (12). At midnight her holographic makeup wears off, exposing a decrepit, unattractive "vieillarde" (14). Not only can appearances not be trusted, but the realm of illusions has been institutionalized. Whenever Difool finds a spare moment he notoriously takes refuge with a holographic prostitute, a "homéopute." Seeking pleasure, Difool constructs virtual prostitutes, choosing, aligning and shaping body parts according to his personal preference.

Throughout the city, ubiquitous television screens continually broadcast news reports and sensational media spectacles. Not only do gigantic screens project from the sides of buildings (a setting later employed in Ridley Scott's film *Blade Runner*), but zombie-like *téléaddicts* sit drinking in their *conapts*, watching televised reports of violence as entertainment. This view of an anesthetized populace riveted to television screens evokes a dystopian version of Marshall McLuhan's "global village." In an interview (about *El Topo*, in 1970) Jodorowsky spoke about the communications media, disagreeing with McLuhan's optimism: "McLuhan says that means of communication have increased.

They have. But those who communicate have diminished" (125). Analogously, in *Las ansias carnívoras de la nada* television represents the ultimate extension of hegemonic control. *El General* speaks to the populace through omnipresent television screens. The general's control is so extensive that he speaks differently to "cada telespectador" (11).[24]

In the *Incal*, a diabolical anchorman, Diavaloo, appears differently in each news report. First appearing as a typical newscaster, the exaggerated Diavaloo next appears in an eighteenth-century-style powdered wig, later as a clown and elsewhere as a writhing contortionist. Diavaloo's broadcasts transcend global boundaries, extending even into the far reaches of the galaxy. The *Incal*'s view of the media and television only slightly exaggerates present-day media spectacles. Jodorowsky depicts what García Canclini, in a study of the role of the media in postmodern politics, has called "la teatralización de lo social" (248).

Rather than providing information, news programming proliferates a narrative of images constituting simulated events. The programming conjures illusions on at least two levels. On a very basic level, the images presented by the media may or may not correspond to the actual situation. This type of misinformation simulates a false situation to gain support among the populace for a particular (usually conflictual) course of action. A second type of simulation constitutes an even more subtle illusion than such incidents of contorted propaganda. As García Canclini points out, the format of special crisis reports generates an extremely subtle form of ideological illusion: "Cuando los problemas parecen irresolubles y los responsables incapaces, se nos ofrece la compensación de una información tan intensa, inmediata y frecuente que *crea la ilusión de que estamos participando*" (emphasis added, 248). In other words media specials create an illusion of democracy. In the *Incal*, when the police cannot detain Difool, the president launches his robotic assassin, la Nécrosonde (89). Significantly, while pursuing Difool the robot televises the entire chase in three-dimensional images. Suffering substantial damage, smaller and smaller components of the robot continue to follow Difool and his companions. Ultimately, only "le nécroclonage presidentiel," the robot's electronic "eye," remains (147). The Nécrosonde underscores the (con)fusion of media and information in contemporary society. The media do not transmit the news (as information or content) but actually create a news spectacle. Rather than presenting information in the form of news, the media re-formats images to produce spectacles of entertainment.

In the *Incal*, where the president exists only as an infinite series of clones, Jodorowsky imagistically constructs a sarcastic commentary on *the power of image*. Early in the story Diavaloo reports on the president's ninth clone operation, during which the president ("Son Ophidite majeure") assumes the body of a two hundred and twenty pound transvestite (26–8). In *Avant l'incal* the president's previous clone transformations convert him from a "nain d'andromède, en état avancé de putréfaction" into "L'homme moyen idéal" (36). In later episodes he alternately takes the form of an old man and a bearded woman. In the world of the *Incal*, political authority surrounds a "figure," a hollow body whose absurd appearance mutates perpetually. The dominant order maintains hegemony through the propagation of meaningless reproduced signs.

The well-shaped city structurally segregates social, economic and racial groups on a vertical scale of privilege according to semiotic and biological determinants. While impoverished mutants occupy the low-level slums, only halo-bearing *aristos* own the right to enter the upper levels.[25] The violence of class struggle also provides prime-time subject matter for the media. At one point Diavaloo remarks snidely to the president, "Si [ces cités revoltes] n'existaient pas, il faudrait les inventées!" (80). The president's *palais volant* (itself divided into stratified layers) hovers above the earth at an almost safe distance from the "city-revolts."

This conflictual dynamic recurs on multiple levels in the novel. When Difool receives *l'incal*, a mysterious crystal-shaped object, he finds himself at the center of an intergalactic power struggle. Everyone—the president's elite paramilitary squad of hunchbacks, the robotic police, the evil Technos (under the direction of the Technopape), squadrons of mutants, revolutionaries and extraterrestrial Berg creatures—pursues Difool in an effort to abscond with the *incal*. At the same time, moreover, the *incal* brings to the surface an *internal* power struggle that surges *within* John Difool. Staring at this "simple pyramide de cristal" (33), Difool refuses to recognize his own fragmented identity. He represses, in other words, the psychic, emotional and sexual struggle put in motion by the "in call." The enigmatically speaking *incal* asks, "Combien sont John Difool?" and then dismembers Difool's body (34). Chopping Difool into pieces, Moebius's drawing represents a Lacanian *corps morcelé avant la lettre*. The experience arouses John's unconscious monsters, embodiments of the psychic struggle between the ego, superego and id (33–4). Difool's personal struggle, then, reiterates the political conflicts surrounding him.

A reading of John Difool's character indicates a marked tension between individual *integrity* and group consciousness. As I have noted elsewhere, Jodorowsky's narratives usually avoid a central character or protagonist. John Difool, on the other hand, represents an archetypal fool character, in part inspired by the Le Mat card from the Marseille tarot, who insists on acting impulsively. Toward the end of the novel, as each of his companions voluntarily yield their personal identities to an advanced state of universal consciousness, the infantile Difool refuses to surrender his individuality: "Je ne veux pas me fondre dans ton unité! Je choisis d'être MOI-MÊME!" (289). *Les aventures de John Difool* corresponds to a graphic "novel of education" in which the protagonist blindly fails to learn his lesson. The episodes of space travel and intergalactic war function allegorically, constituting various tests in Difool's journey toward enlightenment. Difool the anti-hero, a *détective minable de classe R.*, fails to discover the purpose of the *incal* until it is too late. Rather than evolve he repeatedly acts in a selfish, immature and impulsive manner. His negative characteristics become most manifest on *planète Berg* when he finds himself among the competitors for the *Compétition Millénaire et Sacrée de la Fécondation Quinquennale*. In this hilarious adventure, Jodorowsky generates genetic and emotional metaphors via both macro and micro allegories.

Here Difool's duty relegates him to the level of a human sperm cell. He must race to the top of a gigantic ant hill, competing against thousands of human mutants, armed with a variety of medieval-appearing shields and spears. The winner will then descend into the *siège de l'ovulation primordiale* to fertilize *la protoreine*. This "sacred cone," *la fourmilière-matrice originelle*, is situated at the center of an enormous crater. A capacity crowd of Bergs packs the coliseum-crater, watching the "combattants humains" fight tooth and nail to reach the "noyau nuptial." To help John, his six companions (the Meta-Baron, Animah, Tanatah, Solune, Deepo and Kill) become miniaturized, guiding the starship's controls from inside John. With the help of the *incal* (and John's companions, who feed him hormonal and psychic assistance in a manner reminiscent of Woody Allen's film *Everything you wanted to know about sex but were afraid to ask*) Difool ejects himself to the top of the cone and wins the competition (185–91).

On one level, the scene expresses the biological drive toward reproduction in terms of a physical, animalistic urge. At the same time, the throng of Bergs watching the event turns the act of genetic reproduction into a sports spectacle. When Difool finally penetrates the royal (fertilization) chamber, the reader remains watching the scene like a lone voyeur.

Difool's dependence on *images* engages contemporary society's addiction to market-formulated images of beauty. The *protoreine*, a one-eyed liquid mass gelifying in a large vat, repulses John Difool. Because he refuses to enter the vat, she reads his soul to find the appropriate image needed to form his preferred mate. After molding herself into the shape of a large-breasted blond woman (an exact replica of Animah), Difool joins the *protoreine* inside the vat. Copulating with the image of Animah, Difool impregnates the *protoreine* (192–5). The resulting reproduction multiplies Difool's obsession with images. Later, when he returns to the Berg planet, he realizes that he has engendered 78,000 "JDF" clones. One by one his eggs pop out of the sacred cone. As soon as his clones break out of their shells they go screaming in search of a *homéopute* (265–6).[26]

Cloning and mechanically reproducing series of copied bodies plays a pivotal role in the *Incal* narrative. The government, directed by a presidential clone, attempts to enforce its laws with mechanically produced police, the *robofliks*. The president's paramilitary squadron constitutes a mass of identical mindless hunchbacks. In *Avant L'Incal*, the authorities arrest young Difool's father for impersonating an *aristo*. By applying a machine to his back, the authorities essentially lobotomize the elder Difool, giving him a *remodelàge intégral ... le total effacement de sa mémoire* (23). The process not only erases his mind but reconstructs him physically as another hunchbacked *bossu* militiaman.

The political power network that pervades the *Incal* universe evokes images akin to Jean Baudrillard's formula of hyperreal simulation. For Baudrillard, simulation, "la génération par les modèles d'un réel sans origine ni réalité," has subsumed representation (*Simulacres* 10). The most controversial aspect of Baudrillard's theory is the utter lack of a ground zero. Rather than a conspiracy theory wherein media moguls consciously create and propagate images to their advantage, Baudrillard evokes a perpetual loop of simulation effects that renders obsolete the notion of discovering an original referent behind the sign. In the *Incal*'s *cité puits*, as in Baudrillard's theory, the contiguity of signs and referents has been corrupted, leaving series of re-produced signs without referents: "Dans ce passage à un espace dont la courbure n'est plus celle du réel, ni celle de la vérité ... Il ne s'agit plus d'imitation, ni de redoublement ... Il s'agit d'une substitution au réel des signes du réel" (11). In *Ouisky, SPV et homéoputes*, the ever-present Diavaloo also turns out to be a series of disposable clones. This conspicuous lack of authentic political representation[27] becomes a serial spectacle itself: Diavaloo, a clone, broadcasts serial reports of presidential clonings.[28]

What, then, is the strategy behind the representation of clones? Early in this chapter, I underscored the intertextual relationship between Jodorowsky's various graphic novels. After writing the *Incal*, Jodorowsky and Moebius wrote a "meta-chapter" that purportedly takes place within the novel's cycle. Subsequently, Janjetov and Jodorowsky began publishing the *Avant l'Incal* series, which literally copies the physical settings and character traits from the *original*. Later still, Gimenez and Jodorowsky commence *La caste des Méta-Barons* series, which explicitly begins by redrawing the earlier meta-chapter. While perhaps a marketing strategy, it remains noteworthy that Jodorowsky's narratives specifically highlight serial reproduction. *El loro Valdivia's* imitation of Viñas's imitation of Neruña, the clone Diavaloo's broadcasts of presidential cloning, and Difool's propagation of 78,000 clones (all addicted to *homéoputes*) rearticulate an obsession with the notion of serialization.

In the concluding remarks to her book, *Contested Culture: The Image, the Voice, and the Law*, Jane M. Gaines addresses the discursive paradox that complicates the legal control of (re-produced) images in contemporary society: "It is not a question of restoring that subject to a rightful place; rather, *the issue is the contradiction inherent in any rhetoric of originality and authenticity* that becomes evident when there is neither a singular person to produce an original work nor any possibility of the virginal uniqueness of that work" (emphasis added, 240). Both thematically and archetextually, Jodorowsky engages the problem of indefinitely deferred images, which, while perhaps more visible in the context of electronic culture, has always (already) existed. Jodorowsky (con)fuses the order of things with the chaos of narrative, representing again and again a quest for an original copy.

A consideration of the *Incal*'s structure in relation to classic comic books will perhaps help bring Jodorowsky's repetitive narrative strategy into focus. In his essay, "The Myth of Superman," Umberto Eco describes *repetition* as an aspect of industrial society that contributes toward the making of Superman:

> Man becomes a number in the realm of the organization which has usurped his decision-making role, he has no means of production and is thus deprived of his power to decide. Individual strength, if

not exerted in sports activities, is left abased when confronted with the strength of machines which determine man's very movements. In such a society the positive hero must embody to an unthinkable degree the power demands that the average citizen nurtures but cannot satisfy. (107)

"Man," in other words, aspires to break away from his serial condition, fantasizing of his mythic strength and abilities. Although Jodorowsky does critique industrial and postindustrial serialization, his writing turns the superhero motif upside down. Difool represents an anti-hero, a man of less than ideal morals who is intrinsically devoid of superhuman power. This contrast is not merely a divergence on the level of character but is visible structurally as well.

Eco theorizes that Superman comics start anew at the conclusion of each episode in order to maintain the mythic quality of an invincible, eternal hero. There is never any evidence of time passing, because the superhero figure cannot age. He terms this structure an "iterative" scheme, comparing it with the prefigured repetition of detective fiction and other popular narratives. The six volumes that comprise the *Incal*, on the other hand, *progress* where each previous album concludes. This tactic, which keeps readers buying the series of subsequent albums (to find out what happens), also allows for considerable character development within the narrative. Interestingly, John Difool does not essentially change in spite of his adventures. The *Incal* depicts the persistence of his character. His foiled enlightenment at the end of the series duplicates his fall from the opening scene. Instead of breaking the iterative code, the overall series magnifies it to another scale. Time progresses between albums but John Difool remains frozen in his archetypal foolishness, in the same fashion that the couple of *El túnel se come por la boca* circles eternally in their quest for light. Before concluding I would like to examine yet one more example where Jodorowsky reiterates similar obsessions.

LAS ANSIAS CARNÍVORAS DE LA NADA: RE-MEMBERING HISTORY

In *Las ansias carnívoras de la nada*, Jodorowsky represents another *quest*, this time without a definitive narrator, subject or goal. While the reader searches *Las ansias carnívoras de la nada* for meaning, three entities search for their lost memory along a dirt road in Chile. At the novel's conclusion, the three seekers directly encounter the general, the ubiquitous power figure they have been unknowingly pursuing since the beginning. In his final declaration of power, *el general* changes identity and place with one of the three: "De ahora en adelante serás yo ... ¡Ponte mi uniforme y dame tus ropas! ¡Aquí están mis dientes, mi peluca, mis bigotes, mis ojos de fuego para tus cuencas vacías! ¡Yo me pondré el sombrero, los anteojos, el impermeable" (136). One of the seekers assumes the general's position of power by putting on his clothes and his face. His first pronouncement of authority—"¡USTE-DES TRES, PIERDAN LA MEMORIA!" (136)—restarts the narrative of three entities in search for their memory. The ex-general fades into amnesia and anonymity, re-commencing an eternal quest of three entities who have lost their memory.

The question presents itself as to whether Jodorowsky merely indulges in a fictional game or if his art articulates any "real" implications. Are we to conclude that, in life as we know it, our quests for understanding and our negotiations with power figures have no meaning? Are hegemony and oppression merely manifestations of perverse poetry? Finally, what is the role of memory (and memory loss) in a text where only the general has recourse to remember?[29] Ultimately, *Las ansias carnívoras de la nada* simultaneously stages two cyclical narratives that "begin" at the novel's "end." The first of these describes how three subjects lose their memory and traces the steps of their futile quest to remember. To bring Jodorowsky's ideological agenda into relief, consider the leitmotif of amnesia within a political context: To remember is to represent history.

In Chapter 10 of *Las ansias carnívoras de la nada* the general's authorities accuse the three amnesiacs of political subversion. Young soldiers interrogate and torture them to force a confession. The accused are willing but unable to confess:

> —Es muy posible que seamos culpables ...
> —¿Culpables de qué?
> —No lo sabemos ...
> —¡Escarben en sus memorias, boludos!
> —No tenemos memoria. (76)

As they cannot remember where they came from or who they are, the interrogators invent a past for them:

> Para que confiesen tenemos que crearles un pasado ... Ustedes recuerdan una casa blanca ... Jugaban con un oso amarillo ...

> Tenían una madre alta, de cabellera larga y hermosa voz ... Su padre
> vestía de color violeta y tocaba el violín ... Ustedes fueron a la
> escuela ... Comenzaron a fumar ... Hicieron el servicio militar ...
> Se casaron ... Tuvieron hijos ... Fortuna ... Cometieron una falta,
> una terrible falta contra nuestro General. (76)

This invention of memory indicates the common root of narrative that
links history to fiction. Both concepts correspond to representations
whose narratives blend an indeterminate amount of facts and literature.
Later in the novel the three wanderers encounter their mother. She
shows them the house where they were born and the golden bear with
which they played. Their father still dresses in *violeta* and still plays the
violin. It seems, in other words, that the soldiers invented an accurate
memory for them.

Memory, nevertheless, constitutes a cognitive function, that, like
narrative, tends to progress toward chaos. Over time we tend to lose our
memories. Like an iterative function, initial indeterminacies become
magnified over time. People routinely exaggerate their pasts, embellish-
ing incrementally just how long that fish they caught really was. In
cases of childhood memories and memories formed after amnesia (after
an accident, for example), one never knows whether memories reflect
events of the past or memories of what one has been told about the
past. As Jodorowsky writes in *Las ansias carnívoras de la nada*, "la
memoria cambia cada día y como un loro fiel nos obedece, podemos
empobrecerla o llenarla de colores" (98). Writing, for Jodorowsky,
corresponds to a technique for inscribing and illustrating memory.

This scene of inventing a past in *Las ansias carnívoras de la nada*
(1991) repeats almost verbatum a scene from Jodorowsky's play *El
túnel se come por la boca* (from 1965). In the earlier play, three police-
men (1, 2, 3) invent *una memoria* for *un rabino andrajoso* in order to
force a confession:

> A: Soy culpable.
> 1, 2, 3: ¡De qué?!
> A: No sé ... ¿Ah?
> 1: Escarbe en su memoria.
> A: Yo no tengo memoria ...
> 3: ¡Para que confiese hay que crearle una memoria!
> ... Usted recuerda una casa blanca ...
> 1: Usted jugaba con un oso amarillo ...

2: Su madre era alta, caballera larga, hermosa voz …
3: Su padre vestía de negro y tocaba el violín …
1: Usted fue a la escuela …
2: Comenzó a fumar …
3: Conoció a su futura esposa …
1: Tuvo hijos …
2: ¡Fortuna!
3: Cometió un acto …
1: Una falta contra la Ley … (34–5)

What, then, does this scene express and why does Jodorowsky continually repeat himself?[30] Clearly, Jodorowsky did not forget that he had included an episode (about an amnesiac whose past is invented by the authorities) nearly thirty years before. He furthermore elaborates variations of this idea throughout his work. A trivial explanation might posit that the author reiterates this scene as part of his own literary quest, in a sustained effort to achieve a certain expression. At the same time, nevertheless, Jodorowsky's obsessive repetition can be viewed as a mnemonic device that aspires to re-member history through narrative.[31]

Jodorowsky's circular depictions of a perpetual quest without origin, history or end, paradoxically reinscribe a crucial place for subjects. Along with the narrative of amnesia, *Las ansias carnívoras de la nada* also relates how one unconscious entity becomes a subject. Jodorowsky's solution corresponds to an act of mystic awareness—one finds the general by realizing that she or he already is the general. By re-membering oneself one achieves an identity and becomes a subject.[32] Like John Difool in the *Incal*, we too must learn to re-member ourselves as conscious subjects: "Il faut que tu recommences … que tu aprennes à te souvenir" (*Incal* 295–6).

Amnesia, consequently, serves Jodorowsky as an allegory for contemporary (postmodern) disorientation. With the transnational shifts of late capitalism we seem unable to recall who, or where, we are. With the fall of grand narratives we have forgotten where it was we were going. In the ecstasy of semiotic glut we can no longer remember how to read the texts whose interpretation might point a way out of this place. Signs have been hewn from their referents, and we wander aimlessly in a hyperreal (con)fusion of images, reproductions and copies. Postmodern existence can be characterized by the continual perpetuation of images. Jodorowsky responds by reiterating the stream of images by writing novels and comic books, films, pantomimes and theater—texts that explicitly underscore a perpetual play of images *ad infinitum*.

I would like to conclude by returning to the significance of tarot in Jodorowsky's work. Like literature, tarot represents a system of images that, in principle, allow a reader to interpret her or his current situation. Although certain schools of tarot attribute hidden meaning to the images represented on the cards, Jodorowsky rejects the notion of predetermined meaning. For Jodorowsky, meaning originates not within the tarot cards themselves but rather as a product of one's reaction and interpretation, one's reading, of the images.

One could read Jodorowsky's art as a re-presentation of the iconography that is represented on the cards. On an autobiographical level, his writing, like art in general, corresponds to a personal attempt to interpret his own life and situation through literature. Jodorowsky's work, ranging from *El Incal* to *El loro de siete lenguas*, explicitly derives from, interprets and reconfigures specific tarot images. In other words, Jodorowsky's work effectuates a reading and a rewriting of the tarot's symbolism.

For Jodorowsky, everyone must elaborate his or her own interpretation of the cards to find his or her own version of truth. Jodorowsky's mystic perspective, on the one hand, seems apolitical. And yet while he denies the existence of truth, Jodorowsky stacks a preeminently political deck. For years vast numbers of followers have sought out Jodorowsky, asking him for advice and guidance. What can be more political than to encourage these seekers to look inside themselves, to construct their own interpretation of the images that surround them and to find their own truth? This insistence on finding individual truths evokes a subversive political commitment that questions and interrogates all forms of authority, including Jodorowsky's. Awareness and faith in individuality inscribes aesthetic expression with political agency. Only when one consciously directs one's own "reading" can a reader become a subject, rewriting one's own text.

Whereas Jodorowsky distorts the iterative code of popular narrative, he *reiterates* the narrative of a perpetual quest toward an always already copied, translated and narrated narrative. And yet although his work is chaotic there is a significant difference between literary and scientific chaos. As Hayles points out, scientific paradigms "acknowledge that ordered, predictable systems do exist" (183). In a nonlinear equation, for example, the chaos enters at a specific site of origin. Jodorowsky, on the other hand, does not insert indeterminacy at the beginning of his narratives to produce subsequent chaos. In language there neither is nor has there ever been a stable "origin" with which one can meddle. Narrative representation is always already chaotic. Jodorowsky, then, accentuates and reiterates chaos—(con)fusing spiritual, literary and political quests, simultaneously celebrating, critiquing and rattling *la jaula* of representation.

NOTES

1. Flammarion first published Gérard Roero de Cortanze's French translation of *El loro de siete lenguas* in 1985 (under the title *Le Paradis des perroquets*) six years before the original Spanish version of the novel. Flammarion insisted that Jodorowsky cut one hundred pages from the manuscript, which has since been restored in the Chilean version (published by Hachette). *Le Paradis des perroquets* won the Prix de l'Humour Noir in 1985. *Las ansias carnívoras de la nada* was also first published as a French translation as *Enquête sur un chemin de terre* in 1988 by Belfond. *L'Incal* was published with Moebius as a series of albums called *Les aventures de John Difool*. Humanoïdes Associés originally published each volume individually as *L'Incal noir* (1983), *L'Incal lumière* (1983), *Ce qui est en bas* (1985), *Ce qui est en haut* (1985), *La Cinquième essence* 1re partie (1988) and *La Cinquième essence* 2e partie (1989).

2. The published accounts of his birth and various peripetias also seem to problematize the notion of a definitive origin. In interviews Jodorowsky describes leaving Chile in 1953 at the age of 23, but he gives his birth year as 1929. On the jackets of his Hachette novels, the editor prints his birthdate as 1929 and says that he emigrated to France at 22 years of age (1952). Jean Annestay's *Les Mystères de L'Incal* cites his birthday as February 7, 1929 and reports that he first came to Paris in 1955. Michel Larouche's *Alexandre Jodorowsky: Cinéaste panique*, gives his birth year as 1930. His names, furthermore, are subject to various spellings, including Alexandro, Alejandro, Jodorowski and Jodorowsky.

3. For a history of the Panic Movement, see Dominique Sevrain's "Quelques jalons dans l'histoire du panique" in Arrabal's collection, *Le Panique* (1973). In addition to Jodorowsky's manifestos, "Panique et poulet rôti" and "Sortir le théâtre du théâtre," *Le Panique* features related writings by Arrabal and Topor. Jodorowsky first published "Sortir le théâtre du théâtre" in Spanish as the prologue to his book *Teatro pánico* (1965) under the title "Hacia el 'efímero' pánico o ¡Sacar el teatro del teatro!" See also *Les*

Cahiers du silence: Arrabal, which compiles newspaper clippings, photographs and quotations giving an impression of the humor, cynicism and irreverence characterizing the Panic Movement. For a more recent analysis see Francisco Torres Monreal's "Origen y vida del Pánico," the critical introduction to Arrabal's collection *Teatro pánico* (1986). See also the recent anthology, *Alejandro Jodorowsky: antología pánica,* which includes a number of Jodorowsky's early texts, interviews and images.

4. *Fando y Lis* (1968) was a low-budget adaptation of Fernando Arrabal's play of the same title. Jodorowsky directed a version of the play for a year in Mexico before filming. His better known *El Topo* (1971) cost $400,000 to produce and became a cult classic. Jodorowsky wrote, produced, directed, played the lead role and composed the music for this film, which became the first "midnight movie" in New York. The screenplay with photographs (and an interview with Jodorowsky) has been published in *El Topo: A Book of the Film.* Music from the film was released on a phonographic LP titled *Music of "El Topo"/Shades of Joy.* Jodorowsky also wrote, directed, casted and acted in *La montaña sagrada,* which cost $1,500,000. He finished filming *La montaña sagrada* in the United States after the film and crew were banished from Mexico. For a study of these films (and the subsequent *Tusk* [1980, filmed in India]) see Michel Larouche's monograph, *Alexandre Jodorowsky: Cinéaste panique.*

In 1990, Jodorowsky made the film *Santa Sangre* (which he wrote and directed) in México, starring his children, Axel and Adam. Most recently, Jodorowsky directed the film *The Rainbow Thief,* starring Peter O'Toole, Omar Sharif and Christopher Lee.

5. Jodorowsky told me that he now writes his scripts in Spanish and an employee of the editor translates the scenarios into French. The editor also provides translators who follow Jodorowsky's instructions to write dialogues into particular idioms, such as robot-speak or punk slang.

To come as close as possible to an "original" text, I cite the French version of *L'incal.* I note page numbers parenthetically from the collected Geneva edition (encapsulating all six volumes) to take advantage of continuous pagination.

6. On the conception of the *Incal* see the interview with Moebius and Jodorowsky, "L'Homme de l'année: Moebius/Jodorowsky" in *L'Année de la Bande Dessinée.* For Jodorowsky's impressions of the comic book industry see the interview in *Un comic.*

7. Jodorowsky's *Dune* screenplay took great liberties with Herbert's novel. Salvador Dalí agreed to play the Emperor and Pink Floyd was to play the music. For a description of the intended film, see Jodorowsky's "Le film

que vous ne verrez jamais" (14–15) in Jean Annestay's *Les Mystères de l'incal*. See also Paul M. Sammon's article, "Designing 'Dune': Versions of Arrakis you'll never see" in *Cinefantastique* (32–5). Sammon's article reproduces designs that Moebius, Christopher Foss and H.G. Giger created for Jodorowsky's *Dune*.

8. Jodorowsky and Moebius actually collaborated on a digest-size comic book album, *Les Yeux du chat* (1978) after the *Dune* failure and before the *Incal*. Les Humanoïdes Associés published this short story (rendered in full panel drawings) on bright yellow paper and gave copies away as bonus gifts to subscribers. The album became a highly coveted collector's item, purportedly selling for as much as $600 (U.S.). After a number of bootleg editions appeared, Humanoïdes began reissuing editions of *Les Yeux du chat*. See *Taboo 4* (1990) for an English translation of the story, interviews with Moebius and Jodorowsky about *Les Yeux* and a concise but complete summary of the two artists' creative histories.

9. I emphasize that Jodorowsky's *Dune* screenplay, more so than Herbert's novel, represents the *Incal*'s most significant intertext. There exist, at the same time, other "influences" that inform the *Incal* narrative to varying degrees. In the interview in *Un comic*, Jodorowsky explains that he read all of the Mickey Spillane novels in order to work out the appropriate detective story rhythm for the adventures of John Difool. In the interview with *L'Année de la bande dessinée*, Jodorowsky mentions his intent to improvise on the comic book tradition of Tin Tin. Moebius's early work in the science fiction vein, for example *Arzach* and *The Long Tomorrow* (which he produced with Dan O'Bannon, another special effects collaborator in the aborted *Dune* project) clearly prefigures the setting of a not-so-distant future that characterizes the *Incal*.

10. On the relationship between film storyboard and comics see Roger Sabin's chapter, "Adult Comics and Other Media." According to Jodorowsky and Moebius, specific images from the *Dune* storyboard (and the *Incal*) were appropriated in subsequent films. Roger Sabin notes that Ridley Scott's *Blade Runner* and Steven Speilberg's *The Empire Strikes Back*, for example, employed the *Dune* storyboard–*Incal* in an "unofficial capacity" (287). Sabin writes that Humanoïdes Associés (the *Incal*'s publisher) refers to the influence in these films as "homages" (287). It is worth noting that members of the team Jodorowsky had assembled for *Dune* (Moebius, Dan O'Bannon, Chris Foss and H. R. Giger) later worked together on Ridley Scott's film version of *Alien* as well as *Blade Runner*.

11. It is important to note that the *bande dessinée* tradition in France commands much more intellectual and financial respect than American

"pulp" comics. French public libraries maintain substantial collections of hardbound B.D.s, which sell in stores for about $20 (U.S.). Of course, Jodorowsky's commercial success pales in comparison with multinational best-sellers, such as Disney's *Donald Duck* and *Mickey Mouse*, superhero classics (such as *Batman* or *Superman*), or even the mainstream European B.D.s *Tin Tin* and *Asterix*.

Historically the *Incal* emerged from the underground tradition of the 1960s and 1970s that promoted countercultural attitudes and values through comics. For an explanation of the "Underground comix" movement see Roger Sabin's *Adult Comics: An Introduction*.

12. *El tunel se come por la boca* (first performed in 1963) forms part of Jodorowsky's book *Teatro pánico*, published in Mexico (by Era) in 1965. All quotations are cited parenthetically with pagination referring to this edition.

13. Although this movement toward light suggests parallels with Plato's allegory of the cave, Jodorowsky's view does not correspond with a neoplatonic perspective. For Plato, the deception of the senses keeps man imprisoned, gazing at shadows instead of truth. Jodorowsky, on the other hand, sketches a circular cave, essentially eliminating the ideal exit of Platonic knowledge. Rather than trying to escape from the cave, Jodorowsky's narratives advocate enjoying those shadows projected by the light within.

14. For detailed structural analysis of the play see Winifred Harner's article, "Polycentric Framing Devices and Dramatic Structure in Alexandro Jodorowsky's *El túnel se come por la boca*."

15. The text–stage directions of *La jaula* appear on page 84 of *Teatro pánico*. Jodorowsky re-tools the concepts of *la jaula* and *el prisionero* as *microcuentos* in *Sombras al mediodía* (29 and 39). See my interview, "Las prerrogativas de la imaginación: una conversación con Alejandro Jodorowsky" for his description of *La jaula*, as well as his comments on other works.

16. All quotes of *El loro de siete lenguas* are taken from Dolmen's second Chilean edition and are cited parenthetically.

17. For a description of the historical evolution of the concept of chaos in science, see James Gleick's *Chaos: Making a New Science*. For a literary application of chaos theory to the Caribbean, see *The Repeating Island: The Caribbean and the Postmodern Perspective* by Antonio Benítez-Rojo. For more literary approximations, in addition to *Chaos Bound*, by N. Kathryn Hayles, see the collection of essays she edited, *Chaos and Order: Complex Dynamics in Literature and Science*.

18. To iterate, according to the *American Heritage Dictionary*, means

"to say or perform again; repeat" (696). For the adjective "iterative," the *American Heritage* gives two definitions: 1. "repetitious." 2. (in a grammatical context) "frequentive" (696).

19. Peter Brooks underscores the repetitive nature of narrative in his book *Reading for the Plot*:

"Todorov's 'same but different' depends on repetition. If we think of the trebling characteristic of the folk tale, and of all formulaic literature, we may consider that the repetition by three constitutes the minimal repetition ... Narrative must ever present itself as a repetition of events that have already happened ... Repetition in all its literary manifestations may in fact work as a 'binding' ... within the energetic economy of narrative" (288–9).

20. Jodorowsky has studied tarot for forty years. He performs public readings of tarot for a group of devoted followers every Wednesday in the café Saint Fiacre in Paris and then gives a presentation concerning mysticism in a nearby venue (for an audience of 200–600 followers). Virtually all of his novels, comics and films include references to tarot.

21. Chapter 8, where this takes place, bears the title "En busca de un perseguidor."

22. The blending of fact and fiction is also prominent in Jodorowsky's other works. The prologue of *Donde mejor canta un pájaro*, for example, begins by affirming the novel's truth and then immediately describes the act of fictionalizing or transforming the facts into myth: "Todos los personajes, sitios y acontecimientos, (aunque a veces se altere el órden cronológico), son reales. Pero esta realidad es tranformada y exaltada hasta llevarla al mito" (7).

23. Note the contrast between Jodorowsky's chaotic conclusion and the arcadian monologism that René Jara evokes to describe the discourse of (neo)fascism:

Y en el Milenio, en el orden arcádico del futuro podrá lograrse la anulación misma de la historia y de la multiplicidad de los lenguajes; el discurso será uno, el monólogo del poder proyectándose sobre un mundo mítico ... el mundo será otra vez uno, idéntico a sí mismo, una la raza, una la lengua, como en las vísperas de Babel. Este es el diseño del triunfo militar sobre el individuo, la historia y la sociedad humana. (51)

24. In an interview from 1970 (eighteen years prior to the first publication of *Las ansias carnívoras de la nada*) Jodorowsky prefigures the images

of hegemonic media manipulation that appear years later in his graphic and literary novels:

> Maybe the communications media will become extensions of the senses of one man: the President. He'll be like a gigantic octopus who'll put television glasses on your eyes. Yes and sound in your ears and a communicative skin over your skin. (*El Topo: A Book of the Film*, 1974, 125)

25. In the *Avant L'Incal* series, the young detective Difool discovers the mystery of aristocratic halos. The Technos take prostitutes' infants and infect their pineal glands with a mixture of *cocalfol* (an obvious pun on Coca Cola) and genetic material extracted from the nonputrified corpses of Sante Tereze da Villa and Saint Franzoi D'Acide (*Croot* 35–8). To create an aristocratic *auréole*, they transplant this infected gland into the baby of an *aristo* (*Anarco psychotiques* 31–4).

26. Difool's penchant for copulating with images is a leitmotif found throughout the *Incal*. In the *Avant l'Incal* series Animah strategically disguises herself as a *homéopute* to become impregnated with Difool's child, Solune. A real woman disguises herself, in other words, as a virtual woman, an image.

27. With Janjetov in the *Avant l'Incal* series, Jodorowsky represents the "real" authority as a gigantic black machine covered with an enormous brain. The president, Technopape and Diavaloo teleconference with the computer, appearing to each other via gigantic screens. See *Croot*, *Anarco psychotiques* and *Ouisky*, *SPV et homéoputes*.

28. Jodorowsky has produced another graphic novel with artist George Bess titled *Anibal 5: Dix Femmes avant de mourir*. In this story Anibal is a robotic spy who conducts his missions by following the instructions of a man named Pinker. The robot, Anibal, amuses himself with a harem of robotic sex machines. At the conclusion, furthermore, Pinker gives Anibal a collection of Marilyn Monroe robot nurses to lift his spirits. This comic book, then, re-presents Andy Warhol's well-known reproduction of reproduction, perpetuating, en masse, representations of representations.

29. In the *Myth of Eternal Return* Mircea Eliade observes that only "heros" remember their personal history (in archaic societies).

30. *Las ansias carnívoras de la nada* reincorporates several passages from Jodorowsky's earlier published works. The episode in Chapter 8 in which an absurd "master" orders his servants to tell him what to order them (63–6) almost repeats word for word *El túnel*'s pages 38–40. Additionally, Jodorowsky includes his short stories "De como Ori siendo gris se convirtió

en dorado" and "Los hermanos siameses" (from the even earlier *Cuentos pánicos* [1963]) with minor changes in the novel.

31. According to the *American Heritage Dictionary* the word "mnemonic" derives from the Greek term "mnemon" meaning "mindful" (842).

32. This perhaps explains the ubiquitous presence of severed limbs throughout Jodorowsky's artistic production. *El túnel se come por la boca*, *El Topo*, *The Holy Mountain*, *Les Aventures d'Alef-Thau* (whose first installment is titled *L'Enfant Tronc*), *Santa Sangre* and *Las ansias carnívoras de la nada* all feature characters who are missing arms or legs.

CHAPTER 4

Guillermo Gómez-Peña:
Re-Drawing the Borders

¿Cuál es la frontera? ¿El corte? No, es apenas la señal.

—Diamela Eltit

Guillermo Gómez-Peña, a Mexican performance artist living in the United States, explores transculturation at the junctures of opposing societies, cultures and languages. His work hybridizes multiple media combining printed text, video, plastic arts and theater. His performance art blends dramatic techniques from popular theater, "happenings" and political "art actions." He co-founded a performance troup called Poyesis Genética in 1981, which, after several incarnations, became the Taller de Arte Fronterizo/Border Arts Workshop in 1985. These groups staged collaborative, interdisciplinary performance interventions on the U.S.– Mexico border. In 1986 Gómez-Peña began co-editing and publishing a bilingual and binational magazine, *The Broken Line/La Línea Quebrada* with the express purpose of highlighting issues on the border.[1] Additionally, he has collaborated on large-scale installations, photomontages and radio programs.[2] Although Gómez-Peña's performances have been mentioned by various critics in essays on postmodernism (Homi Bhabha, Nestor García Canclini, Jean Franco, Celeste Olalquiaga, Juan Flores), his work remains largely unanalyzed.

Recently at a literature conference I spoke with a scholar who warned me that Gómez-Peña's work would resist rigorous analysis. "How can you possibly analyze him without falling victim to his satire?" he asked. It is true that Gómez-Peña's work imposes a series of logistical complications. His politically confrontational performances make use of a corrosive, oftentimes kitsch brand of parody. His propensity to lick the microphone, babble in "tongues" and scream obscenities at his audience may prove difficult to describe in academic discourse without taking refuge in the hollow imprecision of a term like *enfant terrible*. I sustain, nevertheless, that it is crucial to consider Gómez-Peña's work critically in spite of, and even because of, his iconoclastic hermeticism. Studying Gómez-Peña's unconventional texts demonstrates how performance art can be used as a political instrument in the 1990s, even in the midst of a (postmodern) flood of mass-produced images.

Winner of a 1991 MacArthur Foundation Fellowship,[3] Gómez-Peña directly engages the political and aesthetic factors comprising our present-day "crisis of representation." For Olalquiaga, this crisis results from an oversaturation of images in contemporary culture: "The principles of representation, which worked as long as a certain notion of reality could guarantee their secondary status ... have been overturned by the multiplication of images that has literally left no space for such distinctions" (5–6). If media-produced images do not actually constitute reality, they certainly shape public perception. Gómez-Peña uses performance to contest the vulgar images with which hegemonic culture stereotypes minority "others." In this sense Gómez-Peña's work coincides with the perspective that Hutcheon perceives in postmodern art: "It is a critique ... of the view of representation as reflective (rather than constitutive) of reality and ... it is also an exploitation of those same challenged foundations of representation" (*Politics of Postmodernism* 18). Aware that there is no escape from representation, Gómez-Peña constitutes his critique from the *inside*. Through the embodiment of stereotypes, Gómez-Peña *inhabits* (and de-naturalizes) the dominant images of social contradiction.

Focusing on the question of identity, I primarily explore how Gómez-Peña draws attention to and problematizes complex notions of cultural, political and discursive borders. His use of performance art, furthermore, reiterates his agenda to redraw boundaries. As Elena De Costa writes, the genre of performance art transgresses the borders between different disciplines:

> Performance art disregards boundaries among the arts, blending the visual arts, dance, and music to enhance its means of expression. Its emphasis is not on a plot or story being conveyed ... but rather on the multiple implications which evolve during the dramatic performance via juxtaposed images and actions and spectator interpretations. (25)

Through his interdisciplinary and multimedia performance art Gómez-Peña simultaneously inscribes and transgresses geopolitical, cultural, linguistic and aesthetic borders.

To highlight how Gómez-Peña crosses boundaries, I read a spectrum of his "texts" from several representational media. Literary analysis of his poems "Califas," "Border Brujo," "1992" and "New World Border" reveals a multicoded conflation of textual and intertextual images. These texts, as well as Gómez-Peña's critical articles, provoke and participate in the dialogue concerning immigration and multiculturalism in the United States.[4] "Reading" a video recording of a performance (of his "Border Brujo" poem) allows for an analysis of the manner in which Gómez-Peña creates and articulates his body-as-text. Gómez-Peña's use of vestimentary codes in relation to signs and stereotypes of national and sexual particularity constructs characters who subvert notions of pure identity. His expression of vestimentary "sign language" became most extreme in a performance titled "Two Undiscovered Amerindians Visit ..." Speaking only in tongues and dressed as outlandish tribes people, Gómez-Peña and collaborator Coco Fusco enclosed themselves in a cage. Analyzing Paula Heredia and Fusco's documentary video of the performance, *The Couple in the Cage: A Guatinaui Odyssey*, makes it possible to consider the political repercussions of the performance simultaneously, taking into account both the performance and the dynamics of audience response. As an expert in the technique of (con)fusing signs, Guillermo Gómez-Peña represents an ideal example of a writer-artist-performer through which to explore the paradoxes inherent in the postmodern position. To comprehend Gómez-Peña's discursive positionality it is necessary to consider the thematic nexus between his early work and the U.S.–Mexico border.

FOLLOW THE BOUNCING BORDER: (CON)TEXTS BETWEEN OTHERS

A brief overview of the Border Arts Workshop–El Taller de Arte Fronterizo demonstrates the manner in which Gómez-Peña and his collaborators both underline and undermine the transparent discursive division imposed by the politics of border control. In their *End of the Line* performance on October 12, 1986, the BAW/TAF members met at the border where the "line" intersects with the Pacific Ocean. The performers—an international group of Chicanos, Anglos and Mexicans—were dressed in ostentatious border stereotype costumes. Installing a table that spanned the border, the Mexicans took their place on their side, and the Anglos and Chicanos occupied *el otro lado*. After "illegally" sharing food across the line they rotated the table, producing a coterminous illegal invasion. According to Gómez-Peña, the Mexican media reported the event as news. Some two hundred people, "artists, tourists, journalists, undocumented workers, vendors, surfers, photographers, 'coyotes,' rangers from the park etc.," were present.[5] From the perspective of the performers, the public who (unwittingly) attended the event also participated.[6] This type of intervention on the border functions as a guerrilla theater action. Mounting a spectacle of this kind in public forces passersby to read the performance and to reflect on its meaning.

Much of Gómez-Peña's work involves physical border crossings. In his performance "De Regreso a Aztlán" (1987), Gómez-Peña and a group of collaborating artists attempted to cross the border in costume. The border control agent on duty allowed Gómez-Peña, dressed as a blind man, to cross the border without asking for his documents. According to Gómez-Peña, this crossing marks the only time that he has ever crossed the border without having to produce his papers. He writes in *Warrior for Gringostroika* that he inaugurates all of his performance characters by crossing the border in costume (29). This practice—part playful, part parodic—demonstrates the BAW/TAF conception of the border as an experimental laboratory where they continually attempt to push and explore the limits of the "line." It is precisely on the border that these artists experiment with art and politics, attempting to find the proper combination of provocation, spark and theory that will both call attention to their work and encourage others to reconsider the border critically.[7] Gómez-Peña does not simply reconceptualize the notion of borders but rather employs the concept heuristically, as a means to further investigate the lines of thought that divide and shape the contemporary map of political, economic and ethnic conditions.

By problematizing this map, the BAW/TAF calls attention to the (well-known but often overlooked) fact that geopolitical borders have always been subject to change. The most dramatic of these changes would surely apply to the Spanish conquest of the Americas, which completely redrew the globe. While obviously a military occupation, the conquest can also be cartographically represented as an imposition of political and geographic maps. The *conquistadores* inscribed *their* map onto the New World territory. The borders of the Spanish empire expanded to include *las colonias*. The very process of colonization implies a political gesture of remapping territory.

Of course it is not necessary to look that far back in history to encounter examples of migrating borders. Even in the recent past, the U.S.–Mexico border takes the arbitrary shape of a movable line. In 1848 the Treaty of Guadalupe Hidalgo reduced Mexico's territory by half, placing Arizona, New Mexico, Utah, Nevada, Texas, California and sections of Wyoming, Oklahoma and Colorado within the borders of the United States. Subsequently, in 1853, the Gadsden Purchase pushed the border even farther into Mexican territory, to the Río Grande. Although the actual location of the two thousand-mile border-line has not changed geographically since, the physical obstacles that serve as security markers have been expanded and lengthened. Prior to 1992, a chain link fence demarcating the border petered out on the beach at the intersection of Border Field State Park and Playas de Tijuana. In the year of the quincentenary, however, the U.S. Army and the Immigration and Naturalization Service extended a thirteen-mile steel barrier out into the Pacific Ocean.[8] Until recently, long stretches of the border were fenced by three strands of sagging barbed wire. Now, however, fortified guard towers and stadium-style searchlights have ostensibly built up the image of the border-as-obstruction. The line may be fixed but the border situation continues to fluctuate. Paradoxically, while the presence of the border control becomes more pronounced along the U.S.–Mexico border, current economic trends continue to diminish trade barriers (globally).

Recent international agreements such as the North American Free Trade Act (and formation of the European Commonwealth Community) continue to redesign global economic cartography. Fredric Jameson emphasizes that the evolution of late capitalism has transferred economic power from nation-states to transnational corporations. On the one hand, electronic media and free trade have effectively erased national boundaries from the perspective of transnational corporations. On the other hand, this lack (or loosening) of trade barriers highlights the existence of concrete political and economic boundaries. Corporations cross borders precisely because of significant economic differences. As of 1994, there were more than 2180 foreign-controlled factories operating in Mexico, the bulk of these just on the other side of the border.[9] The commercial logic that drives these *maquiladora* plants is based purely on the existence of economic disparity—they are profitable only because of lower labor costs in the Third World.

One final caveat with respect to the boundary between the so-called Third and First Worlds: While vast economic discontinuities make such distinctions viable on the level of international business, these two different Worlds have, in fact, substantially penetrated each other. In spite of highly visual campaigns to halt illegal immigration into the United States, thousands of undocumented workers have crossed, and continue to cross, the border.[10] In many cases they live in conditions not unlike the poverty of the Third World. Looking just beyond the borders, furthermore, it becomes evident that many nonimmigrant minorities (such as African Americans and Chicanos) live in deplorable conditions of poverty throughout the United States. Gómez-Peña addresses this issue in "Border Bujo:"

> You thought there was a border between the 1st & the 3rd worlds
> & now you're realizing you're part of the 3rd world … (86)

The implication here is that the border is not at all what we thought it was. Gómez-Peña's writing constitutes a critical deconstruction of the concept of a border as a fixed, clearly delineated line. His early work, in particular, interrogates and challenges the hegemonic concept of the U.S.–Mexico border.

NATIONS, BORDERS AND PEOPLE: RE-IMAGINING THE LINES

What is Gómez-Peña's view of the border? The definition offered by Patricio Chávez and Madeleine Grynsztejn in the introduction to *La Frontera/The Border: Art About the Mexico/United States Border Experience* describes the perspective of many border artists:[11]

> The border is not a physical boundary line separating two sovereign nations, but rather a place of its own, defined by a confluence of cultures that is not geographically bounded either to the north or to the south. The border is the specific nexus of an authentic zone of hybridized cultural experience, reflecting the migration and cross-pollination of ideas and images between different cultures that arise from real and constant human, cultural, and sociopolitical movements. (xvii–xviii)

This definition reconceptualizes the border from a dividing line to a zone, or stage, of cultural hybridism. Instead of signifying opposition and exclusion, this account of the border evokes the area's positive potential for cultural and political production. According to this definition, furthermore, the border paradoxically resists the political concept of discrete nations: "[It] is not geographically bounded either to the north or the south" (xviii). The border-as-zone, then, does not divide one culture from another but rather spreads into two overlapping areas.

This image of the border as a fertile locus of cultural hybridism certainly situates Gómez-Peña's work in interdisciplinary, binational and bicultural performance. And yet although Gómez-Peña's writing does arise from this "specific nexus of an authentic zone of hybridized cultural experience" and although he does indeed explore the complex phenomenon of border culture, his critical gaze focuses well beyond the line. He writes in the program notes to "Border Brujo" that "his character puts a mirror between the two countries" (75). By placing mirrors on the border, Gómez-Peña looks both inside and out. In other words, Gómez-Peña casts his gaze at the border and simultaneously examines images of Mexico and the United States. After positioning these mirrors, furthermore, he proceeds to break them.

If the border is not a line that separates two sovereign places, then what is a nation? Benedict Anderson defines a nation as an imagined political community: "It is *imagined* because the members of even the smallest nation will never know most of their fellow members, meet them, or even hear of them, yet in the minds of each lives the image of their communion" (emphasis original, 15). Constructing his texts out of a mosaic of independent characters, Gómez-Peña underscores the imaginary discursive foundation shaping the concept of nation. "Despite the great cultural mirage sponsored by the people in power," he writes, "everywhere we look we find pluralism, crisis, and non-synchronicity" ("Multicultural Paradigm" 46). The variety of characters that he performs—Tijuana barkers, drunks, pachucos, transvestites, *macuarros*, television evangelists, rednecks, news anchormen, tourists, *merolicos*—emphasizes the fact that many others get left out of the picture. The dominant discourse responsible for articulating the (imaginary) national image erases "others." The fragmented composition of Gómez-Peña's writing directly contests the notion of a unified nation.

One of Gómez-Peña's most striking representations of the border takes the place and form of the Border Brujo's "Casa de Cambio": "the place where Tijuana and San Diego se entrepiernan" (80). Playing with the image of a foreign currency exchange as a ubiquitous border fixture, Gómez-Peña satirizes the power of capital. Here at the Casa de Cambio "anything can literally change into something else" (80). With equal ease the Brujo can change nationality, currency or sexuality. With a

Tijuana barker's voice he enumerates the limitless possibilities for change:

> Money exchange kasse
> cambio genético verbal
> cambio de dólar y de nombre
> cambio de esposa y oficio ...
> sin cover charge
> here everything can take place for a very very reasonable fee ...
> Mexicanos can become Chicanos
> overnite
> Chicanos become Hispanics
> Anglo-Saxons become Sandinistas
> & surfers turn into soldiers of fortune ...
>
> I can turn your pesos into dollars
> your 'coke' into flour
> your dreams into nightmares
> your penis into a clitoris
> you name it, Califa ... (80)

Language represents one of the most sweeping of these changes, "because here Spanish becomes English, ipso facto" (80). With respect to language, the border represents a place of vulgar mispronunciation and distortion: "If your name is Guillermo Gómez-Peña I can turn it into Guermo Comes Penis" (80). Names can be translated adroitly into insults, such as "Bill, 'the multimedia beaner'" (80), or (il)legal status, "Indocumentado # 00281431" (80). The "Casa de Cambio" changes currency, "pesos into dollars," as readily as "dreams into nightmares" (80). One's identity, existence and experience on the border is defined by and dependent on the function of financial transaction.

Of course if nations are constructed of imaginary communities then the borders that surround and separate them must also correspond to arbitrarily inscribed lines. As Chon Noriega writes, "the problem with borders is that they are imagined, much like the communities that they are designed to contain" (6). It is by reiterating the cultural ambiguities that surround the political border that Gómez-Peña deconstructs the demarcations of binary thought. Locating his site-specific performance on the U.S.–Mexico border, Gómez-Peña simultaneously engages the imaginary images of nation-ness that persist on both sides. He performs between two nations, perforates the conceptual border line between them and simultaneously interrogates the fictional cohesiveness of both nations.

PERFORMING BETWEEN THE LINES:
READING BETWEEN THE NATIONS

If, following Homi Bhabha, we can conceive of "nation as narration" (142), then Gómez-Peña's "Border Brujo" takes place between two national "texts." Bhabha points out that the traditional concept of nation is predicated on a "progressive metaphor of modern social cohesion—*the many as one*" (emphasis original, 142). In lieu of any homogeneous image of "the people," Gómez-Peña's "disnarrative" and multivoiced performance evokes a nonreducible assembly. Instead of reducing the nation to one homogeneous grouping that can be pedagog- ically fixed, Bhabha posits a "performative" conception of nation as a pluralistic and dynamic process. For Gómez-Peña the border constitutes a place from which to articulate difference: "[Border culture] means to speak from the crevasse, desde acá, desde el medio. The border is the juncture, not the edge, and monoculturalism has been expelled to the margins" (44). Gómez-Peña's metaphor of the border inverts the tradi- tional narrative of nationhood. For Gómez-Peña, consequently, the border-nation could be described as *the many as many*. In a manner consistent with Bhabha's theory, Gómez-Peña attempts to perform the impossibility of a monolithic national culture.

A brief comparison with Gloria Anzaldúa's *Borderlands/La Fron- tera: The New Mestiza* will bring Gómez-Peña's deconstructive impulse into focus. Anzaldúa also evokes the cultural and linguistic hybridism that is native to the U.S.–Mexico border zone. Like Gómez-Peña, Anzaldúa abhors the dynamics of late capitalism. She evokes the image of the border in terms of a bloody conflict: "The U.S.–Mexican border *es una herida abierta* where the Third World grates against the First and bleeds. And before a scab forms it hemorrhages again, the lifeblood of two worlds merging to form a third country—a border culture" (empha- sis original, 3). Anzaldúa also blends the codes of English and Spanish: "A border tongue which developed naturally. Change, *evolución, en- riquecimiento de palabras nuevas por invención o adopción* have created variants of Chicano Spanish, *un nuevo lenguaje*" (emphasis original, 55). In spite of these similarities, there exist significant differences between Gómez-Peña's and Anzaldúa's conceptualizations of the border.

Whereas both Anzaldúa and Gómez-Peña celebrate difference, the ideological agendas of their respective border writings diverge. Anzaldúa's conflation of English and Spanish arises naturally as her native language. Her decision to write *Borderlands/La Frontera* in "Spanglish" constitutes a political challenge to represent herself:

> I am my language. Until I can take pride in my language, I cannot take pride in myself. Until I can accept as legitimate Chicano Texas Spanish, Tex-Mex and all the other languages I speak, I cannot accept the legitimacy of myself. Until I am free to write bilingually and to switch codes without having always to translate … my tongue will be illegitimate. (59)

This quote testifies to Anzaldúa's view that her ethnic and linguistic identities are inextricably related. In essence Anzaldúa's celebration of the borderlands corresponds to a (minority) nationalist cause. In celebrating the mestiza on the border, Anzaldúa imagines a different kind of nation, a "borderlands nation," that will truly represent the sexual and cultural diversity of the regional population.

For Gómez-Peña, on the other hand, his decision to blend Spanish and English reflects a different political agenda. Instead of constructing a borderlands nation, as does Anzaldúa, Gómez-Peña denies the myth of national unity. Referring to himself as a Chicano, Gómez-Peña calls attention to the arbitrary nature of both national and ethnic identity: "I'm just a deterritorialized 'chilango' who claims to be a Chicano" (87). What does it mean for a Mexican performance artist to call himself a Chicano? Besides a political identification with a marginal group, what are the consequences of Gómez-Peña's proclamation of *chicanismo*?[12] To answer these questions it is necessary to analyze the term "Chicano" in the context of Gómez-Peña's notion of border identity.

With respect to identity it should be possible to analyze the word "Chicano" semiotically, as a national or ethnic *sign*. National signs signify through difference. A "Mexican" is a Mexican because he or she is not Canadian, Guatemalan or a citizen of the United States. All of these terms are dependent on the existence of other nationalities but no *specific* frontier defines their articulation. The sign Chicano, on the other hand, takes its linguistic, national and ethnic meaning from a more specific mechanism of difference. Chicano means not Mexican and not Anglo American but rather someone in between.

Unlike generic national signs, the term Chicano is explicitly contingent on the U.S.–Mexico border. According to current usage, only someone whose Mexican ancestors had crossed the border would qualify as a Chicano.[13] And yet while the border represents a critical factor in determining Chicano identity, the imaginary community that the Chicano movement forged in the 1960s and 1970s corresponds to a borderless area spanning from the mythical Aztec utopia called Aztlán to contemporary Latin America.[14] As Gómez-Peña's character El Johnny says in "Califas":

> It's confusing
> we know
> our nation extends
> from the tip of Patagonia
> to the peak of your
> tortured imagination. (71)

This quote bears witness to the pan-American ideology running through Chicano nationalism. The source of this identification is at least as much political as it is ethnic. Dissatisfaction with social and economic disparity—internal colonialism—has led many Chicanos to identify themselves with Latin American culture, history and revolution.

In spite of the pan-American idealism that many Chicanos embrace(d) theoretically, cultural borders problematize such integration in everyday practice. In "Califas," Gómez-Peña's character El Chicano Shaman laments the irresolvable schism that separates Chicanos and Mexicans in California:

> No one was there to imagine
> that this land of encounters
> called Califas
> would be mortally sliced in half
> Chicanos & Mexicanos ... (68)

The mortal "slice" refers to the Treaty of Guadalupe Hidalgo, which allocated half of Mexico's territory and most of California to the United States. The following section of the poem underscores the linguistic rift that resulted from the historic slice:

> nos otros & aquellos
> los amputados
> del más allá
> del what you say ... (68)

Notice how even the first-person plural suffers from a kind of internal exile. The division has left only "others" (nos *otros* & *aquellos*), amputated geographically from Mexico (*el más allá*) and linguistically from Spanish (*del* what you say). Bhabha utilizes a similar image of national cleavage to theorize postcolonial culture: "We are confronted with the nation split within itself, articulating the heterogeneity of its population" (148). By situating himself explicitly on the split of the border, Gómez-Peña underscores the fissures unaccounted for by a concept of national identity as well as the system of cracks emanating from each side of the fault line.

Analyzing this metaphor of the border as a split or crack can clarify Gómez-Peña's adoption of Chicano culture. While distinguishing the peoples of Mexico from the United States, the U.S.–Mexico border divides Chicanos from both. For Gómez-Peña, the border does not signify national identity but rather marks the *trace* of minority cultures obscured by the inscription of hegemonic images from each side.[15] When Gómez-Peña refers to himself as a Chicano, then, he aligns himself with a border or hybrid (non)identity. Commenting on Gómez-Peña's "New World Border," Bhabha describes an "opening out" of interstitial culture:

> What is at issue is the performative nature of differential identities: the regulation and negotiation of those spaces that are … "opening out," remaking the boundaries, exposing the limits of any claim to a singular or autonomous sign of difference—be it class, gender or race … Difference is neither One nor the Other but *something else besides, in-between*. (emphasis original, 219)

By performing at the liminal space between two countries, Gómez-Peña confronts the split between and within two always already split nations. Culturally he locates himself between the space of national signs. In his performances, furthermore, he continually moves *between* the signs of diverse linguistic codes.

BORDER BABEL: (CON)FUSING TONGUES

Although Gómez-Peña primarily performs in English, his characters alternate and fuse Spanish, Spanglish, pseudo-Náhuatl and "tongues," along with a smattering of French and German. This conflation of codes without subtitles or explanation represents one example on a linguistic level of the process I call (con)fusing signs. He begins the "New World

Border" performance by switching between English and Spanish: "Hello querido, yuppies, *turistas, voyeuristas, antropólogos, aficionados*, perplexed citizens of the end of the century" (emphasis original, 125–6). Not only does the text oscillate back and forth between languages but it also incorporates humorous word play. Gómez-Peña directly acknowledges his audience before introducing his collaborating actress, Coco Fusco: "I warn you. This ain't performance art but pure Chicano science fiction. *Anygueyes, comenzamos sin* translation *cha-cha*! Y ahora nuestra corresponsal en los Estamos Undidos" (emphasis original, 127). By fusing "Any" with "gueyes" the speaker sounds out both the English "anyway" and the Mexican slang greeting-insult "gueyes."[16] By removing the d from Estados (and substituting an m) and adding an extra d in Unidos, Gómez-Peña turns the "United States" into the sound of "we are sunk." This type of code switching, or the alternate mixing of different languages, merely reflects the most basic version of his (con)fusion.

In addition to juxtaposing and playing with different languages, Gómez-Peña often recontextualizes a broad range of intertextual citations and concepts. Consider the way in which he evokes postmodernity in his performance "New World Border":

> We are all living in the age of *pus-modernity*, a blistering festering present. In these times, all known political systems and economic structures are dysfunctional ... Many see this as the era of *la desmodernidad*, a term that comes from the Mexican noun *desmadre*, which can mean either being without a mother or living in chaos. The Great Fiction of social order has evaporated and has left us in a state of meta-orphanhood. We are all finally untranslatable *hijos de la chingada*. (emphasis original, 127)

This ironic reading of contemporary chaos superimposes and juxtaposes a vast spectrum of intertextual signs. Thematically his parodic treatise on pus-modernity, re-presents Jean-François Lyotard's well-known definition—"*postmodern* as incredulity toward metanarratives" (emphasis original, xxiv). For Lyotard the postmodern condition reflects the changing status of knowledge in contemporary society. Now that we have lost faith in "Grand Narratives" such as religion or (emancipatory) positivism, we find ourselves drifting confusedly in unknown directions. As Gómez-Peña writes, "The Great Fiction of social order has evaporated and has left us in a state of meta-orphanhood" (127).

In the performance, Coco Fusco pronounces this report on pus-
modernity while playing the role of an anchorwoman. The scene satirizes the generic sound of televised news programming, both through its
content and by its distortion of her voice with echo (127). Her report
immediately evokes the political rhetoric that has surrounded the argument in favor of the North American Free Trade Act: "Imagine a new
American continent without borders" (127). By adding the letter "B" to
the contemporary cliché of "New World Order," nevertheless, Gómez-
Peña's text creates a play on words that inscribes prominent (border)
lines through this rhetorical whitewash: Now the entire continent "has
become a huge border zone. Think of it as the New World Border"
(127). The overall effect simultaneously underlines and undermines the
authority of the news media, political representatives and European
(postmodern) theoreticians.

Gómez-Peña's parody of Lyotard reorients the Eurocentric theory to
an explicitly Mexican point of view. By recontextualizing postmodernism as a "desmadre" and "meta-orphanhood," furthermore, the text draws
Octavio Paz's *El laberinto de la soledad* into the parody as well. Paz
referred to Mexicans as "hijos de la Chingada" in his now classic essay
of 1950. Explaining that the Mexican slang term *chingada* originated
during the conquest as a raped indigenous woman, Paz alludes to "el
mexicano y la mexicanidad" as "orphans" in search of identity (79).
What is perhaps most problematic about Paz's reading (from a 1990s
perspective) is the patriarchal bias with which he accuses La Malinche–
Chingada of passivity and treason:[17] "Su pasividad es abyecta: no ofrece
resistencia a la violencia, es un montón inerte de sangre, huesos y
polvo ... Ella se da voluntariamente al Conquistador" (77). Coco Fusco
as an anchorwoman ironically mocks Paz's infamous essay: "We are ...
hijos de la chingada" (127). Her assertive manipulation of theoretical
discourse and parody, to say nothing of her leopard-skin halter top,
grass skirt, sneakers and sunglasses, highlights the discursive violence
of Paz's (phallocentric) thesis.

Significantly, the text defines these orphaned survivors as "untranslatable *hijos de la chingada*" (127). What is untranslatable is not merely
the expression ("hijos de la chingada," hence the code switch) but the
neocolonial experience of *mexicanidad*. Culture, as Bhabha observes,
cannot be translated: "The migrant culture of the 'in-between,' the
minority position, dramatizes the activity of culture's untranslatability"
(224). Gómez-Peña, consequently, (con)fuses codes again. He expresses
Fusco's "los hijos de" in French and then echoes the last syllable of

chingada: "*Les enfants de la chingada da-da*" (127). Re-presenting the untranslatable "chingada" with a French accent and absorbing "her" into a French sentence, Gómez-Peña crosses yet another series of contextual borders.

Switching into French, the phrase's final "da-da" brings to mind Tristan Tzara's Dada "movement." In this context "la chingada" crosses the grammatical border from feminine noun (la Malinche) to a code-switched adjectival expletive modifying Dada. Although this mention of Dada might at first appear gratuitous, the historical avant-garde plays an important role in Gómez-Peña's intertextual dialogue with European theorists. In critical articles and interviews Gómez-Peña and Fusco have argued against Eurocentric art historians who trace the roots of performance art to Dada.[18] They cite, to the contrary, the Mexican *carpa* tradition and Latin American popular theater as primary influences that developed independently from the Western avant-garde. In ascribing Latin American and Chicano cultural performance to the avant-garde canon of Western art history represents yet another example of Eurocentric conquest and colonialism.

Fusco points out in her article "The Other History of Intercultural Performance" that contextualizing Latino art in Western paradigms represents the continuation of a long-standing practice of colonialism in literary and art criticism. It is a well-known fact that the historical avant-garde appropriated and fetishized primitivism, re-presenting it in a European context. For Fusco, interpreting Latin American performance art as (postmodern) neo-Dada reiterates the colonizing gesture of the avant-garde. It is a practice, she writes, "of appropriating and fetishizing the primitive ... [that] simultaneously erases the original source" (150). By exaggerating the roles of Indians and *brujos*, Gómez-Peña's performance art contests this denial of the original source. This is not to say that he asserts an agenda of *indigenismo*. Gómez-Peña does not represent indigenous peoples but instead underscores the representations through which they have been traditionally erased.[19] He follows his remark (*la chingada da-da*) with prerecorded chants in Quechua. The narrative and soundtrack conflate the *signs* of Europe, Latin America and postmodernity. Investigating how Gómez-Peña relates to his audience will demonstrate another level on which he performs (con)fusion.

(CON)FUSING THE AUDIENCE

In his performances Gómez-Peña sometimes seats members of his audience in separate sections according to the languages that they speak. He delineates borderlines between speakers of English, Spanish, Spanglish and pseudo-Nahuatl.[20] By performing in a mixture of all of these languages, Gómez-Peña crosses over the line separating audience from performer. This is especially obvious when he actually confronts his audience. In "Border Brujo" he interrogates the audience in Spanish, aggressively grilling them about why they have attended his performance:

> ¿a qué vienes extranjero?
> ¿a experimentar 'peligro cultural?'
> ¿a tocarle los pies al brujo? ...
> ¿a ver si te reorienta hacia el poniente? (87)

Referring to his U.S. audience as *extranjero*, Gómez-Peña turns the tables of cultural perspective. As in an act of magic, Gómez-Peña the *brujo* inverts the entire context of his performance. Now, the U.S. citizen-audience plays the role of stranger, straining to understand a performance that has slipped into Spanish. This inversion also questions the audience members' conceptions of their role as passive theater spectators. Why have they come? To receive a sacred reorienting message? If so, their experience cannot fulfill their expectations.

The *brujo* then steps across another border. Empathizing with the audience, the narrator describes the discomfort that the spectators feel toward the Border Brujo: "Sus palabras te confunden aún más te hieren, te desconsuelan" (87). Ironically, a monolingual English speaker cannot even understand this section. Gómez-Peña then (con)fuses the signs once more, switching suddenly to English:

> You can't even understand the guy
> 'cause he speaks in a foreign tongue
> seems real angry and ungrateful
> & you begin to wonder. (87)

He not only confirms the confusion of his monolingual spectators but appropriates their language and perspective, as if he were looking through their eyes. In this brief extract Gómez-Peña-as-Border Brujo crosses a number of diverse conceptual, linguistic and subjective borders. The deconstruction of the performer-spectator opposition acknowledges Gómez-Peña's (Brechtian) approach toward political praxis and art. Clearly there is no illusion of representation here but rather a series of thought-provoking alienation effects. At the end of the performance

Gómez-Peña carries baskets into the audience and asks them to give him "whatever ... [they] no longer need" (95). He warns them that they will not be able to recoup these objects:[21]

> Some objects I will bury right in the
> U.S./México border ditch
> & others will become part of my traveling altar
> damas y caballeros ... ¡aflojen! (95)

At the show's conclusion, then, Gómez-Peña invites the audience to cross the border, as it were, and to add their personal objects to the Border Brujo's altar. The public's participation becomes active. The *brujo* alone cannot create social change. Not only must the audience find the coherence in his performance but they contribute toward the *mise en scène* of the "Border Brujo" *text*. To appreciate the full effect of Gómez-Peña's theatrics, nevertheless, it is crucial to actually view his show. "Reading" one of Gómez-Peña's performances always entails a multimedia approximation.

A MULTIMEDIA BODY:
DRESSING ACROSS THE BORDER

A visual analysis of Isaac Artenstein's video, *Border Brujo* (which documents one of Gómez-Peña's performances), underscores the manner in which Gómez-Peña creates and superimposes a series of interrelated texts. Gómez-Peña's costumes are at least as fragmented and disnarrative as are his performances. He dresses himself with a hodgepodge of ornamentation: a necklace of plastic bananas, a mariachi hat, wrestler masks, dark glasses, a plastic heart, a pachuco hat, a collection of buttons (Batman, a punk skull with a mohawk, "I accept tips," "Enjoy Coca Cola," "FDR" [Frente Democrático Revolucionario], "Illegal," a Catholic virgin), skeleton earrings, feathers, punk spikes on his hand and wrist, an American flag wrist-watch and so forth. By plastering himself with "signs" Gómez-Peña creates a collage-like "text" out of his body. In another performance, as the "Warrior for Gringostroika," he literally writes on his body, scrawling "Please don't discover me!" across his chest.[22] The visual overload stages an interdisciplinary dialogue between (fragmented) literary and visual images.

One might argue that this visual farrago impedes the articulation of a sustained message. What does a Batman button have to do with plastic bananas and the Frente Democrático Revolucionario?[23] Like Jameson in the Bonaventura Hotel, we suffer from a (postmodern) visual overload "that can only be characterized as a milling confusion" (43). A bric-a-brac of props surrounds and grows out of his body-costume–text. Gómez-Peña performs behind an eclectic altar that was built by the Chicano artist Felipe Almada. The altar itself assembles an eccentric mix of objects—shampoo bottles, tequila bottles, televisions, megaphones, knives, doll heads, plastic hamburgers, puppets, votive candles and so forth. Together the performer, costume and altar give rise to a cyclone of visual confusion.

Looking beneath the surface nevertheless reveals a kind of aesthetic logic that recurs throughout much Chicano art. Tomás Ybarra-Frausto describes the cluttered pastiche of home *altares* as an example of an aesthetic sensibility called *rasquachismo*: "The rasquache inclination piles pattern on pattern, filling all available space with bold display ... The composite organization has a sort of wild abandon yet is subtly controlled with precise repetitions, replications, and oppositional orders of colors, patterns, and designs" (157). The *rasquache* effect, furthermore, constitutes a link between Gómez-Peña's aesthetic, thematic and political concerns. As Ybarra-Frausto points out, the home *altar* aesthetic reiterates the milieu of the *barrios*:

> The visual distinctiveness of the barrio unites the improvisational attitude of making do with what's at hand to a traditional and highly evolved decorative sense ... In yards and porches, for example, traditional items like religious shrines (capillas) and pottery mingle with objects from mass culture, such as pink plastic flamingos or plaster animal statuary. Throughout, there is a profusion of textures and colors and a jumble of things. (157)

By juxtaposing objects of mass culture with traditional iconography, the Border Brujo's costumes and (Almada's) *altar* replicate the (con)fusion of urban signs that characterize the *barrio*. The text constitutes a minute representation, or *mise en abyme*, of contemporary urban culture.

Ybarra-Frausto specifically notes that Gómez-Peña manipulates "rasquache artifacts, codes, and sensibilities from both sides of the border" (161). Grynsztejn arrives at a similar interpretation of one of Almada's alters:

> This accretion of material and information accurately conveys a sense of the complexity of the border and the cross-pollination of

ideas and cultures. Almada couches his vision in the formal language of Mexican folk and even of pre-Hispanic art, thus consciously allying himself with his indigenous roots, even as he acknowledges his community's and his art's own hybrid natures. (29)

Collaborating with Almada and performing as part of Almada's altar, Gómez-Peña elaborates a kind of double border *rasquachismo*. He appropriates and merges the Chicano aesthetic with Mexican and Gringo counterparts to engender an intertextual (con)fusion of transnational signs.

If Gómez-Peña's body-text emerges from the altar aesthetic, his performance also stages the process (an alter process) of altar construction. Gómez-Peña's visual text perpetually changes throughout the show. He repeatedly adds and subtracts articles of clothing (wigs, hats, glasses, bandannas) to signify shifts of character. In terms of narrative, the movement does not follow a linear progression. In his preface to "Califas," Gómez-Peña writes that "the structure is disnarrative and modular, like the border experience" (67). This statement could describe any of his performances. As critics we are faced with the problem of determining how to read this ever-changing, but never evolving, text.[24]

In spite of the visual instability, a spectator can focus on specific stages of his corporeal textualization to interpret the performance at large. At several places in "Border Brujo" Gómez-Peña becomes a transvestite. Although gender represents only one of many issues raised by "Border Brujo," processes of transformation recur. The concept of transvestism proposed by Marjorie Garber in her book, *Vested Interests: Cross-Dressing and Cultural Anxiety*, lends itself particularly well to Gómez-Peña's manipulation of vestimentary signifiers because it can be applied to cultural as well as gendered cross-dressing. Garber maintains that transvestism indicates a place of "category crisis" in culture: "a failure of definitional distinction, a borderline that becomes permeable, that permits ... border crossings from one (apparently distinct) category to another" (16). Gómez-Peña transgresses categories precisely to draw into question the existence of clearly delineated cultural classifications. Analyzing his transvestism will underscore the positionality from which Gómez-Peña articulates his critique.

Garber describes cross-dressing as a deconstruction of gender categories: "Drag is the theoretical and deconstructive social practice that analyzes these structures from within, by putting in question the 'naturalness' of gender roles through the discourse of clothing and body parts" (151). The spatial metaphors of this paradigm are striking: Drag constitutes a critique of gender that functions *from within*. One can never get outside of gender. We can change clothes as well as our sexual make-up (the most extreme case being sex-change operations) but we cannot get outside of our bodies. By *crossing boundaries* a drag performer (in this case, Gómez-Peña) simultaneously underscores and effaces the boundary. In Garber's words, "to transgress against one set of boundaries was to call into question the inviolability of both" (32). The Border Brujo problematizes the question of identity in precisely this manner. The performance does not move toward a permanent resolution of binary oppositions but instead delineates a fluid, nonfixed condition that is subject to continuous change. Gender represents only one of the *brujo*'s transformations. As the Border Brujo, Gómez-Peña dresses across a myriad of borders. Oscillating between the signs of pachucos, mariachis, wrestlers, transvestites and other "others," Gómez-Peña employs a brand of parodic transvestism to cross and paradoxically erase sexual, cultural and discursive borders.

Gómez-Peña's use of parody lends a distinct meaning to his transvestism. At the risk of sounding ironic, Gómez-Peña is not a real transvestite as is, for example, Chicano performance artist Luis Alfaro. In "Cuerpo Politizado" Alfaro gives testimony to his experience as a cross-dressing Chicano queer:

> I am a Queer Chicano.
> A native in no land.
> An orphan of Aztlán.
> The *pocho* son of farmworker parents. (235)

Here Alfaro stakes a claim of identity within the doubly marginalized no-place of Chicano transvestites. While the quote above reflects his personal struggle for identity, in "Vistiendo en Drag" he speaks in a collective voice, representing the history of the Chicano transvestites with whom he identifies:

> We all aspired
>   (*los señoritas* of Hype-rion Avenue)
>   to the *Mexicana* icon.
> Preferred long-suffering *mujeres*
>   over *chichona* Jayne Mansfields.
> Drag, it is a man's field ... (217)

Alfaro represents a very different drag than does Gómez-Peña's parody of
a transvestite voice. In contrast to Alfaro, Gómez-Peña's characters do
not represent *him*. There are times when he speaks in a normal voice
and even relates an experience from his own personal history, but he
never entirely identifies with any of his characters. In Gómez-Peña's
performance "1992," he specifically talks about many of his memories.
At one point he flashes back to a radio interview in Berlin. "But Mr.
Gómezz," asked the interviewer, "Where exactly do you live? & Who
are you really?" (117). His answer expresses a perpetual state of
marginality:

> Soy el otro fuera de mí
> el otro dentro de tí
> the other tras de tí. (117)

Rather than speaking from a firm platform of identity, Gómez-Peña
always seems to represent another "other," marginalized between
dominant discourses. He clearly distances his work from a testimonial
perspective. In "1992" he questions his own existence, his direction,
and the supposed link between him and his writing:

> I'm not even sure there is a North really
> not even sure I really exist
> do I?
> do I?
> do I?
> I see my face on the page
> but I hardly recognize it. (116)

By problematizing his own identity while performing that of "others,"
Gómez-Peña underscores the tension between nationalist and counter-
hegemonic discourses. He attempts to uphold the values of the disenfranchised without going so far as to promote an attitude of minority
nationalism.

How is it possible to resist hegemonic nationalism without paradoxically asserting a (counter) discourse of minority nationalism? Instead of predicating resistance on a praxis of identity politics, Gómez-
Peña invokes a parodic posture of collective (non)identity. Appearing in
a leopard-skin wrestling mask, Gómez-Peña disappears behind the ambiguous identity of a wrestler-superhero figure. As Gómez-Peña writes

in his poem "El 7 Máscaras Super Héroe Fronterizo," he really doesn't represent anything or anyone in particular:

> Yo soy el vato relamido
> que sí, que no
> el va todo lamido
> soy nada & en la nada me revuelco. (155)

At the same time, nevertheless, this masked anonymity allows him to conjugate a collective (non)identity that opposes the hegemony of dominant culture:

> En la movida
> me explayo & multiplico. (155)

Gómez-Peña stages this struggle allegorically through the symbolism of wrestling. A contextual consideration of wrestling in Mexico facilitates our analysis of Gómez-Peña's performance texts.

EL 7 MÁSCARAS FRONTERIZO: SUPERHEROES, WRESTLING AND COLLECTIVE NON-IDENTITY

While communicating an aura of absurdity, Gómez-Peña's wrestling mask also functions as a symbolically "loaded" signifier. Yareli Arizmendi describes the complex coding of wrestling in Mexico:[25]

> Mexico's wrestling world is a contained cosmology dealing with the forces of good and evil. Each mask is a modern morality play, a continuation of the Spanish auto sacramental combined with the deeply rooted mask traditions of indigenous cultures and the conventions of the contemporary comic book hero. Also, wrestling is Mexico's most popular working-class family pastime. (108–9)

While wearing a wrestling mask Gómez-Peña simultaneously plays with all of these traditions. The Border Brujo not only raises moral issues but also assumes the voices of an extended spectrum of Mexican characters. He juxtaposes these characters with their cultural rivals from Anglo and Chicano cultures. The mask also alludes specifically to images of Mexico's political superhero—Superbarrio.

Purportedly the idea of Superbarrio first came to a retired wrestler-turned-social-activist–performance artist after hearing an evicted housewife say that only Superman could save her household from evil landlords.[26] What is ironic about her statement is the fact that Superman never defended the claims of the disenfranchised. As Umberto Eco points out in "The Myth of Superman," the real comic book hero consistently defends capitalist ideology, particularly the right to own private property:

> He is busy by preference, not against blackmarket drugs, nor, obviously, against corrupt administrators or politicians, but against bank and mail-truck robbers. In other words, *the only visible form that evil assumes is an attempt on private property.* (emphasis original, 123)

Superbarrio opposes exactly the opposite type of perpetrators, namely corrupt administrators and politicians. With "SB" emblazoned on his chest, the noticeably pudgy Superbarrio emerges from the slums as a counterforce to the myth of a superhero fighting to uphold the hegemonic values (and correlative goods) of "man." Olalquiaga contrasts the escapist perspective of U.S. comic figures with Superbarrio's reappropriation:

> Whereas in the United States superheroes ... do little more than promote consumer goods and reinforce the good guys versus bad guys national ideology, in Mexico City popular appropriation of the superhero has replaced leisure consumption with the need for basic goods and a schematic narrative by a street struggle for the basic rights of the poor. (87)

Superbarrio satirically twists the icons of popular culture as a means to turn the public sphere into a political stage. In the tradition of comic books, Superbarrio conjugates fantasy and entertainment together. In contrast to "real" comic book figures, nevertheless, Superbarrio's telephone hotline, Barriomobile and Barrio Cave draw attention to the everyday needs of the *barrio*.

The mask is more than a detail in Superbarrio's costume. Arizmendi explains that wrestling masks have a crucial sign value in Mexican culture: "In the wrestler's code of honor, taking off your mask means ... that you accept defeat" (109). Furthermore, as Olalquiaga notes, the mask "allows collective identity" (87).[27] In his essay "From Art-Mageddon to Gringostroika: A Manifesto Against Censorship," Gómez-Peña writes about a Catholic priest, Fray Tormenta, who became a professional wrestler to raise money for abandoned children. According to Gómez-Peña, Fray Tormenta wears religious vestments in the wrestling ring and a wrestling mask while performing mass (58). Within the sphere of performance activism in Mexico, masks symbolize collective power. Superbarrio's mask literally amplifies his power by allowing three or four men to play the role of the superhero. Thus, like a real comic book hero, Superbarrio can appear in several places at once.[28]

When Superbarrio visited the Mexico–U.S. border, the BAW/TAF constructed a mock wrestling ring with barbed wire. They encapsulated a performance space and in so doing marked off a border within the border. Representing "border heroes" (*Supermojado*, *Superviviente*, *Chicanosaurio*, and *Saint Frida*), Gómez-Peña and his collaborators interacted with Superbarrio until he "cut the border fence" with pliers (*Warrior* 28). Aside from symbolically refusing the politics of border control, it is worth contemplating the positional paradox of this action. The event took place at the Centro Cultural de la Raza on the San Diego side of the border in September 1988. Severing the wire wrestling ring on the border does not correlate to cutting the border. Instead of perforating the barrier separating Mexico from the United States, this gesture actually opens their performance space from an enclosed wrestling ring to a border zone.

My point is not to raise questions with regard to the space opened by this performance but rather to consider the spatial implications that accompany border art. BAW/TAF catalogues consistently underscore the fact that their performances take place on the border. And yet while the site may appear clearly delineated when visualized in terms of the line, how far must one move to get "off the border"? The relevance of this question becomes apparent in the context of Gómez-Peña's career. In 1989 Gómez-Peña decided to abandon border art, the BAW/TAF and the U.S.–Mexico border.

In an article titled "Death on the Border: A Eulogy to Border Art," Gómez-Peña lamented the co-optation of border art by the art market and the (multi-) culture industry. He declared the border art movement dead in an acidly worded attack: "The border as metaphor has become hollow. Border aesthetics have been gentrified and border culture as a utopian model for dialog is temporarily bankrupt" (9). For Gómez-Peña the so-called Latino Boom that resulted from the institutional recognition of border art resulted in a "consumer monstrosity" (8).[29]

Although it is clear that Gómez-Peña lost faith in the movement that he helped to found, the reification of border culture was only the final factor in his decision to leave the area. For Gómez-Peña, the dominant culture's reception of border art implies a kind of racist, exoticist stereotyping: "For the art world, we are practitioners of distant languages that, in the best of cases, are perceived as exotic" (*Warrior* 40). Framed within the discourses of the (high) art world and the preconceived stereotypes of ethnic art, the border artist remains incarcerated— pre-presented within a matrix of hegemonic images. "We must challenge the anachronistic myth," writes Gómez-Peña, "that as 'artists of color' we are *only* meant to work within the boundaries of our ethnic 'communities'" (emphasis original, 33). In order to escape from these issues Gómez-Peña physically removed himself from the border and the genre of border art. And yet his situation did not, and cannot, essentially change. As García Canclini concludes in his study of contemporary cultural hybridity, "Hoy todas las culturas son de frontera" (325). An analysis of Gómez-Peña's international exhibition with Coco Fusco, "Two Undiscovered Amerindians Visit ..." highlights a web of transparent border lines that extends through and beyond geopolitical sites. No matter where Gómez-Peña carries his art, *borders* perpetually shape and define his images. His performance, accordingly, transgresses and reiterates the confines of the postmodern position.

TWO UNDISCOVERED AMERINDIANS VISIT ...

In a critique of the 500th Anniversary of the "Discovery of America," Gómez-Peña and Cuban-born performance artist Coco Fusco enclosed themselves in a guilded cage for three days in Madrid's Plaza de Colón. Garbed in an absurd pastiche of clothing, trinkets and kitsch, the two artists claimed to be "Amerindians" from an undiscovered island named Guatinaui, hidden somewhere in the Gulf of Mexico. This interactive exhibit allowed spectators to purchase an authentic dance (from the female specimen), a story in Guatinaui (from the male specimen) or a polaroid photograph of themselves posing in front of the cage. Following the exhibition in Spain, Gómez-Peña and Fusco transported their cage around the globe, performing in or outside of major art museums.[30] Viewers often mistook the performance for reality—they believed, in other words, that Gómez-Peña and Fusco were authentic specimens from an exotic, faraway tribe.

   The fact that many spectators were unable to perceive the theatrical component of this performance poses an important question concerning the political effectiveness of the work's intended critique. Some critics assert that the work completely misses its target. Jan Avgikos from *Art Forum*, for example, observed that Fusco's erotic allure superseded the work's political message:

> I can't stand there and suddenly realize that cultural genocide is a horrible thing ... What I did think about was how beautiful (the woman's) scantily clad body was. Which is probably what just about everyone else was thinking too.[31]

It would seem from reactions like this that their performance did not actually accomplish very much, other than giving a mass of spectators around the world the opportunity to stare at (and mentally undress) Fusco and Gómez-Peña. Because Fusco never speaks and Gómez-Peña only tells his "story" in unintelligible Guatinaui "tongues," an objection can be registered that their performance lacks a critical voice.[32] What are the consequences of such enigmatic performances? If a substantial percentage of the viewing public remains essentially blind to the point of this issue-oriented art, do these performances actually articulate political critiques?

By staging mute performance art, the artists self-consciously refuse the pontificating posture of traditional discourse. They are not subjects speaking but rather are self-consciously converting themselves into objects—exposing themselves to an oftentimes uncritical (and frequently hostile)[33] public gaze. The documentation on video of their performances, however, considerably enhances and amplifies the range of their political potential. A close "reading" of the video *The Couple in the Cage: A Guatinaui Odyssey* by Coco Fusco and Paula Heredia (see Figure 4-1) underscores the (con)fusing implications of Gómez-Peña and Fusco's cage.[34]

THE COUPLE IN THE CAGE: GAZING THROUGH BARS

The video opens with a soundtrack of media reports on their performances around the world. Recorded descriptions of the spectacle in varying accents of English and Spanish overlap with one another while the video presents images of the "Indians" on leashes being led into the cage. Significantly, more of the video focuses on public reactions to the exhibit than on the performance itself. We listen to a substantial number of viewers whose comments imply that they believe the theatrical pretense. One young woman is moved to tears, unable to fathom why

Figure 4-1. Publicity flyer for the video documentary
The Couple in the Cage: A Guatinaui Odyssey,
by Coco Fusco and Paula Heredia
(Courtesy of Coco Fusco.)

the museum would display people in a cage. The soundtrack includes a phone call from a man who called the Chicago Field Museum to inform the director that he wanted to retract his membership. His message is as concise as it is caustic: "Hello, this is George Mead. I would like to withdraw my membership. I am shocked and amazed at an exhibit I just saw of two people in a cage. I am disgusted with the museum at this point. Good-bye." The voice of another man pointedly questions and scolds the exhibit, accusing the handlers of taking advantage of their specimens: "Do you realize that these poor people have no idea what they are doing?" Another caller rebukes the manner in which the specimens are cared for: "Feeding people like animals is completely disgusting."

In her subsequent analysis, "The Other History of Intercultural Performance," Fusco explains that the performers had never expected audiences to take them for *real specimens* (143). She estimates in retrospect that roughly half of their spectators failed to recognize the exhibit as a performance. Since a combined 141,000 people viewed the exhibit (*not* including the Madrid and London shows, which were held outdoors in heavily trafficked areas), then well over 70,500 people witnessed the performance and (mis)took it for reality![35]

Aside from general naïveté, why did so many people confuse this exaggerated act of performance art with a real museum curiosity? In essence the performance represents the problematics of reading. Encountering the cage in a plaza or museum, the public must "read" and interpret the cage, its accompanying documentation, and the cage's unusual occupants. Watching the video we witness many spectators in the process of reading these *signs*. After listening to Gómez-Peña's story in unintelligible Guatinaui, a women spectator hazards a partial interpretation: "It seemed to me that he began his story with a private moment that was perhaps a type of prayer or something ... I felt he was very emotional about what he was saying but I couldn't understand it." Notice how her interpretation restates *her* point of view. She *felt* he was "emotional." Fusco observes that viewers projected their own preconceived images: "The cage became a blank screen onto which audiences projected their fantasies of who and what we are" (152).[36] The spectators did not actually read the cage-as-performance but rather inserted it into a previously existing text.

What kinds of clues did the audience have with which to read this performance? Next to the cage the artists displayed a didactic panel listing a selected chronology from the history of exhibiting non-Western peoples from 1493 until 1992. Another panel (displaying a spurious entry from *Encyclopedia Britannica*) provided objectifying data about the two Guatinaui specimens. Not only did the panel list biological and physical information about the Guatinauis (their weight, height, eating habits and sexual customs), but the text provided (simulated) analyses of their habits. It revealed that the male's "frequent pacing in the cage leads experts to believe that he was a political leader on his island" and that the female's "facial and body decorations indicate that she has married into the upper caste of her tribe" (165).[37] Although absurd, these statements resemble real interpretations offered by anthropologists about their objects of study. The public's gullibility can be explained as a result of long-term conditioning. Accustomed to seeing exotic others—Indians, savages or generic primitives—on display in museums and (*National Geographic*-like) magazines, the public read these specimens as real. The long-standing tradition of orientalism shaped the public's horizon of expectations. Ironically, from a hermeneutic perspective, the public encountered a familiar text.

The public's familiarity with the conventions of human exhibition also arises from the tradition of carnival and circus freak shows.[38] The *Couple in the Cage* video highlights this connection by splicing in footage and photographs from sideshow exhibitions. We see, for example, photographs of two microcephalic "pinheads" from El Salvador, Maximo and Bartola, who were touted throughout Europe and the Americas (from 1853 to 1901) as "the last Aztec survivors of a mysterious jungle city called Ixinaya." Another couple of microcephalics, "Flip and Pip," were billed promotionally as "Twins from the Yucatan." On a basic level, Fusco and Gómez-Peña's performance operates through the same voyeuristic mechanism as a freak or human oddity exposition. Their handlers used a voice reminiscent of carnival barkers to hawk photographs, stories and dances to the public. When providing information, on the other hand, they spoke as knowledgeable museum attendants. The cage provided the public with the opportunity to safely observe and discover the curious traits embodied by a pair of Guatinauis.

Gómez-Peña and Fusco's performance further draws attention to the tradition of displaying *indigenous* primitives as freaks. As Fusco points out, an ideological collusion between science and popular culture promoted the racist agenda of European superiority: "With the emergence of scientific rationalisms, the 'aborigines' on display served as proof of the natural superiority of European civilization, of its ability to exert control over and extract knowledge from the 'primitive' world, and ultimately of the genetic inferiority of non-European races" ("The Other History" 146). The video presents documentation from examples in which primitive others were exhibited as ethnological curiosities. Ishi, the last of the Yahi Indians, was captured in 1905 and spent his life living as a specimen in the museum of the University of California. This case, along with several others (for example, The Hottentot Venus [1810–15], Fifteen Ubangis featuring "the nine largest-lipped women in the Congo" [1931], a wild African bushman named Clicko and Truganini, a Tasmanian Aboriginal), underscores the continuity between colonial ideology and human exhibition. Acknowledging this tradition, furthermore, helps us comprehend why spectators believed the fictional pretense of the "Two Amerindians Visit ... " performance.

On the other hand, Gómez-Peña and Fusco's costumes are so ludicrous that one must strain to accept the fact that viewers could really mistake the performance for an ethnological exhibition. Fusco wears sneakers, a grass skirt, a leopard-skin halter top and sunglasses. Gómez-Peña describes himself in a feather headdress, (leopard-skin) wrestling mask, a shimmering breastplate and an ornate loincloth as "an Aztec from Las Vegas" (quoted in Siems 30). Intuitively, one would like to think that contemporary European and U.S. audiences have enough experience to see through such a ruse. And yet, as Edward Said writes in *Orientalism*, electronic communication media have rewritten "the exotic" from the realm of myth into a hodgepodge of stereotypes:

> If the world has become immediately accessible to a Western citizen ... the Orient ... is now less a myth perhaps than a place crisscrossed by Western, especially American interests ... One aspect of the electronic, postmodern world is that there has been a reinforcement of the stereotypes ... Television, the films, and all the media's resources have forced information into more and more standardized molds. (26)

Said's commentary points to the ironic contradiction that characterizes cultural awareness in the age of electronic communication. The public today has unprecedented access to non-Western cultures through television documentaries. Televisual access, nevertheless, does not seem to enhance knowledge about other cultures. In the *Couple in the Cage* video, one woman complains that Fusco's dancing does not match up to something she might see on public television. Rather than demonstrating public awareness, her comment bears witness to the extent of *mediation* in the construction of Indian-ness.

During Gómez-Peña and Fusco's performance, a VCR inside the cage plays video clips from television and film programs that depict indigenous peoples. The absurdity of these true cultural artifacts, many dating from the 1960s and earlier, rivals that of the Guatinauis. Presenting these televised images of caged freaks and overstylized Indians within the cage, Fusco and Gómez-Peña's performance constructs a *mise en abyme*. The *Couple in the Cage* video again re-presents this embedding of images by filming spectators and news crews shooting photographs and videos in front of the cage (which contains both the Guatinauis and the television). These popular images help to explain the public's gullibility. The entertainment industry has so pervasively disseminated stereotypes of pseudo-Indians that the public's threshold of plausibility remains virtually infinite. [39]

To convey the influence of mediation, *The Couple in the Cage* video intersperses a montage of film fragments. By selectively juxtaposing these quotations from historical documentary films with Hollywood renditions of exotic, savage or noble primitives, the video implicates the media as both purveyor and receptor of stereotypes. The border lines between fiction and documentary become blurred. In Hollywood films (such as the clip that concludes the video, following the credits), fictional "anthropologists" explain their desire to present primitives "just as they are," emphasizing that while their subjects are primitive they seem in many ways happier than civilized humans. The Hollywood images invoke the motif of the "noble savage," and they simultaneously exoticize and ridicule their indigenous specimens.

Obviously many spectators were not deceived by the performance. It is striking, nonetheless, to note how those who suspected (or resented) a taint of artifice negotiated the question of the Guatinauis' *authenticity*: "I've studied a lot about Indians but there's something not quite right" said an Australian man. "It just doesn't sound 100 percent," he added. One woman explained her reaction to the performance in terms of a betrayal: "I feel like I'm being put on. And you know it's kind of offensive. It feels like a slap in the face." In Madrid a viewer objected that their skin seems too lightly colored: "Están muy blancos para ser de la selva." The handlers explained that the Guatinauis live very deep in the jungle, "donde los rayos del sol no filtran." For these spectators, the question of whether or not the specimens are real Indians was of paramount importance. The possibility of deception threatens their self-esteem. As Baudrillard wrote of simulation, it "threatens the difference between 'true' and 'false,' between 'real' and 'imaginary'" (*Simulations* 5). The mere prospect of simulation disrupts the public's sense of balance.

And yet the simulation question is not limited to the couple's purported ethnological authenticity. Other spectators, aware of the installation's performative element, raised the question of "authentic art." After watching one of Fusco's fifty-cent Guatinaui dances an audience member retorted: "That to me looks like something for fifty cents." Although she had admittedly been watching the cage for some time, the performance left her with a feeling of cheapness. Near the end of the video, Gómez-Peña, Fusco and their collaborating "handlers" discuss audience reactions toward earlier performances. According to one of the caretakers, a number of critics believed that Gómez-Peña and Fusco were merely employees who had been hired by their artists-handlers to play the role of savages. In addition to staging the practice of human exhibition, consequently, the "Two Undiscovered Amerindians" performance puts on display the question of artistic authenticity. Ironically, Fusco and Gómez-Peña's performance did not strive to stage original art. To the contrary the performance parodically re-presented the images with which the mainstream media presents Amerindians.

This explicit parody of colonialism also indexes the postcolonial practice of exhibiting (a restricted, watered-down and exoticized version) of Latino art. In his essay, "The Multicultural Paradigm," Gómez-Peña directly relates the commercial phenomenon of the Latino Boom to colonial rhetoric: "In 1987, just like in 1492, we were 'discovered' (rediscovered to be precise) ... We are suddenly in, fashionable, and grantable, and our ethnicity is being commodified" (50). Inhabiting the exaggerated images of postcolonial commercialism, Fusco and Gómez-Peña mock the authenticating pretensions of "high art."

The *Couple in the Cage* video records a performance in New York City during which the cage occupied the center of a formal party. In the video we watch as fashionably dressed art critics sip wine and light-heartedly purchase photographs, stories and dances from the Guatinauis as jazzy cocktail music plays in the background. A sudden jump cut in the video splices in black-and-white footage from the 1930s of an elegant dance featuring two nearly naked primitives who stand amongst a tuxedo-clad orchestra. After cutting back to the Guatinauis in New York, the video then returns again to the black-and-white film. An explanatory subtitle, "In 1930 'Cannibals' were transported from Africa to attend a moving picture gala," provides the historical context from which Gómez-Peña and Fusco base their performance. Returning once again to New York, the video washes out the color, emphasizing the continuity between historical and contemporary thought. This juxtaposition of the Guatinauis with an actual case of the entertainment industry's exploitation of a non-Western people brings the polyvalent critique of the "Two Amerindians" performance into sharp focus.

On one level, the cage evokes the economic and social constraints that limit and restrain disenfranchised others throughout the world. At the same time the artists' manipulation of kitsch, and their rendering of exaggerated stereotypes, articulates a critique of contemporary society's fascination and abuse of *images*. In *The Political Unconscious*, Fredric Jameson describes late capitalism as a new, postindustrial model of cage:

> The characteristics of the total system of contemporary world society are less those of political domination than those of cultural programming and penetration: *not the iron cage, but rather the société de consommation* with its consumption of images and simulacra, its free-floating signifiers and its effacement of the older structures of social class and traditional ideological hegemony. (emphasis added, 93)

This postmodern confine is precisely the paradox that Gómez-Peña and Fusco underscore. Obviously Fusco and Gómez-Peña are not really confined; they are performing confinement and using the cage as a narrative frame and intertext. The cage installation draws attention to the performers, to the tradition of human exhibition and especially to the transparent cage of cultural-televisual programming—the *société de consommation*.

At one point in the video of *The Couple in the Cage*, a clip of a reporter for Channel 7's Eyewitness News informs television viewers that the exhibit is fictional: "Okay so it's not for real. Those people in the cage are really actors. And you know what? They are studying us." Although partially correct, the eyewitness informant from the media oversimplifies the performance. While it is true that these experimental artists study the public's reaction, they do not simply reverse the ethnographic process 180 degrees. Conceptualized in this way, analyzing the savagery of civilized spectators, the two pseudosavages would tautologically invert the process of traditional ethnography and leave the system of objectification intact. Inverting an opposition can only produce an inverted opposition. Rather than reversing the conventions of cultural representation, Gómez-Peña and Fusco reappropriate the process at large.

To comprehend how "for real" this performance *is* obliges a consideration of both the performers' and the public's response. By enclosing themselves in the cage, Fusco and Gómez-Peña inhabit mass cultural images of otherness. Staging mute performance art, the artists self-consciously refuse the pontificating posture of traditional discourse. They represent the tribe of the Guatinauis (*Guati-nau-is* even sounds like "what now is") and conjugate a (con)fusion of images that *is* present in contemporary society. By granting viewers the opportunity to photograph themselves in front of the cage, the performance situates the public within the frame of the public's own objectifying gaze. Each photograph of a viewer in front of the cage re-presents an*other* image of otherness. When Eyewitness News reports the event as news about fiction, "Okay so it's not for real," the reporter trivializes both the performance and the historical context with which the installation engages. This (con)fusion underscores the transparent lines of thought that shape and textualize these images.

I began this chapter arguing that Gómez-Peña stages a sustained deconstruction of the concept of border lines. Initially, the "Two Undiscovered Amerindians" performance appears vastly different from Gómez-Peña's earlier border art. Whereas Gómez-Peña's site-specific performances once took place on the U.S.–Mexico border, he and Fusco later transported their cage to exhibition sites and museums around the world. Gómez-Peña moved from performance monologues to collaborative representations of mute presence. A closer analysis, nonetheless, reveals a continuous presence of border lines that "Two Undiscovered Amerindians" re-presents metaphorically through the bars of the cage. Underscoring the borders that surround the Amerindians and their spectators, Gómez-Peña and Fusco redraw the lines from apparently fixed geopolitical locations to less obvious but equally formidable *cultural borders*.

In "Border Brujo" a drunken-voiced Gómez-Peña explicitly delineates his position within the border in terms of incarceration:

I'm here in prison
right in the center of the wound
right in the crack of the 2 countries ... (94)

The "I" speaking represents the entire spectrum of characters who are channeled by the Border Brujo. On one level the situation evokes the confinement of border dwellers to a perpetual existence of poverty and economic exploitation. Gómez-Peña situates the perennial subjugation of indigenous peoples in nearly identical terms in his poem "Oración del indio enjaulado:"

> cansado estoy
> y cansado permanezco
> por los siglos de los siglos
> let me loose
> cansado estoy
> y cansado permanezco
> por los siglos de los siglos
> let me loose
> (ad infinitum) (147)

"Por los siglos de los siglos," the caged (canary-like) *indio* repeats this same "song" to the deaf ears of those holding the key.[40] Since the conquest of "America," colonial and neocolonial powers have confined native peoples to the limits of artificially inscribed geopolitical borders. The native "other" remains stuck between the cracks of the cultures in control.

The Border Brujo addresses the social stereotypes with which (post-colonial) dominant culture pigeonholes Latinos:

> I am a prisoner of thought
> a prisoner of art
> a prisoner of a media war
> I'm each & every bad guy in the film ... (94)

The vilifying images with which the media typecasts Latinos constitutes one more version of objectification. The dominant culture, according to Gómez-Peña, transforms Latinos into pure *images*:

> We are perceived through the folkloric prisms of Hollywood, fad literature, and publicity; or through the ideological filters of mass media. For the average Anglo, *we are nothing but "images," "symbols," "metaphors."* We lack ontological existence ... We are perceived indiscriminately as magic creatures with shamanistic powers ... All this without mentioning the more ordinary myths, which link us with drugs, supersexuality, gratuitous violence, and

terrorism; myths that serve to justify racism and disguise the fear
of cultural otherness. (emphasis added, 40)

These are precisely the images that Gómez-Peña has been inhabiting
since the beginning of his career. He and Fusco utilize the approach that
Linda Hutcheon identifies with (postmodern) complicitous critique.
They reappropriate "existing representations that are effective precisely
because they are loaded with preexisting meaning and [put] them in new
and ironic contexts" (*Politics of Postmodernism* 44). As Hutcheon
points out, this technique of reappropriation indicates the boundaries of
transparent political mechanisms: "While exploiting the power of
familiar images, it also denaturalizes them, makes visible the concealed
mechanisms which work to make them seem transparent, and brings to
the fore their politics" (44). From "Border Brujo" through "Two Amerindians Visit ...," Gómez-Peña's work denaturalizes the repressive
dimensions of hegemonically produced images.

   One last look at the cage will situate the critical *mise en abyme* of
Fusco and Gómez-Peña's installation. As the viewer contemplates the
Guatinauis from straight ahead, the performers' sunglasses reflect the
audience. This added reflective detail might be said to constitute what
Slavoj Zizek (following Lacan) would call the point of anamorphosis:
"This paradoxical point undermines our position as 'neutral,' 'objective'
observer, pinning us to the observed object itself. This is the point at
which the observer is already included, inscribed in the observed scene—
in a way, it is the point from which the picture itself looks back at us"
(91). By inhabiting the images that the dominant culture represents as
"others," Gómez-Peña and Fusco occupy *our* images. Reflecting critically on this reflection leads us to a "discovery." We have met the
other and it is us.[41] Yet there is more at stake to this (con)fusing "box
in a box" than a simply narcissistic *trompe l'oeil*. Rather than invert
the objectifying gaze, the performance reflects our position with(in) a
social *mise en abyme* of spectacle and observation. As one critic has
written of *mise en abyme*, "it upsets the assumed relationship between
subject and object in the scene of representation ... The object cannot
be grasped by the subject, it slips away into infinity ... The subject ...
loses not only its capacity to grasp the object, but ... becomes the
subject of a representation that exceeds it" (28).[42] The image of a cage
in the cage of representation underscores the public's misunderstanding
as well as the performance's silent deconstructive critique of representational discourse. Fusco and Gómez-Peña's performance has redrawn the

last invisible border line that separates and links the positions of "subject" and object-other. We not only encounter ourselves within the cage but, more specifically, we confront ourselves in the process of observation. It is not enough to recognize our images within the cage. We-the-public are the "Couple" *and* the "Cage."

NOTES

1. Gómez-Peña originally worked with the Mexican journalist Marco Vinicio Gonzalez on this project. After Vinicio moved away from the border in 1987, Gómez-Peña coedited a series of issues with Emily Hicks, Harry Polkinhorn, César Espinosa and Isaac Artenstein. For Gómez-Peña's perspective on the journal, see the section titled "Breaking the Line" in *Warrior for Gringostroika* (26–7). See also García Canclini's *Culturas híbridas* (301–2).

2. In 1984 Gómez-Peña and Marco Vinicio Gonzalez started a bilingual radio show in the San Diego–Tijuana area called "Diálogos Fronterizos." Subsequently he has worked with National Public Radio and several other radio production companies. From 1990 to 1992 he continued to experiment with radio, including live broadcasts of his performances and what he terms "pirate radio interventions." Most recently Gómez-Peña released a compact disc titled *Borderless Radio* (Word of Mouth Productions: 1994), compiling solo and collaborative works from 1985 to 1993. The accompanying documentation that markets the project as "a double CD of Spanglish Radio and Spoken Word Pieces" includes an essay by Gómez-Peña chronicling his work in radio.

3. Gómez-Peña also won the Prix de la Parole at the International Theater Festival of the Americas and the New York Bessie Award in 1989. His most recent book, *The New World Border: Prophecies, Poems and Loqueras for the End of the Century* (San Francisco: City Lights, 1996), was awarded the American Book Award in 1997.

4. Gómez-Peña has published several versions of each of these texts. "Border Brujo," "Califas" and "1992" are compiled in his book *Warrior for Gringostroika*, which also presents the bulk of Gómez-Peña's critical articles. All Gómez-Peña quotes correspond to pagination in *Warrior for Gringostroika* unless otherwise noted. All references for "New World Border" pertain to the text printed in *The Drama Review*.

5. For a description of the *End of the Line* performance and accompanying photographs see the BAW/TAF 1989 catalogue (14–17), which documents the preceding five years of performances. The stereotype designs for

the costumes were created by Chicano artist Victor Ochoa. Ochoa's stereo-type designs are reproduced on pages 28–30 of the same catalogue. See also Gómez-Peña's commentary in *Warrior for Gringostroika* (27–8).

6. In another BAW/TAF performance the artists solicited participation from a group of Mexicans, some of whom were waiting until nightfall to cross the border illegally. Intersecting the border with a black rope they enacted a tug-of-war between participants in "Migra" border control masks and others wearing wrestling masks. Attempting to pull a map of the Western Hemisphere (at the center of the rope) completely onto one side, they playfully enacted border politics as an uneven line of power. Allegedly, U.S. border control agents observed the scene from their vantage point on a nearby mesa. For a description of this performance, see C. Carr's *On Edge: Performance at the End of the Twentieth Century* (191–2).

7. Gómez-Peña resigned from the BAW/TAF in 1989 due to internal conflict and a growing feeling that border art was becoming co-opted by institutions. I return to this subject at a later point in this chapter. The BAW/TAF continues to perform on the border, although now with different members.

8. This barrier was constructed from recycled Desert Storm landing material. Not only does the construction demarcate the border between the United States and Mexico but, ironically, it calls attention to the network of transnational interests transcending national boundaries. The Gulf War, which began as a border dispute between Iraq and Kuwait, became the (tele-visual and military) stage for establishing an international "World Order."

9. On the economic, social and political situation surrounding *maquiladoras*, see Augusta Dwyers, *On the Line: Life on the U.S.–Mexican Border*.

10. The growing Hispanic population in the United States correlates to the fourth or fifth largest Spanish-speaking group in the world. Needless to say, illegal aliens are only one of many groups of Spanish-speaking immigrants of vastly variable socioeconomic status.

11. I should note that Gómez-Peña specifically refused to participate in the exhibition from which this text was created. Chávez and Grynsztejn, nonetheless, describe the border in terms that are consistent with Gómez-Peña's work. I address Gómez-Peña's conflicts with other border artists at a later point in this chapter.

12. In an article in the *Utne Reader*, "Going Gangsta, Choosn' Cholita," Nell Bernstein describes a growing trend especially among Caucasian adolescents in the United States to claim another racial identity: "Identity is not a matter of where you come from, what you were born into, what color your skin is. It's what you wear, the music you listen to, the words you use"

(87). Gómez-Peña's claim to be a *Chicano* reflects a political statement that parodies frivolous fads of "claiming." The history of the term *Chicano*, furthermore, would allow for certain flexibility in its use (see following note).

13. I emphasize a contemporary context because the word *Chicano* has evolved considerably over time. For an exhaustive analysis of the term's history, see Tino Villanueva's prologue to his anthology *Chicanos: Antología histórica y literaria.* Although the etymology of the term is still open to debate, Villanueva observes that at the beginning of the twentieth century *Chicano* was used to designate a *Mexican* laborer who had recently arrived in the United States: "Se refería al obrero mexicano no calificado y recién llegado a los Estados Unidos" (7). Over time, *Chicano* became a pejorative name for Mexican Americans. Finally, in the 1960s, Villanueva writes that young Mexican Americans in the Chicano movement reappropriated the (formerly negative) term as a symbol of their right to ethnic and political agency: "El término *chicano* abarca todo un universo ideológico que sugiere no sólo la audaz postura de autodefinición y desafío, sino también el empuje regenerativo de autovoluntad y de autodeterminación, potenciado todo ello por el latido vital de una conciencia de crítica social; de orgullo étnico-cultural; de concientización de clase y de política" (17).

14. Chicanos adopted the idea of Aztlán from an Aztec legend referring to Aztlán as a paradise in the north. For a definition of Aztlán and a history of the Chicano movement, see the chapter titled "Aztlán: Geografía, Demografía e Historia" in Juan Gutierrez Martínez-Conde's *Literatura y sociedad en el mundo chicano.*

15. D. Emily Hicks describes the border in terms of a holographic interference pattern: "If we conceive of the border as a multidimensional or holographic text created from the interference pattern formed by two dominant cultural codes, we will find that no links among any two signifiers can all hold. All signifiers and their binary oppositions *al otro lado* will continually struggle for dominance and be dismantled" (110).

16. "Buey," Spanish for ox, is a common slang term among Mexicans and Chicanos. Depending on context, *buey* can mean "dude" or "stupid."

17. In *Marvelous Possessions: The Wonder of the New World*, Stephen Greenblatt argues against a passive denial of Doña Marina/La Malinche. Greenblatt describes her as a "go between" who played a crucial role in the "New World" as both a linguistic and cultural translator.

18. Consider, too, the actual word "Dada" instead of the Movement. Although Tzara's manifestos denied any single significance for the term, the suggestion of a child's pronunciation of "father" remains audible. This implication of Dada as father enters as well into the passage's themes of

"*desmadre*," "being without a mother" and "meta-orphanhood."

19. Gómez-Peña does not aspire to speak for the "other" as did, for example, Neruda, in "Las Alturas de Machu Picchu," but rather attempts to call attention to the fact that others are "others" only because of hegemonic discourses.

20. Gómez-Peña's "Nahuatl" is a simulation that attempts to imitate the tonality of indigenous languages. In the program notes to "1992" he refers to it as *tongues*: "The 'tongues' are a personal 'esperanto' that experiments with the phonetic structures of indigenous language, and sounds like shamanistic tongues" (98). Often while speaking tongues he inserts the names of well-known multinational corporations.

21. Gómez-Peña and Coco Fusco also ask the audience to contribute "objects" for the "New World Border" performance. In this case the performers ask for the objects before the show at a "Pre-Performance Event in the Lobby" (125). Here again the event breaks down traditional theater dichotomies: Lobby-Theater, Life-Performance and Actors-Spectators.

22. See the photograph on page 138 of *Warrior for Gringostroika*.

23. The Batman icon can suggest a Chicano superhero (Vatoman) with only a slight adjustment in pronunciation. The bananas refer to neocolonial exploitation in Latin America which resulted in the creation of "banana republics." But how is the viewer to read them all together within the immense jumble of other buttons, slogans and props?

24. D. Emily Hicks (a former collaborator of Gómez-Peña's) evokes a Barthesian metaphor to describe the paradoxical cohesion that characterizes border writing: "Border narratives are decentered: there is no identity between the reader and the individual character, but rather, an invitation to listen to a Voice of the Person that arises from an overlay of codes out of which characters and events emerge" (xxviii). On the other hand, perhaps it is not necessary to synthesize any *single* voice from the overlay but rather to recognize that there are always many voices.

25. Arizmendi's article, "Whatever Happened to the Sleepy Mexican? One Way to Be a Contemporary Mexican in a Changing World Order," analyzes the work of Mexican performance artist Sergio Arau, who wears wrestling masks while performing with his band "La venganza de Moctezuma." For semiotic analysis of the wrestling spectacle in a European context, see Roland Barthes's "The World of Wrestling" in *Mythologies* (15–25).

26. Luis Camnitzer discusses the origin of Superbarrio in his article, "Art and Politics: The Aesthetics of Resistance."

27. The Zapatista Liberation Army (EZLN) utilizes a very similar strategy by having its members wear anonymous black ski masks in public. That
the Zedillo government went to great lengths to "unmask" Subcomandante
Marcos bears witness to the extent that the mask as a code of honor pervades Mexican culture. The government hoped that by unveiling Marcos's
true identity with a photograph, the rebel leader would lose his popular
appeal. Zapatista supporters insist on the collective goal of the rebellion,
nevertheless, retorting in demonstrations, "Somos todos Marcos."

28. Although Superbarrio's comic book aesthetic might appear frivolous, the effectiveness of his performance activism is noteworthy. According to Camnitzer, Superbarrio prevented more than 1500 evictions in five
years. Gómez-Peña underscores the consequences of Superbarrio's interventions by noting the governmental response: "The Mexican government
responded to the popularity of Superbarrio by creating a performance rival:
Superpueblo" (*Warrior* 59).

29. Ironically, it was a $350,000 MacArthur Foundation Fellowship in
1991 that allowed Gómez-Peña to move his performance base away from the
border. The institutional praise awarded to Gómez-Peña's work is a point of
contention among his former Chicano collaborators. In an informal interview, Victor Ochoa told me that he and other members of the original BAW/
TAF do not feel that Gómez-Peña sufficiently acknowledges their contribu-
tion to border art or his career. Ochoa also disapproved of Gómez-Peña
traveling around the world performing for predominantly white audiences
while his former Mexican and Chicano collaborators remained "in the
trenches," struggling with the still extant issue of border control.

30. Before performing in Madrid in May 1992 Gómez-Peña and Fusco
conducted a test performance in the Art Gallery of U.C.–Irvine. Following
the exhibition in Madrid, they performed "Two Undiscovered Amerindians"
in Covent Garden in London, the Walker Art Center in Minneapolis, the
Smithsonian's National Museum of Natural History, the Australian Museum
of Natural History in Sydney, the Field Museum in Chicago and the Whitney
Museum in New York.

31. This quote (from *Art Forum*, May 1993) appears as part of the
Couple in the Cage video. By isolating Avgikos's comment and presenting
it between images, the video text reproduces both the performance and its
manifest "problems."

32. This is not the first time that Gómez-Peña has presented an essentially mute performance. In 1979 in a "ritual performance" titled "The Lone-
liness of the Immigrant," Gómez-Peña spent twenty-four hours in a public

elevator wrapped in a batik cloth. According to his own account, he was "kicked, fondled ... cursed by strangers, and peed on by a dog" (*Gringostroika* 20).

33. In Irvine, a woman spectator reached for Gómez-Peña's crotch. Male viewers often made sexual innuendoes to Fusco. In Madrid, teenagers handed the performers containers of urine instead of beer. They also offered them cigarettes, attempting to burn the performers' arms through the bars. See Fusco's "The Other History of Intercultural Performance." See also Larry Siems's article about Gómez-Peña, "Just Who Does He Think He Is?" in the *San Diego Weekly Reader*.

34. For two recent interpretations of Fusco and Gómez-Peña's performance and video, see Diana Taylor's "A Savage Performance: Guillermo Gómez-Peña and Coco Fusco's "Couple in the Cage" and Barbara Kirshenblatt-Gimblett's response, "The Ethnographic Burlesque." These articles came to my attention when this book was in the final stages of editing.

35. These statistics were reported by Fusco in her article, "The Other History of Intercultural Performance" in *The Drama Review*.

36. In the video one of the handlers explains that another spectator interpreted the performance as a satire of an American family in which the male spends his time watching television.

37. A facsimile of the "didactic panel" appears on pages 164–5 of Fusco's *The Drama Review* article. This information is also displayed in the *Couple in the Cage* video.

38. For an analysis and history of human exhibition, see Leslie Fiedler's *Freaks: Myths and Images of the Secret Self*. For another source that documents the exposition of human oddities, see Daniel Mannix's *Freaks: We Who Are Not As Others*. See also the chronology of human display in Fusco's article "The Other History of Intercultural Performance" (146–7).

39. The practice of *zapping* between stations (or videos) exacerbates this confusion by allowing viewers to (con)fuse documentaries (whether they are accurate, inaccurate or exoticized) with fictional images from television and Hollywood. See the chapter on zapping in Beatriz Sarlo's *Escenas de la vida posmoderna: Intelectuales, arte y videocultura en la Argentina* (Buenos Aires: Ariel, 1994) 57–73.

40. Gómez-Peña frequently reminds us that Columbus caged six Arawak Indians and brought them back to Spain. One was left on display for two years until he died. See "1992" (105).

41. Leslie Fiedler comes to a similar conclusion when contemplating an exhibition of freak Siamese twins: "The distinction between audience and

exhibit, we and them, normal and Freak, is revealed as an illusion, desperately, perhaps even necessarily, defended, but untenable in the end" (36).

42. This quote is taken from Diane Elam's *Feminism and Deconstruction: Ms. en Abyme.* Elam uses the trope of *mise en abyme* to describe the never-ending task of feminism to represent women through representation in culture. Her point that there is no "original woman" that feminism can unproblematically reproduce can certainly be applied to the subject-object dialectic of any "other."

CHAPTER 5

Conclusion

I have explored in this book a variety of approaches that Spanish American writers use to critique postmodern political and social conditions at a time when poststructuralist sensibilities have rendered the concept of critical distance obsolete. I have analyzed the manner in which Diamela Eltit, Alejandro Jodorowsky and Guillermo Gómez-Peña employ a strategy of interdisciplinary semiotic (con)fusion to deconstruct the panoptic strictures of hegemonic representation. Through a series of close readings I have attempted to demonstrate how these three Spanish American writers-artists-performers *(con)fuse signs* across a spectrum of nontraditional multimedia texts from which they encounter and critique the inescapable sociopolitical confusion of postmodernity.

A word of caution is in order here. It would be reductive to limit Eltit, Jodorowsky and Gómez-Peña's work to postmodernism *tout court.* As I said earlier, I am not arguing that their work is necessarily postmodern. Analysis of their work sheds light on methods and strategies that writers use to construct political critique from within the confounding context and confines of postmodernity. What I have attempted to demonstrate in this book is analogous, on a metacritical level, to the process of internal critique that I have observed within Eltit's, Jodorowsky's and Gómez-Peña's individual works. By (con)fusing the signs of three Spanish American writers, I have attempted to situate a theoretical position capable of representing an interior space for critique in contemporary political culture.

Theorists of postmodernism encounter endless continua of representational limitations. Jameson critiques the impasse in terms of circularity: "[It is] a kind of bad reflexivity that eats its own tail without ever squaring the circle. Postmodernism theory seems indeed to be a ceaseless process of internal rollover in which the position of the observer is turned inside out" (*Postmodernism* 64). It is not that postmodernism completely eludes critical understanding, however, but rather that the collection of issues shaping postmodern theory can only be approached selectively and internally. As José David Saldívar concludes, "theory is now written not from a condition of critical 'distance,' but rather from a place of hybridity and *betweenness* in our global Borderlands" (emphasis original 153). Without defining the whole, my purpose has been to cast light on the "ceiling" of the postmodern complex from the inside.

Jodorowsky and Gómez-Peña evoke political, social and psychic confusion as a sign of contemporary existence; my reading of Eltit highlights a very different phenomenon. Far from an attempt to reflect societal confusion, the disorientation of *Lumpérica* corresponds to a demystification of the "order" proclaimed by the Pinochet regime. By manipulating an allegory of corporeal rhetoric, the dictatorship claimed to excise the malignant tumor of Marxism from the Chilean *cuerpo nacional*. Like the Harrow of Kafka's "Penal Colony," the military carved punishment directly into the bodies of those who dared to disagree. Maiming, disfiguring and killing, the *régimen* transformed the bodies (or corpses) of their victims into message-bearing signs. Unable to find a safe place or "distance" from which to denounce the Pinochet dictatorship, Eltit staged a (con)fusion of narrative and corporeal mutilation. By inscribing her skin as text, Eltit symbolically rearticulated a discursive *body* that had been appropriated by the regime. In the absence of a space from which to speak, Eltit claimed her body as a site for political inscription. While mutilating the dominant notion of unity Eltit simultaneously constituted a political critique within narrative discourse. She effaced the image of (neo)fascist order without evoking an essentializing counternarrative.

Although I have primarily underscored the (con)fusion of Eltit's first and most fragmented book, her recent novel, *Los vigilantes*, further attests to her continual use of linguistic and narrative fragmentation in what appears to be democratic Chile. *Lumpérica*'s narrative "hermeticism" certainly coincided with the danger of censorship and physical reprisal during the dictatorship. And yet, although her subsequent writing may show some increasing tendency toward linear exposition, she continues to write in a markedly experimental vein.

Let us briefly consider another recent project of Eltit's, *El infarto del alma* (1994), to underscore her effort to articulate unfixed, always already internal postmodern positions. In *El infarto del alma* Eltit recounts her impressions of a journey through a public hospital for the chronically insane. The text juxtaposes Eltit's prose with photographer

Paz Errázuriz's images of confined indigent couples.[7] The combination of Eltit's narrative and Errázuriz's photographs weaves an interdisciplinary dialogue that this time clearly takes place in contemporary Chile. It is crucial to reiterate the conflictual political conditions that characterize contemporary Chile: Although human rights violations no longer constitute the norm, Pinochet only resigned from his position of commander and chief of the armed forces in March 1998 and was subsequently named "Honorary Commander and Chief" by these same forces. As it looks now he will retain his self-appointed position of Senator for Life. The neoliberal policies that began under the dictatorship, furthermore, now form the economic backbone of the country.[1]

Obviously in *Lumpérica* and *El infarto del alma,* Diamela Eltit constructs two very different texts that respond to two different time periods and realities. *Lumpérica,* her first novel, critiques the physical and discursive repression of the Pinochet dictatorship through narrative "shredding," imagistic (con)fusion and literary circumlocution. *El infarto del alma,* on the other hand, frames photographs of real people living on the margins of contemporary Chilean society. Both texts, nevertheless, highlight spectacle, conflating the gaze of observer and observed. *Lumpérica* encloses transient characters within the margins of an abandoned public square. Eleven years later *El infarto del alma* focuses on society's mental pariahs, confined within the walls of a state institution. And, in some regards, very little has changed over the course of Eltit's career. In Raquel Olea's reading, Eltit consistently and persistently interrogates the manner in which society represses those at the margins—sometimes by dictatorship, and other times by democracy: "Eltit repite el mismo gesto político con que se marca la totalidad de su obra; ... ella ilumina ... sujetos parias, desasidos, excluidos de los poderes que, en dictadura o democracia—lo mismo da" (*Lengua* 80). The official image and figurehead of the Chilean government have changed but the dynamics and structures of power remain the same. As Moulian writes, the contemporary Chilean system functions as, and in, a cage, "opera como una jaula de hierro" (51). In *El infarto del alma,* we ponder the hollow void surrounded by the now "democratic" institution. In the aftermath of the dictatorship, when the oppressor is no longer so readily recognizable, Eltit evokes confusion as a metaphor for contemporary conditions.

My research on Jodorowsky encountered an extraordinary spectrum of texts ranging from novels and plays to films, comic books and pantomime routines. Although his works initially appear vastly different from one another, reading them in series revealed an obsessive repetition of narrative *quests*. Comparing Jodorowsky's narrative to a chaotic iterative equation brought forth the author's obsession with the narrative origin of truth, and the indeterminate origins of narrative.

In her introduction to *Freedom and Interpretation: The Oxford Amnesty Lectures*, Barbara Johnson deconstructs the notion of *truth* as a consequence of narrative: "What we know as 'facts' are always themselves constructed, always already in some way a 'facsimile,' a 'version' of something in whose real presence we come to believe only through the ways in which its absence is pointed to" (6). The search for the original language in *El loro de siete lenguas* culminates with the image of a *loro* parroting fragments of always already copied language. For Jodorowsky, in the absence of truth, there are only truths, and it is up to the individual to find or make sense out of his or her quest.

And yet while he celebrates individuality, Jodorowsky de-emphasizes the relative significance of the individual. As in chaotic systems, order becomes noticeable on a systemic level. Jodorowsky's work interprets everything (including history) as a function of narrative. He evokes amnesia as a metaphor for contemporary disorientation. Jodorowsky writes as a means to re-member the subject with a place from which to take charge of his or her own life. Rather than seek truth, sense or guidance from "authorities," Jodorowsky denies the existence of any such authorities. He does not supply answers but instead leaves a space for the reader to find his or her own place in the iterative series of narrative. The sum result of these analyses across Jodorowsky's *oeuvre* reveals a sustained critique of the panoptic "order" hidden beneath the confused signs of contemporary postmodern disorientation.

My chapter on Gómez-Peña explicated the manner in which he (con)fuses literary, vestimentary and hegemonic cultural signs to problematize the essentializing notions of national and ethnic purity. Site-specific performances on the U.S.–Mexico border (in which he participated as a member of BAW/TAF) suggested a complex rereading of the border as a space or laboratory for cultural critique rather than as a line that divides two sovereign nations. Deconstructing this line reveals two opposing social texts: imaginary images of national unity at one extreme and minority discourses predicated on difference at the other.

Gómez-Peña's performances of "New World Border," "1992" and "Two Amerindians Visit ..." (with Coco Fusco) de-territorialize the postcolonial position from which Gómez-Peña writes. The parodic wordplay of his written pieces emphasizes the ultimate untranslatability of culture. Gómez-Peña's (con)fusion of European theories of post-modernism and Mexican culture exemplifies the ideological borders that continue to shape culture, including both popular and "high" culture. His manipulation of stereotypes and kitsch in all of his performances underscores the process through which academia, science and popular culture tag minority "others" with absurd stigmatizing images.

Gómez-Peña's recent work continues to explore the complicity that complicates the relationship among political artists, art and art institutions. In the performance/installation, "The Temple of Confessions," he and collaborator Roberto Sifuentes enclose themselves in Plexiglas boxes in museums.[2] Performing inside of dioramas, Gómez-Peña and Sifuentes literally inhabit the position of the other as object-of-the-gaze, object and text-to-be-discovered. In "Two Amerindians Visit ...," Gómez-Peña and Fusco moved away form the geopolitical border and, in so doing, emphasized the de-territorialized, global and confining aspects of discursive representation. In "Temple of Confessions," these artists move the cage (this time, a smaller transparent box) back inside of the museum. Gómez-Peña, Fusco and Sifuentes use art to corrode the institution of art. Although only partially successful, these gestures ex-emplify the awareness that the only position from which to constitute critique of contemporary culture remains situated on the inside.

One of the most prevalent threads connecting the work of Jodorow-sky, Gómez-Peña and Eltit is their use and conception of *performance*. To (con)fuse signs—to juxtapose, conflate and contrast signs of culture, power and politics—combines the processes of semiotic performance and political intervention. Jodorowsky's notion of the *efímero pánico* aimed to break out of the "box" of theatrical representation. Unrehearsed and unrepeatable, the *efímeros* were free-form "happenings" that took place in public, aspiring to "sacar el teatro del teatro." Eltit's perform-ance perspective, developed while participating with CADA, also aspired to (con)fuse barriers between spectators and participants as well as art and politics. In contrast to Jodorowsky's orgiastic *pánicos* of the 1960s, Eltit's performances critically contested the codes of a specific political institution: the dictatorship. Gómez-Peña, in turn, denounces the ideological repression of U.S. immigration policy and the related role of the media in ethnic stereotyping. From the "guerrilla" interven-tions of the BAW/TAF to his performance monologues, Gómez-Peña engages the public in a critical dialogue with(in) the performance.

In the case of Eltit, her performance needed to clear some physical "space" within an occupied country in order to denounce the dictatorship. Because the regime had projected an allegorical discourse of order that was predicated on corporeal rhetoric, any counterdiscourse could only predicate another inherently limited representation.[3] Rather than oppose the dictatorship via some sort of testimonial counterdiscourse, Eltit contested the order of discourse itself. Unable to get "outside," Eltit inscribed herself and mutilated her narrative. Her performance articulated a position that tied together the signs of body, text, plaza and nation.

By representing characters that perennially seek the center "elsewhere," Jodorowsky allegorizes the confusion of identity as a question of orientation. Directing the search *within* the self, Jodorowsky refuses a localizable answer. His *quête du soi* is a continuous narrative that moves and changes according to the subject's "place" and situation at any given time. Writing is the medium through which Jodorowsky seeks and defines his position. He criticizes the disorientation of contemporary society and consistently denounces the oppression of man by "man," social and economic inequalities, political corruption and market capitalism. Realizing the futility of traditional emancipation narratives, Jodorowsky sees himself as a part of the very systems that he critiques. Rather than seeking a "paradise lost" somewhere else, Jodorowsky invokes a mystical paradigm of memory. For Jodorowsky, when people re-member the self, they realize that they already embody the position that is sought.

My analysis of Gómez-Peña encountered a nomadic performance praxis. His early site-specific performances converted the border into a site of contention. When he removed himself from the border, Gómez-Peña relocated himself between images rather than national borders. Performing in a cage around the world, Fusco and Gómez-Peña mimed the racist performance of hegemonic culture. Gómez-Peña dramatizes an always moving position, one that slips perennially within the markers of identity politics and hegemonic representation.

In conclusion, I would like to address the farther-reaching significance of the metaphor of confinement, which recurs throughout this study. Bringing together the work of Diamela Eltit, Alejandro Jodorowsky and Guillermo Gómez-Peña in this study, I have constructed a narrative of internal confinement that is contextualized within the theoretical "locker" of the postmodern position. From Eltit's L. Iluminada who spends the entire night enclosed within an "open" plaza within a city and country that is under siege to Jodorowsky's cyclical quests for an origin that proves forever to be another copy to Gómez-Peña's movement from the confines of a border between two countries to an international exhibition of caged "Indians," these three writers-artists-performers allegorize the *aporia* that true critical distance remains forever *outside* their grasp. By (con)fusing the signs of self-other, inside-outside and reality-fiction, these three artists-writers-performers constitute their critiques with(in) the regime of discourses containing them. While significant, their "escape" remains admittedly partial. Foucault described this position in terms of panopticism—cage-like partitions divide and order every part of modern society. We can move from cell to cell but true escape proves impossible. I would like to conclude this encounter, then, by reading a series of cages from across the history of literature and art, both inside and outside of the contexts of postmodernity and Latin America.

Don Quijote was placed in a cage by society's self-appointed gendarmes because he insisted on living the life of a *caballero andante*. Still bent on interpreting life through the prism of *libros de caballería*, Don Quijote believes himself to be the enchanted victim of evil magic. For my purposes, what is most striking about this episode is the logic with which Sancho Panza dispels his master's fantasy: "Acaso después que vuestra merced va enjaulado ... le ha venido gana y voluntad de hacer aguas" (491). As Sancho so persuasively argues, if Don Quijote needs to urinate he surely could not be *encantado*. The cage, therefore, is real, and Don Quijote finds himself in a position of unglamorous, grotesque incarceration. Don Quijote remains imprisoned within the cage, the (hegemonic) narrative norms of society and, not least of which, his body. No matter how strong his propensity toward literature and fantasy might be, the character cannot escape from organic, biological exigencies.

In spite of the epistemological changes characterizing contemporary cultural sensibilities, the situation of Eltit's characters in *Lumpérica* bears much in common with Don Quijote's cage. In post-coup Chile, the regime transformed city plazas into open "cages" for those who had nowhere to hide. While the military immobilized individuals with a *toque de queda*, (neo)fascist ideologues attempted to inscribe social order onto the *patria*. Desirous to denounce this occupation, Eltit found herself surrounded by military repression *and* transparent authoritarian discourse. Through interdisciplinary "art actions," Eltit's performances *solicit* the framework of (neo)fascist discourse.

Explicit cage imagery emerges with frequency in literature responding to conditions of military repression. Argentine Manuel Puig's

novel, *El beso de la mujer araña* (1976), also indicts a specific dictatorship while at the same time questioning the authoritarian nature of
discourse in general. The novel begins *in medias res* as a character, later
known as Molina, narrates a scene from a film: In this film, a man
watches a woman who is in the process of drawing, representing, in
other words, a caged panther in a zoo. Several pages later we glimpse
hints that our narrator and his interlocutor are themselves caged men,
one imprisoned for revolutionary activities and the other for sexual
deviancy. Throughout the novel the reader passes in and out of narrated
films and dialogue in the prison cell, elsewhere "leaving" the narrative
to read a series of enigmatic footnotes. These footnotes (which explicitly explore the limits of (homo)sexuality) ultimately cause the reader
to question the separation of fiction and reality, as well as the division
of the inside from the outside of the text. Cages within cages, Puig's
(con)fusion of representational frames expands beyond the scope of the
novel. The novel's characters *and* readers are caught in a web of images
that shape their respective sexual and ideological identities.

    Although in the context of southern cone dictatorships the "cage"
of incarceration is self-evident, there are other cases where the structure
of a disciplinary institution is less visible. Kafka, in his story "A Report to an Academy," evokes another striking narrative of confinement.
The story presents the image of a man-ape who is transported in a cage
after being captured on the Gold Coast of Africa. Within the narrative,
this man tells his story—he presents a report on his former life as an
ape in a cage.[4] The cage is even penned in, wedged between decks on a
steamer ship: "It was not a four-sided barred cage; it was only a three-
sided cage nailed to a locker" (247). The narrator emphasizes the scope
of his imprisonment by enumerating the progressively wider but
equally limiting confinements:

> I could certainly have managed by degrees to bite through the lock
> of my cage ... What good would it have done me? ... I should have
> been caught again and put in a worse cage; or ... supposing I had
> actually succeeded in sneaking out as far as the deck and leaping
> overboard ... and then been drowned. (250)

Caged in a boxed-in cage on a ship at sea, his story traces a *mise
en abyme*, a box in a box in a box, of total enclosure. With time, the
ape discovers a way out of his cage by imitating the behavior of his
captors. By becoming a performer and working on a variety stage, he
avoids the captivity of a zoo. After having "managed to reach the cul-

tural level of an average European" the ape's highest achievement is to file a report to the Academy (254–5). The narrator's escape, consequently, is infinitely limited. He finds a way out of the three-sided cage but that "spacious feeling of freedom on all sides" (249) remains permanently beyond reach. Notice how Kafka's story of confinement evokes each of the disciplinary applications proposed by Bentham for the Panopticon as described by Foucault in *Discipline and Punish*. The ape is initially incarcerated. His progress is so stunning that one of his trainers ends up interned in a mental hospital. Ultimately the ape-man files a report to the Academy, thus assuming his place inside the society of discipline.

Kafka's allegory of society as cage points to the perpetually changing but always present dimensions of social and metaphysical confinement. Like Jodorowsky's mime in "La jaula," one breaks out of a cage only to realize that he has "progressed" to another, larger box. Similarly, in *El túnel se come por la boca*, Jodorowsky collapses binary spatiality. No matter where they start, all of the characters remain perennially *inside* the bars on the inside of a circular tunnel. This confinement evokes our position within narrative, the "prisonhouse of language." Like Eltit and Gómez-Peña, Jodorowsky can only work with(in) narrative structures, yet as a mystic he focuses on a different realm of internal positionality. For Jodorowsky the cage ultimately corresponds to a narrative *illusion* of structure and order. Through his filmic, literary and graphic texts Jodorowsky (con)fuses spiritual, literary and political quests for truth. He reiterates the chaotic indeterminacies of narrative, maintaining that our imprisonment within the panoptic mechanism is self-imposed.

Gómez-Peña does not share Jodorowsky's conviction that our confinements derive primarily from self-imposed limitations. Gómez-Peña's performances, from "Border Brujo" to "Two Amerindians Visit …," underscore the monetary cage of neocolonial economics. He highlights, furthermore, the virtual cage of postmodern simulation. Ultimately, Gómez-Peña calls attention to the mass media's role in shaping contemporary cultural beliefs. If "facts" are constructed of narrative, Gómez-Peña's parodic appropriations point to the manner in which the media constructs and propagates cultural perceptions of reality.

The cage effect of socioeconomic factors is immediately recognizable in the architectural partitioning of urban cities. Contemporary Puerto Rican artist Antonio Martorell used actual wrought-iron bars in his installation titled "Tras las Rejas" (1986).[5] While deriving from the traditional use of andiron grating in Latin American architecture, Martorell's *rejas* highlight the central practice of enclosure at every stratum of urban life. The upper classes bar themselves in—they live in cages—to protect themselves and their deluxe possessions from "others." The lower classes, accordingly, are *caged outside* in the streets, confined to a daily struggle for scraps of food and work, hoping, like Kafka's ape, for a way out into a bigger, more comfortable enclosure.

Although each articulates the theme differently, Eltit, Jodorowsky and Gómez-Peña all highlight the fact that the media, advertising and culture industries play a crucial role in the (con)fusing construction of contemporary identities. L. Iluminada spends an entire night looking between a neon sign (*el luminoso*) and the reflection of her face in a mirror. In presenting L. Iluminada as a grotesque image, Eltit interferes with the dominant cultural projection of a cosmetically beautified woman. To seduce Jodorowsky's Difool, a woman (Animah) must disguise herself as a holographic copy, a *homéopute*. Entertainment, news and government have become irredeemably (con)fused in an endless cycle of reproduced images. Gómez-Peña, in turn, reappropriates the codes of advertising and Hollywood into his performances, calling attention to the racist overtones produced by these "colorized" images. Eltit, Gómez-Peña and Jodorowsky do not merely explore representation but, more important, they underscore what representation *does* to "others."

I would like to offer just one more example of cage images, this time from a genre of contemporary popular "literature"—advertising. In a Diesel Jeans and Workwear advertisement (reprinted on *Ms. Magazine*'s "No Comment" page),[6] two men saunter through a room full of caged women (see Figure 5-1). The women, garbed in a variety of furs and feathers, give the impression of animals. The ad's implication is as straightforward as it is sexist. These caged "animals" reach out through the bars, each begging to become a house pet. Allegedly, if a man wears Diesel clothing he can pick his woman like a pet at a pet store. The advertisement implies clear-cut divisions of hierarchy that separate the merchandise on the inside, women-animals, from the men who look at and consume them from a safe exterior vantage point.

At the center of the room, a saleswoman in a miniskirt sits on a stool. Behind her, a male shopkeeper occupies his place by the cash register. Although the initially blatant binary couplings, man-woman, master-pet and inside-outside define the Diesel ad's narrative, there exist

Figure 5-1. Diesel Jeans advertisement, "Pet Shop" (Fall/Winter 1994).
(Courtesy of Diesel S.p.A.)

other elements that override this merchandising "fairy tale." A closer reading reveals that the dimensions of the cage stretch far wider than they first appear. Is this sexy sales "girl" that removed from the products she sells? Notice how her fishnet stockings mesh intertextually with the cages throughout the store. As a sales "person," she occupies the very center of the shop and works from the inside of a socioeconomic cage. Walls of cages pen her in. And what of the men? The male shop owner wears a leopard-skin shirt. He, too, wears an animal motif, coyly smiling while he promotes his pets. He is the merchant-"owner," but is he really *outside* or does he occupy a different link within the cage of marketing? And what about the male "customers"? One of them passes his hand through a cage offering food to a feather-covered "bird." Walking through a room full of cages in Diesel jeans, seeking out their ideal pet, are these male customers (or at another level, the male "models" who work for Diesel) any more outside the prison house of images? And finally, what about the viewer, no matter how critical, who gazes into this scene? Stacks of cages line all three of the walls within sight. Dare we turn around?

I have given this example in order to situate myself, this book and my readers *within* the inescapable dimensions of the postmodern cage.

In any analysis, but especially in a study of critical distance, it seems that one must stake a claim for the place that he or she occupies. There is no escape from what Adorno refers to as our "open-air prison." Fusco evokes this position in her analysis of her "Two Amerindians" perform-ance: "Even though I know I can get out of the cage, I can never quite escape" (166). Fully aware of this situation, Eltit, Jodorowsky and Gómez-Peña work within and against the boundaries of postmodern representation and in the process articulate internal positions. Identity is and always has been a product of images. Don Quijote appropriated his identity from *libros de caballería*. Kafka's ape, in turn, adopted an iden-tity by mimicking the gestures of his spectators, acting out the roles of his public like a contemporary politician who models his image on public opinion polls. Today, "technological images have become the mirrors in which to look for an identity" (Olalquiaga 4). There is no degree zero to which we can return for a pure, unadulterated origin of authenticity. By (con)fusing signs, nevertheless, Eltit, Jodorowsky and Gómez-Peña articulate critical interrogations of image production as a process in the construction and representation of reality.

I have suggested in this book that Eltit's, Gómez-Peña's, and Jodo-rowsky's works constitute efforts to use (con)fusion as a strategy to orient themselves within postmodern confusion. If postmodernity, as Jameson writes, has transcended the ability of the individual to "locate itself, to organize its immediate surroundings perceptually, and cogni-tively to map its position in a mappable external world" (*Postmodern-ism* 44), this does not preclude the possibility of occupying the "belly of the beast," (con)fusing the signs of power, and inhabiting representa-tion from the inside. Although there is no "way out," an awareness of our inability to get outside can constitute an awareness of where and who we are, or it at least might suggest how the images that we inhabit cohere.

Contemporary sensibilities have erased the myth of critical *distance* and left us with the need to encounter and critique reality internally. And yet, though we can never escape, observing our positions *within* cultur-al texts can help elucidate the dimensions of the cage. By encountering the limits of our enclosures, we might move toward a critical under-standing of our postmodern position. It is this position, always relative and ever changing, that defines our place in history, literature and that incomprehensible, inapprehendable phenomenon called reality. From the comprehension and articulation of this position, furthermore, emerges political critique.

NOTES

1. On October 16, 1998 Pinochet was arrested in London when a Spanish judge served an extradition request and charged the former dictator with genocide, crimes against humanity and torture. At present it is impossible to predict whether Pinochet will be extradited and tried. I will not attempt to summarize the very complicated legal and political issues in this case. The fact that the democratic Chilean government argues that Pinochet should be granted diplomatic immunity, however, bears witness to the extent of Pinochet's influence in contemporary Chile.

2. See Gómez-Peña's discussion of this performance in "Mexican Beasts and Living Santos," *The Drama Review* 41.1 (1997): 135–46.

3. For a theoretical discussion of the paradox inherent to discursive resistance see the preface and (extensive) introduction to Richard Terdiman's *Discourse/Counter-Discourse: The Theory and Practice of Symbolic Resistance in Nineteenth-Century France.*

4. In "The Other History of Intercultural Performance," Coco Fusco compares her retrospective analysis of the "Two Amerindians Visit ..." performance to Kafka's "Report to an Academy." Identifying her role with that of Kafka's narrator, Fusco offers her "reflections on performing the role of a noble savage behind the bars of a golden cage" (143).

5. For a brief discussion of "Tras las Rejas," see Juan Flores and Jean Franco's interview with Martorell, "La Casa de Todos Nosotros: Talking to Antonio Martorell" in *The America's Review* (189–91).

6. According to *Ms.*'s information (Volume 5, Number 5, 1995), the Diesel advertisement originally appeared in a magazine called *Details.*

7. For an analysis of the ethical implications of Eltit's aestheticized testimonial in *El infarto del alma* (and *El padre mío*), see Mary Beth Tierney-Tello's article, "Testimony, Ethics and the Aesthetic in Diamela Eltit." This article was published when my book was in the final stages of editing.

WORKS CITED

Adorno, Theodor W. *Prisms*. Trans. Samuel and Shierry Weber. Cambridge: MIT U P, 1982.

Ahmad, Aijaz. "Jameson's Rhetoric of Otherness and the 'National Allegory.'" *Social Text* 15 (Fall 1986): 65–88.

Alfaro, Luis. "Cuerpo Politizado." *Uncontrollable Bodies: Testimonies of Identity and Culture*. Ed. Rodney Sappington and Tyler Stallings. Seattle: Bay P, 1994. 217–41.

The American Heritage Dictionary of the English Language: New College Edition. Boston: Houghton Mifflin Company. 1979 ed.

Anderson, Benedict. *Imagined Communities: Reflections on the Origin and Spread of Nationalism*. London: Verso Editions, 1983.

Annestay, Jean. *Les mystères de L'Incal*. Paris: Les Humanoïdes Associés, 1989.

Anzaldúa, Gloria. *Borderlands/La Frontera: The New Mestiza*. San Francisco: Aunt Lute Books, 1987.

Arizmendi, Yareli. "Whatever Happened to the Sleepy Mexican?: One Way to Be a Contemporary Mexican in a Changing World Order." *The Drama Review* 38.1 (1994): 106–18.

Arrabal, Fernando. *Teatro pánico*. Madrid: Ediciones Cátedra, 1986.

Bakhtin, Mikhail. *Rabelais and His World*. Trans. Helene Iswolsky. Bloomington: Indiana U P, 1984.

Barthes, Roland. *Mythologies*. Trans. Jonathan Cape Ltd. New York: Hill and Wang, 1972.

———. "The Photographic Message." *The Responsibility of Forms: Critical Essays on Music, Art, and Representation*. Trans. Richard Howard. New York: Hill and Wang, 1985. 3–20.

———. *Le plaisir du texte*. Paris: Editions du Seuil, 1973.

———. *S/Z*. Paris: Editions du Seuil, 1970.

Baudrillard, Jean. *Simulacres et simulation*. Paris: Editions Galilé, 1981.

———. *Simulations*. Trans. Paul Foss, Paul Patton and Philip Beitchman. New York: Semiotext(e), 1983.

Benítez-Rojo, Antonio. *The Repeating Island: The Caribbean and the Postmodern Perspective*. Durham and London: Duke U P, 1992.

Benjamin, Walter. *Illuminations*. New York: Schocken, 1969.

Bernstein, Neil. "Goin' Gansta, Choosn' Cholita." *The Utne Reader* (March-April 1995): 87–90.

Berthens, Hans. *The Idea of the Postmodern: A History*. London: Routledge, 1995.

Bhabha, Homi K. *The Location of Culture*. London and New York: Routledge, 1994.

Boal, Augusto. *Theatre of the Oppressed*. Trans. Charles A. and María-Odilia Leal McBride. New York: Theatre Communications Group, 1985.

Booth, Wayne C. "Distance and Point-of-View: An Essay in Classification." *Twentieth-Century Literary Theory: An Introductory Anthology*. Ed. Vassilis Lambropoulos and David Neal Miller. Albany: State U of New York P, 1987. 269–84.

Brecht, Bertolt. *Brecht on Theatre*. Ed. and Trans. John Willet. London: Methuen, 1986.

Brito, Eugenia. "La narrativa de Diamela Eltit: Un nuevo paradigma socio-literario de lectura." *Campos minados: (Literatura post–golpe en Chile)*. Santiago: Editorial Cuarto Propio, 1990. 167–218.

Brooks, Peter. *Body Work: Objects of Desire in Modern Narrative*. Cambridge: Harvard U P, 1993.

———. *Reading for the Plot: Design and Interaction in Narrative*. New York: A.A. Knopf, 1984.

Brunner, José Joaquín. "Un espejo trizado." *Un espejo trizado: Ensayos sobre cultura y políticas culturales*. Santiago: FLASCO, 1988. 15–41.

Burgos, Fernando. *La novela moderna hispanoamericana: Un ensayo sobre el concepto de modernidad*. Madrid: Orígenes, 1985.

Camnitzer, Luis. "Art and Politics: The Aesthetics of Resistance." *NACLA: Report on the Americas* 28.2 (1994): 38–43.

Carr, Cynthia. *On Edge: Performance at the End of the Twentieth Century*. Hanover and London: U P of New England, 1993.

Castro-Klarén, Sara. "Escritura y cuerpo en *Lumpérica*." *Una poética de literatura menor: La narrativa de Diamela Eltit*. Ed. Juan Carlos Lértora. Santiago: Editorial Cuarto Propio, 1993. 97–110.

———. "Del Recuerdo y el Olvido: El Sujeto en *Breve Carcel* y *Lumpérica*." *Escritura, transgresión y sujeto en la literatura latinoamericana*. Mexico: La Red de Jonás, 1989. 196–207.

Cervantes Saavedra, Miguel. *Don Quijote de la Mancha*. Madrid: Editorial Juventud, 1979.

Chávez, Patricio, and Madeleine Grynsztejn. "La Frontera/The Border: Art About the Mexico/United States Border Experience." *La Frontera/The Border: Art About the Mexico/United States Border Experience*. San Diego: Centro Cultural de la Raza, 1993. 23–39.

Collins, Jim. *Uncommon Cultures: Popular Culture and Post-Modernism*. New York and London: Routledge, 1989.

De Costa, Elena. *Collaborative Latin American Popular Theater: From Theory to Form, from Text to Stage.* New York: Peter Lang, 1992.

De la Parra, Marco Antonio. *Carta abierta a Pinochet: Monólogo de la clase media chilena con su padre.* Santiago: Editorial Planeta Chilena, 1998.

———. *La mala memoria: Historia personal de Chile contemporáneo.* Santiago: Editorial Planeta Chilena, 1997.

De Lauretis, Teresa. "Imaging." *Alice Does–N'T.* Bloomington: Indiana U P, 1982. 37–69.

De Saussure, Ferdinand. *Course in General Linguistics.* Trans. Wade Baskin. New York: McGraw-Hill, 1966.

Deleuze, Gilles, and Félix Guattari. *Anti–Oedipus: Capitalism and Schizophrenia.* Trans. Robert Hurley, Mark Seem and Helen R. Lane. Minneapolis: U of Minnesota P, 1992.

Derrida, Jacques. *Of Grammatology.* Trans. Gayatri Chakrovorty Spivak. Baltimore: John Hopkins U P, 1984.

Dwyer, Augusta. *On the Line: Life on the U.S.–Mexican Border.* London: Latin American Bureau, 1994.

Eco, Umberto. *The Role of the Reader: Explorations in the Semiotics of Texts.* Bloomington: Indiana U P, 1984.

Elam, Diane. *Feminism and Deconstruction: Ms. en Abyme.* London and New York: Routledge, 1994.

Eliade, Mircea. *The Myth of the Eternal Return or, Cosmos and History.* Trans. Willard R. Trask. Princeton: Princeton U P, 1974.

Eltit, Diamela. *El cuarto mundo.* Santiago: Editorial Planeta Chilena, 1988.

———. Interview. "Diamela Eltit: 'Me interesa todo aquello que está a contrapelo del poder.'" By Ana María Foxley. *Literatura y Libros*, supplement for *La Epoca.* November 20, 1988. 4–5.

———. Interview. "Interrogando los signos: Conversando con Diamela Eltit." By Robert Neustadt. *Inti: Revista de Literatura Hispánica* 46–7 (1998): 293–305.

———. Interview. "Narrativa chilena joven: Diamela Eltit y su novela *Lumpérica.*" By Sonia Riquelme. *Foro literario* 18 (1989): 46–50.

———. Interview. "Resistencia y sujeto femenino: Entrevista con Diamela Eltit." By Julio Ortega. *La Torre: Revista de la Universidad de Puerto Rico* 4.14 (April-June 1990): 229–41.

———. *Lumpérica.* Santiago: Editorial Planeta Chilena, 1991.

———. *Los trabajadores de la muerte.* Santiago: Editorial Planeta Chilena, 1998.

———. *Los vigilantes.* Santiago: Sudamericana, 1994.

————. *El padre mío.* Santiago: Francisco Zegers Editor, 1989.

Eltit, Diamela, and Paz Errázuriz. *El infarto del alma.* Santiago: Francisco Zegers Editor, 1994.

Eltit, Diamela, and Lotty Rosenfeld. *Maipu.* Videocassette. 1980.

Fernández Retamar, Roberto. "Antipoesía y poesía conversacional en Hispanoamérica." *Para una teoría de la literatura hispanoamericana.* Mexico: Editorial Nuestro Tiempo, 1981. 140–58.

Fiedler, Leslie. *Freaks: Myths and Images of the Secret Self.* New York: Simon and Schuster, 1978.

Flores, Juan, and Jean Franco. "La Casa de Todos Nosotros: Talking to Antonio Martorell." *The Americas Review: A Review of Hispanic Literature and Art of the USA* 22.1–2 (1994): 183–211.

Foster, David William. "Popular Culture: The Roots of Literary Tradition." *Imagination, Emblems and Expressions: Essays on Latin American, Caribbean, and Continental Culture and Identity.* Ed. Helen Ryan-Ransom. Bowling Green, OH: Bowling Green State U Popular P, 1993.

Foster, Hal, ed. *The Anti-Aesthetic: Essays on Postmodern Culture.* Seattle: Bay P, 1983.

Foucault, Michel. *The Archaeology of Knowledge.* Trans. A. M. Sheridan Smith. New York: Pantheon, 1972.

————. *Discipline and Punish. The Birth of the Prison.* Trans. Alan Sheridan. New York: Vintage Books, 1979.

————. *The Order of Things: An Archeology of the Human Sciences.* New York: Vintage Books, 1994.

————. *Power/Knowledge: Selected Interviews and Other Writings 1972–1977.* Trans. Colin Gordon, Leo Marshall, John Mepham, and Kate Soper. New York: Pantheon, 1980.

Franco, Jean. "Afterword: From Romance to Refractory Aesthetic." *Latin American Women's Writing: Feminist Readings in Theory and Crisis.* Eds. Anny Brooksbank Jones and Catherine Davies. Oxford: Clarendon P, 1996. 226–37.

————. "Going Public: Reinhabiting the Private." *On Edge: The Crisis of Contemporary Latin American Culture.* Ed. George Yúdice, Jean Franco, and Juan Flores. Minneapolis and London: U of Minnesota P, 1992. 65–83.

————. "Remapping Culture." *Americas: New Interpretive Essays.* Ed. Alfred Stepan. New York and Oxford: Oxford U P, 1992. 172–88.

Fuentes, Carlos. *Valiente mundo nuevo: Épica, utopía y mito en la novela hispanoamericana.* Mexico: Fondo de Cultura Económica, 1990.

Fusco, Coco. "The Other History of Intercultural Performance." *The Drama Review* 38.1 (1994): 143–67.

Fusco, Coco, and Paula Heredia. *The Couple in the Cage: A Guatinaui Odyssey.* Videocassette. Authentic Documentary Productions, 1993.

Gaines, Jane M. *Contested Culture: The Image, the Voice, and the Law.* Chapel Hill and London: U of North Carolina P, 1991.

Garber, Marjorie. *Vested Interests: Cross-Dressing & Cultural Anxiety.* New York: HarperPerennial, 1993.

García Canclini, Nestor. *Culturas híbridas: Estrategias para entrar y salir de la modernidad.* México: Grijalbo, 1990.

Gleick, James. *Chaos: Making a New Science.* New York: Penguin Books, 1987.

Gómez-Peña, Guillermo. *Border Brujo.* Videocassette. Dir. Isaac Artenstein. San Diego: Cinewest Productions: Sushi , 1990.

———. "Death on the Border: A Eulogy to Border Art." *High Performance* Spring (1991): 8–9.

———. "The New World Border: Prophecies for the End of the Century." *The Drama Review* 38.1 (1994): 119–42.

———. *Warrior for Gringostroika.* Saint Paul: Graywolf Press, 1993.

Graziano, Frank. *Divine Violence: Spectacle, Psychosexuality, & Radical Christianity in the Argentine "Dirty War."* Boulder: Westview P, 1992.

Greenblatt, Stephen. *Marvelous Possessions: The Wonder of the New World.* Chicago: U of Chicago P, 1991.

Grosz, Elizabeth. "Bodies-Cities." *Sexuality and Space.* Ed. Beatriz Colomina. New York: Princeton Architectural P, 1992.

Gugelberger, Georg, and Michael Kearney. "Voices for the Voiceless: Testimonial Literature in Latin America." *Latin American Perspectives* 18.70 (1991): 3–14.

Harner, Winfred. "Polycentric Framing Devices and Dramatic Structure in Alexander Jodorowsky's 'El túnel se come por la boca.'" *Tinta* 1.3 (1983): 11–17.

Hayles, N. Kathryn. *Chaos Bound: Orderly Disorder in Contemporary Literature and Science.* Ithaca: Cornell U P, 1990.

———. *Chaos and Order: Complex Dynamics in Literature and Science.* Chicago: U of Chicago P, 1991.

Hicks, D. Emily. *Border Writing: The Multidimensional Text.* Minneapolis and Oxford: U of Minnesota P, 1991.

Hutcheon, Linda. *A Poetics of Postmodernism.* London: Routledge, 1988.

———. *The Politics of Postmodernism.* London: Routledge, 1989.

Huyssen, Andreas. *After the Great Divide: Modernism, Mass Culture, Postmodernism*. Bloomington and Indianapolis: Indiana U P, 1986.

———. "Mapping the Postmodern." *New German Critique* 33 (1984): 5–52.

Irigaray, Luce. *This Sex Which is Not One*. Trans. Catherine Porter with Carolyn Burke. Ithaca: Cornell U P, 1985.

Jameson, Fredric. *The Political Unconscious: Narrative As a Socially Symbolic Act*. Ithaca: Cornell U P, 1981.

———. *Postmodernism or the Logic of Late Capitalism*. Durham: Duke U P, 1991.

———. "Third-World Literature in the Era of Multinational Capitalism." *Social Text: Theory/Culture/Ideology* 15 (1986): 65–88.

Jara, René. *Los límites de la representación: La novela chilena del golpe*. Madrid: Fundación Instituto Shakespeare, 1985.

Jodorowsky, Alejandro. *Las ansias carnívoras de la nada*. Santiago: Hachette, 1991.

———. *Antología pánica*. México: Joaquín Mortiz, 1996.

———. *Canciones, metapoemas y un arte de pensar*. Santiago: Dolmen Ediciones, 1997.

———. *Cuentos pánicos*. México: Ediciones Era, 1963.

———. *Donde mejor canta un pájaro*. Santiago: Hachette, 1992.

———. "Hablando de comics con Alejandro Jodorowsky." *Un comic*. Ed. Edita Pablo Brodsky, 1992.

———. *El loro de siete lenguas*. Santiago: Hachette, 1991.

———. *Teatro pánico*. México: Ediciones Era, 1965.

———. *El Topo: A Book of the Film*. Trans. Joanne Pottlitzer. London: Calder & Boyars, 1974.

Jodorowsky, Alejandro, and George Bess. *Anibal 5: Dix femmes avant de mourir*. Paris: Les Humanoïdes Associés, 1993.

Jodorowsky, Alejandro, and Juan Gimenez. *La caste des Méta-Barons: Honorata La Trisaïeule*. Paris: Les Humanoïdes Associés, 1993.

———. *La caste des Méta-Barons: Othon le Trisaïeul*. Paris: Les Humanoïdes Associés, 1992.

Jodorowsky, Alejandro, and Zoran Janjetov. *Anarco psychotiques*. Paris: Les Humanoïdes Associés, 1992.

———. *Avant l'incal*. Paris: Les Humanoïdes Associés, 1991.

———. *Croot*. Paris: Les Humanoïdes Associés, 1991.

———. *Détective privé de class 'R'*. Paris: Les Humanoïdes Associés, 1991.

———. *Ousky, SPV et homéoputes*. Paris: Les Humanoïdes Associés, 1993.

———. *Suicide Allée*. Geneva: Les Humanoïdes Associés, 1995.

Jodorowsky, Alejandro, and Moebius. "Un chapitre inédit de l'incal." *Les mystères de L'Incal.* Paris: Les Humanoïdes Associés, 1989. 58–66.

———. *L'Incal.* Geneva: Les Humanoïdes Associés, 1994.

Johnson, Barbara, ed. *Freedom and Interpretation: The Oxford Amnesty Lectures 1992.* New York: BasicBooks, 1993.

Kafka, Franz. "A Report to an Academy." *The Basic Kafka.* Trans. Willa and Edwin Muir. New York: Pocket Books, 1979. 245–55.

Kirshenblatt-Gimblett, Barbara. "The Ethnographic Burlesque." *The Drama Review.* 42.2 (1998): 175–80.

Lacan, Jacques. "Le Stade du miroir comme formateur de la fonction du je." *Ecrits I.* Paris: Editions du Seuil, 1966. 89–97.

Laclau, Ernesto, and Chantal Mouffe. *Hegemony and Socialist Strategy: Towards a Radical Democratic Politics.* London and New York: Verso, 1985.

Lagos, María Inés. "Reflexiones sobre la representación del sujeto en dos textos de Diamela Eltit: *Lumpérica* y *El Cuarto mundo.*" *Una poética de literatura menor: La narrativa de Diamela Eltit.* Ed. Juan Carlos Lértora. Santiago: Editorial Cuarto Propio, 1993. 127–40.

Larouche, Michel. *Alexandre Jodorowsky: Cinéaste panique.* Paris: Editions Albatros, 1985.

Lértora, Juan Carlos, "Categorías postmodernistas en la narrativa de Diamela Eltit." Unpublished essay presented at the Second Conference on Hispanic Cultures of the Pacific Coast of the Americas, U of Oregon, Eugene, 1992.

———. "Diamela Eltit: Hacia una poética de literatura menor." *Una poética de literatura menor: La narrativa de Diamela Eltit.* Ed. Juan Carlos Lértora. Santiago: Editorial Cuarto Propio, 1993. 27–35.

Lyotard, Jean-François. *The Postmodern Condition: A Report on Knowledge.* Trans. Geoff Bennington and Brian Massumi. Minneapolis: U of Minnesota P, 1989.

Maíz-Peña, Magdalena. "Hibridez textual y disidencia cultural: *Los vigilantes* de Diamela Eltit." *South Eastern Latin Americanist* 40.1–2 (1996): 27–34.

Mannix, Daniel. *Freaks: We Who Are Not As Others.* San Francisco: Re/Search Publications, 1990.

Martínez-Conde, Juan Gutierrez. *Literatura y sociedad en el mundo chicano.* Madrid: Ediciones de la Torre, 1992.

Michie, Helena. *The Flesh Made Word: Female Figures and Women's Bodies.* New York and Oxford: Oxford U P, 1987.

Montecino, Sonia. *Madres y huachos: Alegorías del mestizaje chileno*. Santiago: Editorial Cuarto Propio, 1993.

Moulian, Tomás. *Chile Actual: Anatomía de un mito*. Santiago: LOM-ARCIS, 1997.

Mulvey, Laura. "Visual Pleasure and Narrative Cinema." *Visual and Other Pleasures*. Bloomington and Indianapolis: Indiana U P, 1989. 14–26.

Neruda, Pablo. *Canto general*. Barcelona: Seix Barral, 1982.

Olalquiaga, Celeste. *Megalopolis: Contemporary Cultural Sensibilities*. Minneapolis and Oxford: U of Minnesota P, 1992.

Olea, Raquel. "El cuerpo-mujer. Un recorte de lectura en la narrativa de Diamela Eltit." *Una poética de literatura menor: La narrativa de Diamela Eltit*. Ed. Juan Carlos Lértora. Santiago: Editorial Cuarto Propio, 1993. 83–95.

———. *Lengua víbora: Producciones de lo femenino en la escritura de mujeres chilenas*. Santiago: Editorial Cuarto Propio, 1998.

Ortega, Julio. "Diamela Eltit y el imaginario de la virtualidad." *Una poética de literatura menor: La narrativa de Diamela Eltit*. Ed. Juan Carlos Lértora. Santiago: Editorial Cuarto Propio, 1993. 53–81.

Paz, Octavio. *El laberinto de la soledad*. Mexico: Fondo de Cultura Económica, 1984.

Piña, Juan Andres. *Conversaciones con la narrativa chilena: Fernando Alegría, José Donoso, Guillermo Blanco, Jorge Edwards, Antonio Skarmeta, Isabel Allende, Diamela Eltit*. Santiago: Editorial Los Andes, 1991. 225–54.

Pratt, Mary Louise. "Overwriting Pinochet: Undoing the Culture of Fear in Chile." *Modern Language Quarterly* 57:2 (1996): 151–63.

Prince, Gerald. *Dictionary of Narratology*. Lincoln and London: U Nebraska P, 1987.

Puig, Manuel. *El beso de la mujer araña*. Barcelona: Editorial Seix Barral, 1988.

Richard, Nelly. "Estéticas y políticas del signo." *Masculino/Femenino: Prácticas de la diferencia y cultura democrática*. Santiago: Francisco Zegers Editor, 1993. 47–63.

———. *La estratificación de los márgenes*. Santiago: Francisco Zegers Editor, 1989.

———. *Margins and Institutions: Art in Chile since 1973*. Melbourne: Art & Text, 1986.

———. "Reply to Vidal (From Chile)." *boundary 2* 20.3 (1993): 228–31.

————. "Tres funciones de escritura: Desconstrucción, simulación, hibrida-
ción." *Una poética de literatura menor: La narrativa de Diamela Eltit.*
Ed. Juan Carlos Lértora. Santiago: Editorial Cuarto Propio, 1993. 37–
51.

Sabin, Roger. *Adult Comics: An introduction.* London and New York: Routledge, 1993.

Said, Edward. *Orientalism.* New York: Vintage Books, 1979.

Saldívar, José David. *The Dialectics of Our America: Genealogy, Cultural
Critique, and Literary History.* Durham and London: Duke U P, 1991.

Samaniego, José Luis. "Discurso Entrega Premio José Nuez a Diamela Eltit."
Taller de letras 24 (1995): 202–4.

Santos, Susana. "Diamela Eltit: Una ruptura ejemplar." *Feminaria* 5.9 (November 1992): 7–9.

Shaviro, Steven. *The Cinematic Body.* Minneapolis and London: U of Minnesota P, 1993.

Siems, Larry. "Just Who Does He Think He Is?" *San Diego Reader* June 9,
1994: 1–32.

Silva Donoso, María de la Luz. *La participación política de la mujer en
Chile: Las organizaciones de mujeres.* Buenos Aires: Fundación Fried-
rich Naumann, 1987.

Smart, Barry. *Modern Conditions, Postmodern Contraversies.* London and
New York: Routledge, 1992.

Sosnoski, James J. *Modern Skeletons in Postmodern Closets: A Cultural
Studies Alternative.* Charlottsville: U P of Virginia, 1995.

Taylor, Diana. "A Savage Performance: Guillermo Gómez-Peña and Coco
Fusco's 'Couple in the Cage.'" *The Drama Review* 42.2 (1998): 160–
75.

Terdiman, Richard. *Discourse/Counter-Discourse: The Theory and Practice
of Symbolic Resistance in Nineteenth-Century France.* Ithaca: Cornell
U P, 1985.

Tierney-Tello, Mary Beth. "Testimony, Ethics and the Aesthetic in Diamela
Eltit." *PMLA* 114.1 (1999): 78–96.

Trevizán, Liliana. *Política/sexualidad: Nudo en la escritura de mujeres
latinoamericanas.* Lanham: U P of America, 1997.

Vidal, Hernán. *Poética de la población marginal: Fundamentos materialistas
para una historiografía estética.* Minneapolis: Prisma Institute, 1987.

————. "Postmodernism, Postleftism, Neo-Avant-Gardism: The Case of
Chile's *Revista de Crítica Cultural.*" *boundary 2* 20.3 (1993): 203–27.

Villanueva, Tino. "Sobre el término 'Chicano.'" *Chicanos: Antología histórica y literaria.* Mexico: Fondo de Cultura Económica, 1980.

Williams, Raymond Leslie. "Women Writing in the Americas." *The Novel in the Americas*. Niwot: U P of Colorado, 1992. 119–31.

Wittgenstein, Ludwig. *The Blue and the Brown Books: Preliminary Studies for the 'Philosophical Investigations'*. New York: Harper Torchbooks, 1965.

Ybarra-Frausto, Tomás. "Rasquachismo: A Chicano Sensibility." *Chicano Art: Resistance and Affirmation, 1965–1985*. Ed. Teresa McKenna, Yvonne Yarbro-Bejarano, and Richard Griswold del Castillo. Los Angeles: Wight Art Gallery, 1991. 155–62.

Yúdice, George. "*Testimonio* and Postmodernism." *Latin American Perspectives* 18.70 (1991): 15–31.

Zizek, Slavoj. *Looking Awry: An Introduction to Jaques Lacan through Popular Culture*. Cambridge: MIT P, 1993.

INDEX